Chinese Clothing
An Illustrated Guide

Valery M. Garrett

HONG KONG
OXFORD UNIVERSITY PRESS
OXFORD   NEW YORK

Oxford University Press

Oxford   New York
Athens Auckland Bangkok Bogotá Buenos Aires Calcutta
Cape Town Chennai Dar es Salaam Delhi Florence Hong Kong Istanbul
Karachi Kuala Lumpur Madrid Melbourne Mexico City Mumbai
Nairobi Paris São Paulo Singapore Taipei Tokyo Toronto Warsaw

and associated companies in
Berlin   Ibadan

Oxford is a registered trade mark of Oxford University Press

First published 1994
This impression (lowest digit)
10 9 8 7 6 5 4 3

Published in the United States
by Oxford University Press, New York

British Library Cataloguing in Publication Data
available

Library of Congress Cataloging-in-Publication Data

Garrett, Valery M., date.
    Chinese clothing: an illustrated guide / Valery M. Garrett.
        p.   cm.
    Includes bibliographical references and index.
    ISBN 0-19-586426-3 (alk.paper)
        1. Costume — China — History   2. Chinese — Costume.   I. Title.
GT1555.G36 1993
391'. 00951 — dc20

                                            98-42487
                                            CIP

Printed in Hong Kong
Published by Oxford University Press (China) Ltd

For Richard, James, Ruth, and Vivienne

Preface

The second half of the twentieth century has seen unprecedented changes in China, changes which have also affected dress. In the 1940s the loose-fitting jacket and trousers worn by working people, the slim *qi pao* favoured by fashionable women, and the long gown with skullcap and fan adopted by gentlemen were the accepted forms of dress and stemmed from traditions dating back centuries. But the tumultuous effects of the Cultural Revolution in the mid-1960s caused a strict utilitarian dress code to be imposed on all the populace, with the result that by the early 1980s traditional dress had virtually disappeared, particularly in urban areas. Outside the mainland, rapid urbanization in the associated territories of Hong Kong, Macau, and Taiwan at this time accelerated the pace of life, with Western dress taking the place of traditional Chinese style.

Regulations governing Chinese dress were imposed as long ago as the Zhou dynasty (1027–771BC) and continued to be adhered to, in one form or another, well into the twentieth century. Dress and textile remains from before the Ming dynasty are scarce, but recently there have been many exciting discoveries of Ming textiles and embroideries in Tibet where they were sent by Chinese rulers as gifts. Centuries of near-perfect conditions in cool, dark monasteries helped preserve them and, in many cases, such discoveries have increased the scholarly understanding of Ming official dress. Some features of dress from the Ming dynasty have carried on into the twentieth century, underlining the respect and nostalgia the Chinese have accorded this period, coming as it did between two episodes of alien rule.

In recent years much has been written about official clothing worn during the Qing dynasty; imperial robes, in particular, have been well documented. The Manchu race, who accounted for a mere 2 per cent of the total population of China, imposed their own dress code on the Han literati as a means of exercising control. Little attention, however, has been paid to the traditional dress of Han people during this period. Certain images come to mind: the tiny feet of the Han Chinese women, the rich embroidery on their voluminous jackets, the auspicious symbolism associated with brightly coloured children's clothing. These areas, and others which have been overlooked in the past—celebration dress for weddings and burials, and military uniforms among them—are here examined in detail. Moreover, now that the twentieth century is drawing to a close, attention has been given to those turbulent times and their effects on Chinese clothing.

This book has benefitted greatly from the help of many friends and colleagues in Hong Kong and elsewhere, and particularly from the generous loan of items, many illustrated here for the first time. My sincere thanks go especially to Dr James Hayes for reading a part of the manuscript and offering helpful advice and comments. Grateful thanks are also due to Teresa Coleman, Gary Dickinson, Chris Hall, Shirley Johnson, and Christina Wong Yan Chau. Errors and short-comings remain my own responsibility.

VALERY GARRETT
Hong Kong, 1993

Contents

Chronological Table of Ming and Qing Reigns

Ming Dynasty (1368–1644)

Reign Title	Dates of Reign
Hongwu	AD 1368–1398
Jianwen	1398–1402
Yongle	1402–1424
Hongxi	1424–1425
Xuande	1425–1435
Zhengtong	1435–1449
Jingtai	1449–1457
Tianshun	1457–1464
Chenghua	1464–1487
Hongzhi	1487–1505
Zhengde	1505–1521
Jiajing	1521–1567
Longqing	1567–1572
Wanli	1572–1620
Taichang	1620
Tianqi	1620–1627
Chongzhen	1627–1644

Qing Dynasty (1644–1911)

Reign Title	*Dates of Reign*
Shunzhi	1644–1661
Kangxi	1662–1722
Yongzheng	1723–1735
Qianlong	1736–1795
Jiaqing	1796–1820
Daoguang	1821–1850
Xianfeng	1851–1861
Tongzhi	1862–1874
Guangxu	1875–1908
Xuantong	1909–1911

Republic (1912–1949)

People's Republic (1949–   )

Introduction

The territory of China is vast, some 9.6 million square kilometres, covering an area almost as large as the combined nations of Europe. The population, which has already passed 1.13 billion, is composed of 56 ethnic groups. The Han race totalled 1,042,482,187 according to a 1990 census, making it the largest ethnic group in the world.

Throughout most of China's long history there has been a common style of dress within each social stratum of the Han people, unlike other countries where traditional dress often varied greatly from region to region. The reasons for this uniformity stem from the approach to life evolved by the Chinese. To the Han Chinese man, his place within the clan, the extended family descending from one male ancestor, was and remains of vital importance. He was keenly aware of his responsibilities, not only to future generations and the importance of producing male heirs to continue the lineage, but also of his great obligation to those who went before, his ancestors. Filial piety and success in terms of bringing wealth and honour to the clan were his duty. In doing this he was required to act in a way worthy of his ancestors. His clothes, especially, were a 'uniform', donned to show his place in the hierarchy. Everyone—man and woman—had a designated place in society, in part due to a complex system of dress regulations which was imposed, in one form or another, over the centuries.

These regulations governing the style of dress were enforced by the rulers of the state as far back as the Zhou dynasty. This was done to differentiate between the various levels of society, and to control the populace as a whole. Awards to men of merit were visible to everyone. Successive dynasties followed tradition, with regulations being enacted and adopted right up to the second half of the twentieth century. Such regulations also served to help unite the country, especially as China was attacked, conquered, and several times governed by invaders such as the Mongols and Manchus. Once established, however, the foreign rulers imposed their own set of stringent regulations. During eras of foreign domination the dress of the native Chinese dynasties of the Han, Tang, Song, and Ming were regarded by the Han Chinese with nostalgia and reverence as being the fundamentally correct styles, with the Ming rulers losing no time in restoring earlier Chinese rules for dress once the Yuan dynasty (1271–1368) had been overthrown.

Colour, too, was used a means of indicating a new order or regime, and colour regulations for officials' robes distinguished them from the imperial rulers as well as from the lower classes. Of the five main colours used, yellow was considered a symbol of central authority, while black represented the north, red stood for south, blue for east, and white for west. In 1912 these were depicted on the Republican flag as the official colours of China, only to be replaced in 1949 by a People's Republic flag of red with five yellow stars representing the country's five main nationalities: Han, Manchu, Mongolian, Muslim, and Tibetan.

Performance of ritual worship was one of the most important obligations of both government and people. In elaborate ceremonial sacrifices to Heaven and Earth performed by emperors, as well as those rituals carried out by local government officials and senior family members, a strict dress code was observed. The emperor's responsibilities for ensuring the well-being of his people were tied to the performance of ceremonies paying respect to the heavens, and to the ancestors of the dynasty. It was believed that if an emperor ruled well, Heaven, which cared about the welfare of the people, would smile on earth, and send good weather and abundant crops; if the ruler was incompetent or corrupt, droughts, famines, and floods would devastate the land. This then gave the people the right to overthrow the emperor, thus indicating that the 'mandate of Heaven' had been withdrawn.

The Mongol rulers of the Yuan dynasty fell in this manner. The emperor raised taxes and swamped the country with worthless currency resulting in high inflation. Food shortages brought about by drought, floods, and earthquakes, and worst of all the killer disease, the Black Death, making its way across Asia from Europe, caused the death of millions of people. The suffering caused by poor rule, and the belief that the natural disasters were judgement on a bad ruler, caused a popular revolt. At first the rebellion was disorganized, then an unconventional leader emerged, General Zhu Yuanzhang, a commoner, an orphan, and a former Buddhist novice.

Zhu unified the peasant resistance and began to liberate southern China from Mongol rule. By 1368 he and his troops were strong enough to attack the capital. The Mongol emperor fled north across the frontier, and the dynasty fell. Zhu and his forces occupied Beijing, establishing a new Chinese dynasty which the new emperor named the Ming, literally meaning 'brilliant'. Not since 1127 had one Chinese government ruled the whole country.

Part I
The Ming Dynasty (1368–1644)

1 Official Dress for Men

General Zhu Yuanzhang, the first emperor of the Ming dynasty, took the reign title of Hongwu and ruled for thirty years during which time he fortified the northern frontier, and enlarged China's boundaries to incorporate Manchuria and Korea. Initially, the court and seat of government were maintained in Nanjing, the southern capital, as it was further from the homeland of the Mongols. It remained there until 1421 when the Yongle emperor moved it back to Beijing, or northern capital, and the Forbidden City was laid out. The Mongols continued to raid, and at one point in 1449 captured the reigning Emperor and attacked Beijing. Eventually, however, the Ming armies managed to hold the Mongols in check, even persuading them to honour a treaty to live in peace. As a consequence of such strength the country became stable, and the Chinese were able to re-establish their traditions largely untroubled by events taking place outside their borders.

Amid the unsettled conditions of the beginning of the Ming era, however, the Chinese continued to wear the close-fitting Mongol robes of the previous Yuan dynasty. Nevertheless, the Hongwu Emperor tried to undermine foreign Mongol influences by stressing the importance of a return to the customs and costumes of earlier Chinese dynasties, particularly the Han, Tang, and Song. Some statutes relating to dress were laid down in the third and sixteenth years of Hongwu, and again in the twenty-fourth year of his reign in 1391, when more precise costume regulations were established.[1] The Wanli edition (1587) of the *Da ming hui dian*, the dynastic statutes, brought the regulations up to date by incorporating changes and additions made during the reigns of the Yongle (r.1402–24) and Jiajing (r.1521–67) emperors.

Dress of the Emperor

Clothing for the emperor was classified into five main groups:[2] ceremonial attire, leather military attire, regular military attire, formal attire, and ordinary attire.

Ceremonial Attire

Known as *gun mian*, ceremonial attire was worn when performing sacrificial rites at the temples to Heaven and Earth, at the imperial ancestral temple, on the first day of the Lunar New Year, and at the winter solstice (**fig. 1.1**). On these ceremonial occasions the emperor's head was covered by a black silk hat lined with red, flat-topped and tied under the chin, like those worn by emperors of the Han dynasty. Twelve strings of white jade hung down at the back and front to shield the face.[3] A wide-sleeved, black silk jacket was worn fastening over to the right side and reaching down to hip level. Edged with wide borders and decorated on the sleeves with dragons and pheasants, it was partnered with a seven-panelled skirt, or *shang*, in yellow. Underneath was an inner robe with a neckband decorated with the *fu* symbol (like capital Es back to back), one of the Twelve Symbols.

The full Twelve Symbols of Imperial Authority which first appeared on sacrificial robes in the Zhou dynasty, and then in the Han dynasty (206 BC–AD 220), were placed on the outer jacket and skirt. Only the emperor could wear all twelve symbols which, when placed on a robe, assumed cosmic significance and established the emperor as Ruler of the Universe. Woven into the jacket were six symbols: the sun disc on the left shoulder and the moon on the right, the constellation of seven stars of the Big Dipper above the mountain on the back, and dragons and pheasants on each sleeve. Embroidered on the silk gauze skirt were a further six symbols, each appearing in a pair and together forming four columns: the sacrificial cup, water weed, grains of millet, flames, sacrificial axe, and *fu* symbol, representing the forces of good and evil.

A leather belt with jade plaques was slotted through a long narrow panel called a *bi xi*, sometimes translated as 'knee cover'. This was made of yellow silk gauze embroidered with a gold dragon and flames, and worn at the front of the skirt from the waist to below the knees. This was a tradition dating back to the Zhou dynasty, and

Fig. 1.1 Zhu Yuanzhang (1328–98), the first Ming emperor, in a caricature showing his attire for sacrificial ceremonies. National Palace Museum.

comprised part of the ceremonial dress of the Han dynasty. To complete his attire, the emperor wore shoes with wooden soles and turned-up toes bisected in the centre.

Leather Military Attire

Leather military attire was worn by the emperor during audiences on the first and fifteenth days of the lunar month, when he made proclamations, and when he received envoys and tribute from foreign nations. The name was derived from the hat, called a *pi bian*, originally made of the skin of the white reindeer but after the Sui and Tang dynasties, made of woven rattan covered with gauze (**fig. 1.2, 1.3**). The hat design for the emperor incorporated twelve ridges; princes' hats had nine. The robe had very wide sleeves with a neck opening which fastened to the right side and was worn over a pleated skirt. Around the waist was a leather belt with a *bi xi* and ribbons hanging from it. Underneath was an inner robe; its neckband decorated with the *fu* symbol was visible when all the elements were worn.

Regular Military Attire

Regular military attire was worn on military expeditions and when dispatching troops. The robe was cut as the leather military robe but was made of deep red gauze, worn over a skirt in a different shade of red. The shoes were also red. The helmet had twelve ridges around the crown.

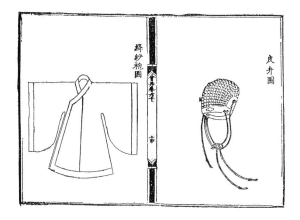

Formal Attire

For feasting courtiers and officials and at all formal events, the emperor wore a dark robe with the sun and moon discs on the shoulders, a dragon medallion at the front, and a dragon square

Fig. 1.2   Pages from the *Da ming hui dian* depicting leather military attire.

at the back. The wide border, in a contrasting colour edging the collar and side fastening, the hem, and the sleeves were embroidered with 189 dragons. The robe was worn with a black silk hat with twelve ridges which was decorated with gold thread and jade and held in place with a jade hairpin (**fig. 1.4**).

The dark robe was worn over an under-robe known as a *shen yi*, or 'deep garment', whose origins dated back to the Zhou dynasty and which, during the Han and Song, had been worn both for sacrificial ceremonies and for social gatherings. The *shen yi* had a straight collar band fastening over to the right, full sleeves ending in narrow cuffs, and a panelled skirt attached to a waistseam. The upper and lower parts of the garment were required to total twelve pieces.

Fig. 1.3   Ridged hat of woven rattan covered with gauze, known as a *pi bian*, and hairpin worn with leather military attire.

Fig. 1.4   Black silk gauze hat with twelve ridges, decorated with gold thread and jade beads, and a jade hairpin worn with formal attire. From the Dingling tomb of the Wanli Emperor. Museum of Dingling.

Ordinary Attire

For informal occasions the emperor wore a yellow robe with a round neck and full sleeves ending in narrow cuffs. Four gold embroidered dragon medallions were placed at chest, back, and each shoulder (**fig. 1.5**). A leather belt with jade plaques encircled it, and the emperor wore leather boots. The headdress comprised a black gauze turban; two wings at the back pointed upwards (**fig. 1.6**). The emperor also wore a crown in the same shape as the turban, but this was made of gold mesh decorated with two profile dragons chasing a flaming pearl, and wings like rounded horns standing up at the back (**fig. 1.7**).

Fig. 1.5 The Yongle Emperor wearing ordinary attire, a robe with four dragon medallions. National Palace Museum.

Fig. 1.6 Black lacquered gauze cap with two upright wings worn with ordinary attire.

Fig. 1.7 Gold-mesh helmet, with dragons chasing a flaming pearl, worn by the Wanli Emperor. From the Dingling tomb near Beijing. Museum of Dingling.

Development of the Dragon Robes

Robes with dragons on them were first recorded in the Tang dynasty and then again in the Song. It was the Mongols of the Yuan dynasty, however, who established the use of dragon robes; consequently, the Ming did not adopt them officially. Even so, dragon robes were worn, constituting the bulk of the material evidence surviving from the Ming dynasty. It was through these robes for 'ordinary attire', or informal wear, that regulations were eventually codified for lower-ranking noblemen and officials. A portrait of the first Ming emperor shows him wearing a robe similar to those worn by Yuan officials: in yellow, it depicts two principal dragons, the head of the first on the chest with its body looping over the left shoulder, the tail finishing on the back, while the head of the other dragon is on the back, the tail appearing over the right shoulder forming what appears to be a large collar. Around the skirt is a horizontal band with a pair of dragons. The heads of the dragons on the upper part are facing front, and this marks the initiation of the tradition for the emperor, and later his most favoured courtiers, to wear dragons which faced the onlooker, while other noblemen and officials wore profile dragons.

Dragons coiled in medallions, a design feature which had possibly died out during the Yuan dynasty, was revived in 1405 with the official announcement that 'ordinary attire' for the emperor should be yellow with gold dragon medallions on each shoulder and on the chest and back (**fig. 1.8**). There are, however, portraits of the Hongwu Emperor painted during his reign which show him wearing robes with these four medallions. The emperor's sons, and grandsons by those sons, wore the dragon medallions on red robes. Then, in the reign of the Xuande Emperor (r.1425–35) twelve large medallions were worn: four on the upper part as before, plus four on the skirt at front and back and each side, and one on the front and back of each wide sleeve.

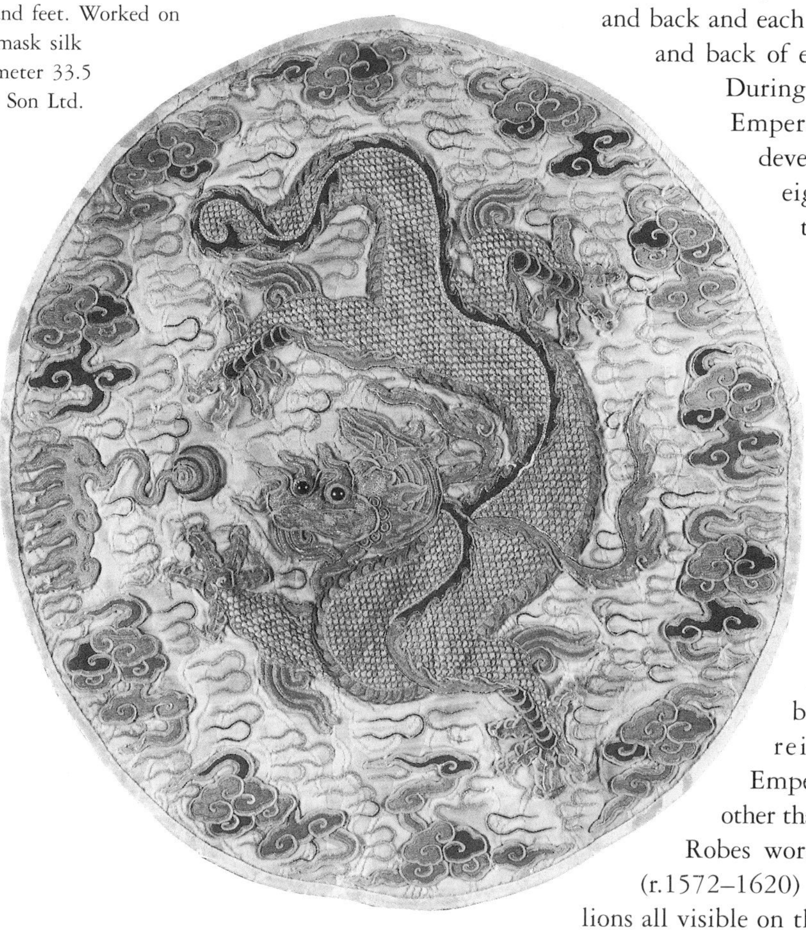

Fig. 1.8   A dragon medallion, possibly placed originally on the shoulder of the robe, with profile dragon, the scales worked in couched gold thread and padded to make it three-dimensional, with rare needlelooping on the spine, legs, and feet. Worked on pale gold damask silk ground. Diameter 33.5 cm. Spink & Son Ltd.

During the reign of the Tianshun Emperor (r.1457–64) a further development commenced, with eight medallions visible on the outer robe and four on the under-robe. These were arranged with the four on the upper body of chest, back, and shoulders; two on the front and back of the skirt, arranged vertically; and the other four placed vertically in pairs at the sides of the under-robe. The Twelve Symbols were used on medallion robes (**fig. 1.9**), and had been introduced during the reign of the Zhengtong Emperor (r.1435–49) for robes other than for sacrificial ceremonies. Robes worn by the Wanli Emperor (r.1572–1620) show the twelve medallions all visible on the outer robe, placed with

four on the upper body as before, two on the front and back of the skirt, and two more on each side of the skirt.

Robes for Noblemen and Officials

The emperor and his sons wore several styles of robes, and gradually other types of dragon robes returned to general use among nobles and officials. Five-clawed dragons known as *long* were worn by the emperor, his sons by the empress, other high-ranking princes, as well as those high nobles and officials whom the emperor wished to reward. Four-clawed dragons called *mang* were worn by other princes, noble-

Fig. 1.9 The Taichang Emperor (r.1620) wearing a robe with eight dragon medallions on the outer robe and four on the under-skirt, and bearing the Twelve Symbols. The *fu* symbol is visible on the neckband of the under-robe. Palace Museum.

men, and all those holding senior appointments in the court and household. They were also given as presentation robes for chief courtiers and high officials. In addition, a custom became established during the early part of the reign of the Yongle Emperor of presenting dragon robes to tribute-bearing nations to encourage trade, or as bribes to stop raids. The results were mixed as at least one Mongol chieftain accepted several dragon robes but did not cease his incursions into Chinese territory.[4]

The standard form of dragon robe had a round neck fastening over to the right, falling straight to the ground, with the two main dragons on front and back extending over the shoulders (**fig. 1.10**) and later down the sleeves also. More important, and therefore more coveted, was a style which had the two dragons on the chest and back, with two more on the outside of the sleeves, while above the hem of the skirt was a horizontal band with pairs of smaller dragons at back and front (**fig. 1.11, plates 1, 2, 3**). Waves curled beneath them, while in the centre, between the dragons, a mountain rose from the waves. At first, the robes were a dark colour while the background colour of the band indicated status—yellow for the highest, with red for the others—but later the band was the same colour as the robe, which was often red, the dynastic colour. However, dragon robes in other colours were also worn. Imperial bodyguards in procession wore green, black, and white, while those eunuchs

Fig. 1.10 Li Zhen, also known as Duke Cao, wearing the first type five-clawed dragon robe. Early Ming. Nanjing Museum.

Fig. 1.11 Usual type of dragon robe showing the horizontal band of dragons around the skirt. From the Li family history, *Ch'i-yang Wang-shih-chia wen-wu t'u-hsiang*.

Fig. 1.12 A nobleman's presentation robe showing what may be the *qilin*. From the Wu family history, *Shan-yin-chou-shan Wu-shih chih-p'u*.

who were the principal attendants to the emperor wore black *mang* robes.[5] A further style had a seam around the waist from which pleats fell.

At the beginning of the dynasty, many dragon robes were made of brocade or *kesi*, but later, especially by the time of the Wanli Emperor, more were embroidered all over on silk or silk gauze, particularly in satin stitch or counted stitch, with no background cloth visible. A great many people and resources were devoted to the production of these robes: a typical one had approximately 250 stitches per square centimetre, totalling more than 6.5 million stitches for the whole garment and taking up to eight work-years to complete (plate 4). Dragon robes became very fashionable in the early years of the sixteenth century, with many officials ordering them freely, and ignoring the laws of 1459 which forbade anyone from having dragon robes made for himself. A decree of 1537 reiterated this, so officials tried harder to get allowances conferred by the emperor, but by the beginning of the seventeenth century laxity of enforcement was rife. Few Ming dragon robes have survived intact, probably because, as it was an honour to own one, the owners were buried in them. Many of those that have survived had been taken into Tibet as gifts and recut into the narrower-sleeved Tibetan *chuba* style. Others were recut during the following dynasty into the slimmer Manchu style, with the exception of the official red robes which were considered to be unlucky.

Presentation Robes

In 1518 the Zhengde Emperor (r.1505–21) began the custom of giving presentation robes to noblemen and members of the court. Each gown was embroidered according to rank with mythical creatures dispersed as on the other dragon robes, but with many smaller animals on chest, back, each shoulder, and a band around the skirt (fig. 1.12, plate 5).

The first rank was stated in the *Ming Shi*, the official history of the Ming dynasty, as being the *dou niu*, literally 'dipper ox': a three-, and later four-clawed dragon with down-curving horns like those of the oxen of northern China, and a tail ending in two curving outward projections. The second rank was the *fei yu* meaning 'flying fish', in fact a winged dragon with a forked fishtail. (These two mythical beasts did not appear after the end of the Ming dynasty.) The third rank was listed as the four-clawed *mang*; however, it is thought that this placement was incorrect as the *mang* would have taken precedence over the *fei yu* and the *dou niu* in that order.[6] The fourth and fifth ranks wore the *qilin*, commonly but erroneously described in the West as a unicorn. It was a composite creature, however, with a dragon's head with two horns, a scaly body, slender legs with cloven hooves, and a bushy tail. Sixth and seventh ranks wore the *bai ze*, a name originally given to the lion, but by the Ming it had become quite a different animal. Like the *qilin*, it had a dragon's head with two horns and a scaly body, but unlike the deer-like *qilin*, the *bai ze* had a lion's body with cat-like paws, and it was usually rendered in white with a coloured mane and a bushy tail.

Robes for Other Occasions

For everyday official business the *pao* or gown was worn. Such robes were cut with a plain round neck and a side-fastening opening based on the style of the earlier Chinese dynasties (**fig. 1.13**). The sleeves were deep and long enough to cover the hands on formal occasions. At each side of the skirt was an additional piece called a *bai* to add greater bulk. A second style had a straight lapel collar fastening to the side, and a gathered skirt from a seam at the lower hip. Round the waist was a stiff-hooped belt with ornamental plaques denoting rank. Made of twelve metres of silk brocade or self-coloured damask the robes were a display of dignity, wealth, and status as the length of the robe and the size of the sleeve indicated the wearer's importance. Movement was restricted because of the bulk of the robe, and they were quite impractical garments, in consequence, being only suitable for a sedentary life at court.

Fig. 1.13 Shen Du (1357–1434), an expert calligrapher and chancellor of the Hanlin Academy, wearing a red *pao* with an insignia badge depicting the crane. Nanjing Museum.

Differences between ranks were indicated in several ways, one being by the length of the robe, as defined by the distance from the ground, and the width of the sleeves. High-ranking officials from the first to the fourth rank, for instance, wore red robes with sleeves three *chi* wide (one *chi*, or one Chinese foot, measured 35 centimetres). Officials from the fifth to the seventh rank wore dark blue robes, and eighth- and ninth-rank officials wore green ones. Even the woven designs in the silk were regulated, with the first grade having a large single floral pattern and the second grade, a small single floral design; the third grade had a scattered floral pattern with no leaves; fourth and fifth grades had a small cluster of mixed flowers; sixth and seventh grades were similar but with slightly smaller clusters; while the eighth grade and below were of plain fabric. Materials used were silk brocade and gauze, satin, and ramie.

The robes worn by scholars taking the civil service examinations prior to becoming officials were cut like the robes of officials. The colour, however, was cream or pale green with wide bands of blue or black at cuffs, neck opening, *bai*, and round the hem (**fig. 1.14**).

For informal wear, or as an under-robe, a man wore a *bei zi*, a narrower robe which met edge-to-edge down the centre front and was fastened with ties at the chest (**plate 6**). These robes were decorated with dragons or other beasts according to the regulations for more formal robes, but they could also be in other designs. Underwear consisted of a thinner robe of silk, worn with a sash around the waist. Beneath this was a short jacket with long wide sleeves and a pair of loose trousers. In summer these were worn alone; in winter they were covered by a pair of leggings, fitting close to the ankles. Black knee-high boots made of felt or leather were worn by the imperial family and high officials, while scholars and students wore black shoes.

Fig. 1.14 A scholar in his light-coloured robe with a black border. Nanjing Museum.

Dress of the Lower Classes

Common people wore clothing made from cotton, as the cultivation of this plant was officially encouraged; prior to the Ming period hemp was the fibre normally used. Colours were restricted because the five official colours of yellow, red, blue, white, and black were the province of the ruling elite. The mass of the population could wear colours which were a mixture, such as brown, green, or paler shades. The wearing of embroidery on silk or satin was also discouraged, so cotton clothing was decorated with stencilled patterns. Tradesmen, craftsmen, and farmers were not allowed to wear boots; those in the north wore leather shoes, while those in the south wore straw sandals.

Accessories

Headwear

Men wore their hair coiled up in a topknot which was kept in place with hairpins and a black net cap made of knitted horsehair. The cap signified manhood, and a special ceremony was held to mark this

Fig. 1.15 A family ritual scene showing the son of a noble family about to have a cap placed upon his head at his coming-of-age ceremony. Late Ming. Bernard Vuilleumier.

when a young man reached twenty (**fig. 1.15**). The net cap could be worn alone or under any type of hat. Noblemen and officials wore the *fu tou* at important court meetings held in the presence of the emperor. Dating back to the Sui and Tang periods, this was the principal official hat during the Ming dynasty. Shaped like a rounded cap, it had two stiff wings at the back which projected apart at the sides. It was made of gauze, lacquered black for added durability. For all important ceremonies coronets were worn by officials, the rank being indicated by a diminishing number of rows of ridges on the crown (**chart 1.1**). For less formal events a four-sided square black satin or gauze hat with ribbons down the back was worn by officials and scholars. A black gauze or satin hexagonal skullcap was worn by men of the lower classes, a style which was echoed by those still worn in the early twentieth century.

Chart 1.1

Officials' Coronet Ridges and Girdle Plaques		
Rank	*Coronet*	*Girdle Plaques and Ribbons*
First	seven ridges	jade plaque; ribbon with four-colour motif of clouds and phoenix
Second	six ridges	rhinoceros horn plaque; ribbon as for first rank
Third	five ridges	gold plaque; ribbon with motif of clouds and crane
Fourth	four ridges	gold plaque; ribbon as for third rank
Fifth	three ridges	silver plaque; ribbon with eagle motif
Sixth/ Seventh	two ridges	silver plaque; ribbon with three-colour motif of magpie
Eighth/ Ninth	one ridge	black horn plaque; ribbon with two-colour motif of mandarin ducks

Belts and Clasps

Unlike the tight belts of the Yuan dynasty, Ming robes were worn with stiff hoop-like belts which stood away from the body. These girdles were made of leather, ornamented with horn, jade, gold, and silver plaques, and decorated with ribbons and motifs. The plaques denoted the wearer's rank, and this was the only regulated identification imposed at the beginning of the Ming dynasty. An emperor's belt had a greater number of plaques than an official's. There were five different shapes of plaque on the belt: the centre plaque, smaller ones to the sides, then side ones with openings underneath to hold the ribbons.

Insignia Badges

Insignia badges, *pu zi*, made their appearance in 1391 and were the only major innovation to costume introduced during this very conservative dynasty. Persian miniatures and Chinese woodblock prints depict Mongol nobles of the Yuan dynasty wearing squares with floral or bird and animal scenes woven directly onto the fabric of their robe at chest and back. These decorative squares did not denote rank, but the Ming court must have been influenced by them when they decided, twenty years after seizing power, to introduce badges of rank.

The emperor and his sons wore the circular medallions mentioned earlier, with coiled five-clawed dragons woven or embroidered in gold directly onto the robe and placed at chest, back, and at each shoulder. A further type of five-clawed dragon with huge bat-like wings, the *ying long*, was also worn by the emperor.[7] Only the emperor and his sons could wear the circular form, so the lower ranks wore square insignia which followed the order laid down for the presentation dragon robes. Badges were worn on the chest and back of the *pao* coat, and were very broad, with no real border, but the top edge of the square was often 3 to 6 centimetres narrower than the bottom edge to ensure that the sides of the square would not be hidden by the wearer's arms. Embroidered or tapestry-woven badges were made in one piece, but the brocade ones made for lower-ranking members of the imperial family, or presented as awards for merit, were woven directly into the robes and incorporated the centre back or front seam of the robe.

Other strange beasts such as the *dou niu* (**plate 7**), the *fei yu*, and the *mang* were bestowed by the emperor on high officials such as the chief eunuchs and others who merited them, and were a mark of imperial favour. These officials were forbidden to wear the five-clawed dragon unless it had, as was often the case, been awarded by the emperor to those especially deserving (**fig. 1.16**). Sons-in-law of the emperor, and dukes, marquises, and earls created by merit, wore a square which depicted the *qilin* (**plate 8**) or *bai ze*.

Officials' Badges

Officials were graded into nine ranks with the civil group distinguished by birds and the military by animals (**chart 1.2**). A further badge worn by officials with civil responsibilities was that belonging to the censors, those guardians of custom and fundamental laws who wore the *xie zhai*, a mythical animal with a white body and a horn to gore wrongdo-

Fig. 1.16 Imperial five-clawed, full-face dragon badge, satin stitch embroidery on silk gauze, gold couched dragon. 36 cm(H) x 35 cm(W), Wanli period. Private collection.

ers, which symbolized justice and roared when it encountered anyone flouting a law (**plate 9**).

The right to wear such insignia was bestowed by the emperor, but the official had to have it made. Badges were created separately in one piece then sewn to

Chart 1.2

Civil and Military Officials' Rank Badges			
	Civil		*Military*
Rank	1391–1527	1527–1644	1391–1644
First	crane or	crane	lion
Second	golden pheasant	golden pheasant	lion
Third	peacock or	peacock	tiger and/or
Fourth	wild goose	wild goose	leopard
Fifth	silver pheasant	silver pheasant	bear
Sixth	egret or	egret	panther
Seventh	mandarin duck	mandarin duck	panther
Eighth	oriole or	oriole	rhinoceros
Ninth	quail or	quail or	sea-horse
Unclassed officials	paradise flycatcher	paradise flycatcher	
Source: Cammann, *China's Dragon Robes*			

Fig. 1.17 Jiang Shunfu (1453–1504), a minister in the reign of the Hongzhi Emperor, wearing a first-rank civil badge depicting a pair of cranes. Nanjing Museum.

the robe so that they could be replaced if the wearer's rank changed. At first, some ranks had a choice of two birds or animals. This was because the square could be very costly, especially where the background was of gold thread, and so an official who was temporarily promoted, or who could expect promotion, could wear either the higher-ranking square or continue to wear the lower-ranking one. However, the gain in 'face' was considered worth the extra expense and the higher rank was almost always worn. The element of choice was abolished when it was found certain ambitious officials were taking advantage of the situation. The Jiajing Emperor instituted new laws in 1527 and all were ordered to wear insignia only of their own rank. At the same time, only one bird could depict each rank, though regulations for military ranks remained unchanged.

At first two birds were shown in a balanced composition, poised in flight (**fig. 1.17**), but later in the dynasty this was replaced by one bird perched on a rock or branch while the other was placed above, flying down. Initially, only sky formed the background of the badges, but later peonies and other flowers filled out the square, and towards the end of the dynasty many auspicious symbols were added. Once the idea of the two balanced birds was changed in the late Ming period, single birds began to appear and a highly stylized bird was seen. Some military ranks displayed two animals in a natural setting while others showed only one animal standing in heraldic pose on a rock (**plate 10**).

Imperial Festival Badges

Festival squares and roundels were popular towards the end of the dynasty, especially during the reign of the Wanli Emperor. These badges, which were worn by members of the imperial family and their household, appeared on many occasions throughout the year: Lunar New Year, the Lantern Festival, the Dragon Boat Festival, the meeting of the Oxherd and the Spinning Maiden, the Mid-Autumn Festival, Chong Yang, and the Winter Solstice, as well as the emperor's birthday (**fig. 1.18**). Symbols on the badges related to the festival being celebrated as well as evoking good fortune and long life. Often two symbols were combined to make the badge suitable for both occasions. A gourd on a New Year badge, for example, might have a canopy placed over it to resemble a lantern, thus making it appropriate for the Lantern Festival held two weeks later (**plate 11**).

Reasons given for the abundance of festivals throughout the year include the suggestion that the Mongol rulers of the preceding Yuan dynasty had suppressed Chinese festivals to the extent that none were celebrated officially. Secondly, continued pressure from Mongol and Manchu forces in the north during the latter part of the dynasty meant that celebrations were seen as relaxing diversions by the beleaguered Ming officials. Finally, the court eunuchs, who controlled household affairs and usually exerted great power and influence over the imperial family, enjoyed the relief festivals brought from monotony and hoped that through the attendant preparation the court would have less time for intrigue which might be to the eunuchs' detriment.

Fig. 1.18 An official or eunuch's front badge worn on the occasion of the emperor's birthday. Embroidered with two couched gold thread *shou* characters, satin stitch plum blossom, chrysanthemum, and *wan* symbol. 31 cm(W)(top), 35 cm(W)(bottom) x 35 cm(H), Wanli period. Private collection.

Notes

1   Although there is some argument as to whether the costume regulations were laid down in the twenty-fourth or the twenty-sixth year of the reign, the twenty-fourth appears correct as the *Ming Shi*, the dynastic history of the Ming dynasty '. . . under the date of July 5th, 1391, states that on that day it was announced that the officials and scholars of the Six Boards, the Censorate, and the Hanlin Academy, had assembled and again determined the laws for clothing; and this is followed by a detailed list of the costume prescribed....' Schuyler Cammann, 'The Development of the Mandarin Square', *Harvard Journal of Asiatic Studies*, 8 (1944–5): 76.

2   *Da Ming Hui Dian*, Wanli edition, vol. 2, compiled by Li Dong-yang et al, revised by Shen Shi-xing et al, reprint, 1989.

3   The number twelve occurs frequently in Chinese regulations as it was considered to be the number of Heaven, and a complete and auspicious number.

4   Schuyler Cammann, *China's Dragon Robes*, New York: Ronald Press, 1952, p. 14.

5   Cammann, *China's Dragon Robes*, p. 14.

6   Cammann, *China's Dragon Robes*, p. 17.

7   Schuyler Cammann, *Chinese Mandarin Squares: Brief Catalogue of the Letcher Collection*, Philadelphia: University of Pennsylvania, 1953, fig. 17.

Plate 1   Blue brocade dragon robe with seven *mang* in gold, placed one large on each of the front and back, two in profile on the front and back skirt, and one on the inside front skirt. Lined red hemp. 150 cm(L) x 190 cm(W), c.17th cent. Hong Kong Museum of Art.

Plate 2   Portrait of Wang Ao (1450–1524), a high-ranking official wearing a four-clawed dragon presentation robe. Nanjing Museum.

Plate 3   An attendant in a blue dragon robe leading the Jiajing Emperor's horse. National Palace Museum.

Plate 4   Back view of a four-clawed informal dragon robe with sleeves recut in narrower Tibetan style. Centre-opening with original collar and cuffs, counted stitch (250 stitches/cm^2) in indigo blue, green, yellow, red, and white on silk gauze. 121 cm(L), c.1450. Private collection.

Plate 5   Eunuchs and members of the Jiajing Emperor's court lighting firecrackers on a barge. National Palace Museum.

Plate 6   An informal robe, or *bei zi*, showing the *ying long* or winged dragon in profile each side of the centre-front opening. Embroidered onto red silk gauze and recut in the style of a Tibetan *chuba* with gussets at the underarms. 136 cm(L), Wanli reign. Private collection.

Plate 7   *Kesi* rank badge in polychrome silks on a gold background depicting a *dou niu*. Worn by a third-rank courtier.
33 cm(H) x 37 cm(W), 16th cent. Spink & Son Ltd.

Plate 8   Silk gauze rank badge of the *qilin* embroidered with counted stitch and interlaced strips of gilded paper. Worn by imperial noblemen. 40 cm square, 15th cent. Spink & Son Ltd.

Plate 9   Censor's rank badge depicting the *xie zhai* embroidered on dark blue silk background. 40 cm(W) x 38 cm(H), 15th cent. Private collection.

Plate 10   Third-rank military badge of a tiger, embroidered in couched gold thread onto a blue damask silk ground, with padded satin stitch clouds. 38 cm square, 17th cent. Private collection.

Plate 11   Festival badge for the Lantern Festival, embroidered on silk gauze and worn by a member of the imperial family. Diameter 36 cm, Wanli period. Private collection.

2 Women's Dress

An emperor was not limited in the number of wives and consorts he might have, although only one at any time could be designated empress. Emperors chose their wives and consorts from daughters of lower-ranking military officials and commoners to avoid the possibility of relatives of women from higher-ranking families gaining political power.[1] Furthermore, women at court were prevented from gaining too much influence by being secluded in their own apartments in the Forbidden City. No men apart from the eunuchs were allowed into their quarters, not even their physicians. This isolated the court ladies: they were trapped like birds in a gilded cage, spending their days painting and plotting, sewing and scheming amongst themselves **(fig. 2.1)**.

Fig. 2.1   Painting on a scroll of women embroidering and ironing. c.1494–1552. National Palace Museum.

Imperial Women's Dress

Ceremonial dress worn by the empress was made of deep blue silk with very wide sleeves almost sweeping the ground, a plain neck fastening over to the right side, and a long skirt. The robe was decorated with pairs of pheasants, while bands of dragons edged the neck, cuffs and hem **(fig. 2.2)**. A hooped belt with jewelled plaques was placed around the waist from which a *bi xi* hung in colour and fabric matching the robe. Rank was denoted by an

Fig. 2.2   Empress Tu (d.1554), mother of the Longqing Emperor, wearing a phoenix crown and robe decorated with pairs of pheasants. National Palace Museum.

embroidered neckband decorated with gold and jade which covered the chest. This was called a *xia pei*, and was the forerunner to the ceremonial vest worn by Han Chinese women in the Qing dynasty. Worn as early as the fifth century AD, it grew in popularity in the Sui and Tang dynasties, and was worn by members of the Ming imperial family as well as wives of officials on ceremonial occasions, and with semi-formal dress later in the dynasty (**chart 2.1**).

Chart 2.1

Women's Xia Pei *Pattern as an Indication of Rank*	
Rank	*Pattern*
Empress	dragons
Imperial concubines, wives of princes, and princesses	phoenixes
Wives of dukes, marquises, earls, and first- and second-rank officials	tartar pheasants
Wives of third- and fourth-rank officials	peacocks
Wives of fifth-rank officials	mandarin ducks
Wives of sixth- and seventh-rank officials	paradise flycatchers
Wives of eighth- and ninth-rank officials	flowers
Source: Schuyler Cammann, *China's Dragon Robes*, New York: Ronald Press, 1952.	

Fig. 2.3   Phoenix crown of six dragons and three phoenixes made of kingfisher feathers, enamel, and precious stones. From the tomb of the Wanli Emperor and his consorts. Museum of Dingling.

On formal occasions the empress wore a red gown which opened down the centre, had wide sleeves, and was decorated with pheasants and edged with bands of dragons. With it she wore a red *xia pei*. At less important occasions such as birthday celebrations, she wore a long gathered skirt and a *bei zi*. There were many styles of *bei zi*: some had narrow sleeves, while others were sleeveless, but the main characteristic was the front opening which met edge to edge down the centre-front. Reaching down to mid-calf and often with high side slits, the *bei zi* was an over-garment usually worn in the cooler months. They were made usually in red or blue silk embroidered with dragons (**plate 12**), and worn over a loose-sleeved red silk blouse (**plate 13**), also decorated with dragons. In the winter the *bei zi* was made of wadded silk or cotton.

A phoenix crown made of kingfisher feathers, pale blue enamel, and strings of pearls was embellished with nine dragons and four phoenixes, in addition to twelve flowers. For non-ceremonial occasions, the empress wore a crown which incorporated fewer phoenixes (**fig. 2.3**). At other times she might wear a coral phoenix crown and a yellow voluminous robe in silk or gauze, with a *xia pei*

in deep blue-green, embroidered with gold clouds and dragons (**fig. 2.4**).

Fig. 2.4   Phoenix crown and *xia pei*, with the dragon under-robe showing at the open neck. The Commercial Press Ltd., Hong Kong.

Dress of Noblewomen and Officials' Wives

Noblewomen and wives of officials wore robes with wide sleeves and a full skirt on formal occasions (**fig. 2.5**), or alternatively, a loose-sleeved blouse and a sleeveless overdress of red or dark blue. Attached to the robe was the insignia square bearing the rank of her husband. The *xia pei* was also worn, as well as the phoenix crown. Dragon robes corresponding in rank to those of their husbands' were worn, but the

Fig. 2.5   Blouse and skirt worn by noblewomen. The Commercial Press Ltd., Hong Kong.

Fig. 2.6   Wife of a prince wearing a four-clawed dragon robe and *xia pei* with phoenixes. The Commercial Press Ltd., Hong Kong.

main dragons faced the opposite direction, the front one over the right shoulder and the rear one over the left shoulder (**fig. 2.6**).

The informal robes worn by women were quite close-fitting by comparison with the masculine equivalent. For less formal wear a jacket with long sleeves was worn with a long flowing skirt which trailed on the ground (**fig. 2.7**). Light colours were popular for the skirt which became fuller as the dynasty progressed. By the seventeenth century the skirts were very full at the hem with many coloured ruffles. Waist sashes with small perfume pouches attached had ends which trailed to the floor.

Wives of courtiers, noblemen, and attendants to the imperial family also wore the slim fitting *bei zi*, either sleeveless, which was preferred as it gave greater movement, or with sleeves which became wider later in the dynasty. This garment was also worn as ceremonial dress by lower-class women. Decorated bands outlined the front edges and the cuffs (**fig. 2.8, 2.9**).

An unusual style of gown reaching to mid-calf was made up of small pieces of differently coloured cloth in a patchwork design. It fastened to the side like a Buddhist monk's robe. Initially, the patchwork pattern was balanced and the patches cut in rectangles, but later in the dynasty the patches became very irregular and were made of many different types of cloth. Because of its resemblance to the patchiness of paddy fields, the gown was called *shui tian yi*, meaning 'paddy field dress.' It continued to be worn into the early Qing.

Underwear for women was a pair of loose trousers fastened round the waist with a cord; the legs were tucked into stockings. A broad bodice, fastened in front with buttons or at the back with tapes attached to the corners, was worn over the breasts (**fig. 2.10**). Over this the woman wore a short, front-buttoning jacket with a high collar, in addition to the outer robes.

There were many different hairstyles for women; the majority involved binding the hair into a bun using jewelled pins or a net cap. If the hair was not long enough, detachable ready-made hairbuns

Fig. 2.7   Four ladies in waiting wearing the long-sleeved *bei zi*.

could be purchased. A headcloth made from black satin, or gauze for summer, was also used by young and old alike.

Fig. 2.8   Portrait of one of the Zhengtong Emperor's concubines wearing the *bei zi* and flowing skirt, with a diadem around her forehead. Palace Museum.

Insignia Badges

The empress and the highest noble-women, such as the wife of the heir-apparent, wore a square badge with the phoenix, or *feng huang*, a mythical bird. The phoenix was regarded as the king of birds which only appeared in times of prosperity and peace. Depicted as having a hen's head, a serpent's neck, a tortoise's back, and long wavy tail plumes, it was considered a divine bird able to fly to heaven, a product of the sun or fire and often shown look-ing at the sun.[2]

The birds were shown in pairs, with one bird, *feng*, having long serrated tail feathers representing the feminine aspect, and the other, *huang*, having curling plumes representing the masculine aspect (**plate 14**). Lower-ranking princesses wore the lesser female phoenix, called *luan*, against a floral background. Noblemen's wives and princesses outside the emperor's immediate family circle wore the pheasant, while wives of civil and military officials wore the same rank of bird or animal as their husbands (**fig. 2.11, plate 15**).

Fig. 2.9   A couple in the bed-room, the woman wearing a sleeveless overdress, or *bei zi*, over a wide-sleeved blouse. Palace Museum.

Fig. 2.10 Women undressing, wearing the bib brassiere and loose trousers, with the ends of the trousers tucked inside leg-gings. From the Ming block print *Lieh-nu-chuan*.

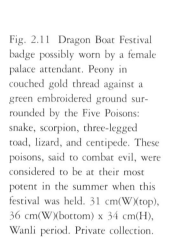

Fig. 2.11 Dragon Boat Festival badge possibly worn by a female palace attendant. Peony in couched gold thread against a green embroidered ground surrounded by the Five Poisons: snake, scorpion, three-legged toad, lizard, and centipede. These poisons, said to combat evil, were considered to be at their most potent in the summer when this festival was held. 31 cm(W)(top), 36 cm(W)(bottom) x 34 cm(H), Wanli period. Private collection.

Footwear

The cult of binding the feet to make them very small was already practised in China by this time. It is thought to have started in the fifty or so years between the end of the Tang dynasty and the beginning of the Song. One of the rulers of this period was Li Yu, and tradition relates that his favourite consort, Yao-niang, while dancing, bound her feet to represent a new moon. The fashion grew among the women at court, but following the Song dynasty the binding became so tight that dancing was impossible. During the Ming dynasty, the custom flourished and gradually the style spread to women outside court circles until it was almost universal in China. 'Lotus hooks', 'golden lilies', and 'golden lotus' were some of the euphemisms used to describe bound feet, and this exceedingly painful fashion lasted right up to the beginning of the twentieth century.

To cover the swollen ankles caused by binding the feet, leggings were worn. These were made of plain silk with an embroidered hem which hung over the shoe. They were fastened with ties around the calf, with the under-trouser legs tucked inside the leggings. Binding cloths were changed after bathing, but the

Fig. 2.12 Small shoes with embroidered uppers and stitched soles made for bound feet. Joint Publishing Co.

shoes and leggings were traditionally the last items of clothing to be removed inside the curtained bedchamber during lovemaking as the small feet and their smell were regarded as a strong aphrodisiac.

A pair of high-heeled bound-feet shoes, belonging to the secondary empress Xiaojing, was found in the Wanli tomb. The uppers are made of satin and embroidered with the symbols of longevity, pine and bamboo, while the heels are made of layers of paper covered with plain satin. Some high heels were made of camphor wood. Flat-heeled shoes with soles made of layers of stitched cotton and embroidered uppers with curving pointed toes were also worn (fig. 2.12).

Notes

1 Relatives of noblewomen in earlier dynasties had exerted great influence, and even usurped the throne. The taking of measures to avoid this problem was considered one of the great achievements of the Ming. Charles O. Hucker, *The Traditional Chinese State in Ming Times (1368–1644)*, Tucson: The University of Arizona Press, 1972, p. 43.

2 It is also a symbol of the empress and is depicted on traditional bride's clothing even in the 1990s, especially in Hong Kong.

Part II
The Qing Dynasty (1644–1911)

3 Manchu Men's Court Dress

The Great Wall, an achievement of the Qin dynasty, had been constructed to protect the fertile regions of central China from the barbaric nomads who lived to the north. Invasion from the north was a continual fear during the Ming era as the country began to be threatened by the Manchus, a confederation of settled tribesmen of Tungusic descent, together with some semi-nomadic Eastern Mongolian herdsmen from the region now called Manchuria. The Manchus raised reindeer, hunted, fished, and trapped animals for a living, and later set up an agrarian civilization similar to that of China. They traded sable furs and ginseng with the Ming army along the Liaodong Peninsula and, as a means of control, the Ming bribed the Manchus with dragon robes and silks as well as titles and favours.

Fighting between the Manchus made Nurhachi from the Aisin Gioro clan the head of the numerous clans, and the title of brigadier bestowed by Ming Chinese made him supreme chieftain of all Tungusic tribes in Manchuria. The first Manchurian chieftain of his time strong enough to be a great military leader, he was able to forge a new nation from people of differing origins and abilities. He drove the Ming forces out of the Liaodong Peninsula but died in 1626. His successor, Abahai, formally took the name Manchu for the collective tribes and attracted Chinese border troops into the Manchu army. After his death in 1643 his younger brother, Dorgon, acted as regent for Abahai's seven-year-old son.

By this time a Chinese rebel army had captured Beijing, an event which culminated with the Chongzhen Emperor (r.1627–44) committing suicide in the palace gardens on Coal Hill. Ming border troops from the Great Wall returned to Beijing to defend it, and Dorgon bribed the defending general Wu Sangui with a princely title and promised punishment for the rebels. General Wu allowed the Manchus through the Great Wall, and Dorgon and his army entered Beijing in June 1644, setting up his nephew as the first Manchu emperor, Shunzhi.

The Manchus named their new empire Qing, meaning 'pure'. The Manchus' intention was to remove the threat of invasion by taking control of the north and west borders, and to improve the quality of life by injecting better standards into an inefficient and corrupt government. During this dynasty China was to reach its greatest size to include Tibet, Inner and Outer Mongolia, and Taiwan. The descendants of Nurhachi maintained the fiction of a 'Manchu race' both in order to hold together an amalgam of people of differing origins and as a means of keeping their trusted followers from being sinicised.

Manchu Dress Regulations

In order to establish full control over the Han Chinese people, the Manchu emperors decreed that their customs, language, and especially their style of clothing should be adopted by the conquered race. In particular, all Chinese males were compelled to shave the front of their heads and wear their hair in a single plait, or 'queue'. Regulations first set down in 1636 before the conquest were revised and extended in 1644. As in preceding dynasties, the system of dress regulations was established to embrace and unite the country, but additionally they were enforced to make the Han Chinese indistinguishable from their Manchu rulers.

By 1759 the Qianlong Emperor (r.1736–95) was sufficiently concerned that the Manchu costume was being diluted by the Chinese style that he commissioned 'Illustrated Precedents for the Ritual Paraphernalia of the Imperial Court' (*Huangchao liqi tushi*), which was published and enforced in 1766. This was a series of illustrated regulations governing the style of dress for all official occasions for everyone, both Manchu and Han Chinese, who was employed in the service of the Manchu government. It included the clothing worn by the members of the imperial family down to clothing worn by officials employed in all aspects of the government. Clothing was divided into official and non-official, then subdivided according to the degree of formality. Thus official formal and semi-formal clothing would be worn at court and indicate rank, while official informal dress was for official travel, some court entertainment, and for important domestic events.

Additionally, there were rules governing the changing of clothing according to season, the timing of which was dictated by the Official Gazette from Beijing. When the month, day, and hour that the emperor would change his clothing from winter to summer and back was announced, anyone entitled to wear official dress had to follow suit, with those found not wearing the correct clothes at the correct time subjected to severe punishment.

The five colours favoured by the Ming continued to have symbolic properties for the Manchus. Blue was adopted by the Manchus as their dynastic colour, but red was generally avoided as it had been the official colour of the preceding dynasty, although it was worn occasionally by the emperor for the sacrifice to the Sun. However, because of its connections with the Ming rulers, red was considered a lucky colour by the Han Chinese and used extensively for weddings and celebrations. White was considered unlucky because of its association with death.

Robe colours were carefully controlled, and certain colours were reserved for the emperor and his immediate family. Bright yellow, representing central authority, was reserved for the emperor, although he could wear other colours if he wished or if the occasion demanded it; 'apricot yellow' was for the heir apparent; 'golden yellow', *jin huang*, actually orange, was worn by the emperor's sons. Imperial princes and noblemen wore blue or brown, unless they had been given the honour of wearing golden yellow by the emperor. Civil and military officials wore blue or blue-black.

Court Dress

Ming robes were already familiar to the Manchus as gifts in exchange for tribute to the Ming court, and despite their determination to impose their own culture and customs on the Han Chinese, they did adopt the pattern of the dragon robes, if not the style of them. The Manchus, having been hunters, had developed their own style of clothing using skins of the animals they caught, and they altered the cumbersome and impractical Ming robes to suit their more active way of life.

The *chao fu*, literally 'court dress', was official formal wear comprising the *chao pao* or court robe, *pi ling* or collar, hat, girdle, necklace, and boots. The wearing of the court robe for all important ceremonies and rituals was restricted to the very highest in the land: members of the imperial family, princes, nobles, dukes and high-ranking mandarins at court. The robe consisted of a short side-fastening jacket, which was attached to a skirt formed by a pair of pleated aprons to give the necessary impression of the bulk traditionally associated with festival garments. It is likely the garment was cut down from the voluminous Ming robes given to the Manchus before the conquest, with the dragons in cloud collar formation on the upper body, and the pleated skirt with the horizontal band of dragons around it. It has been suggested that the *chao pao* was originally made in two parts with a short riding jacket and a pair of pleated aprons worn over trousers, but it is a most un-Manchu-like garment as the bulky skirt with no slits at front and back would have been impractical for riding.[1] In any event, by the end of the eighteenth century the top and skirt were joined together as one, with a small flap called a *ren* at the side whose original function was to cover the fastening.

The Manchus imposed some of their nomadic features on the *chao pao* in the form of a curved overlapping right front, a shape derived from animal skins which was added for extra covering and protection and which fastened with loops and toggles, again nomadic in origin. One alteration, which became a standard feature of Manchu robes, was made to the sleeves which were cut above the elbow, the lower portion of the sleeves being replaced with ribbed silk, thought to have developed so that the wearer could bend his arm more easily when hunting. The sleeves ended in horse-hoof cuffs, originally intended to protect the hands when riding in bad weather and, during the Qing, to cover the hands, especially on formal occasions when it was considered impolite for them to be shown.

Fig. 3.1   Painting on silk of the emperor's first style of winter court robe, faced on the cuffs, collar, side opening, and hem with sable. Victoria and Albert Museum.

There were two styles of winter *chao pao* and one style of summer *chao pao* listed in the *Huangchao liqi tushi*. The first winter style was lined and lavishly faced with sable on the cuffs, side-fastening edge, *pi ling* collar, and with a deep band round the hem (**fig. 3.1**). Its use was restricted to the imperial family, the first three ranks of civil officials, or mandarins, and the first two ranks of military mandarins because of the amount of fur used and its sub-

Chart 3.1

First Style of Winter Court Robe		
Rank	*Colour*	*Dragon Placement*
Emperor	yellow (blue for ceremony at the Altar of Heaven)	four front-facing *long* placed on chest, back and shoulders; six *long* on front and back of skirt, placed as one front-facing and two profile; Twelve Symbols on upper part
Heir Apparent	apricot yellow	as above, but without the Twelve Symbols
Emperor's sons	golden yellow	four front-facing *long* on upper body; four profile *long* on skirt: two on front and two on back
First- and second-rank princes	blue, brown, or any colour unless golden yellow was conferred by emperor	as above
Third- and fourth-rank princes and imperial dukes	as above	four front-facing *mang* on upper body; four profile *mang* on skirt unless conferred *long* type
Chinese dukes and other nobles; first- to third-rank civil officials; first- and second-rank military officials; first-rank imperial guardsmen	blue-black	four profile *mang* on upper body; two profile *mang* on front and back of skirt

sequent scarcity. Both the second style of winter *chao pao* and the summer version were similar in design; only the fabrics were different. The second winter style was trimmed with otter fur (**fig. 3.2**), while the summer one was made of satin or gauze and trimmed with brocade (**fig. 3.3, plates 16, 17**) (**charts 3.1, 3.2, 3.3**). Those worn by the emperor and crown prince had a row of nine and seven medallions, respectively, above the band of dragons on the front and back of the skirt. Lower-ranking officials were restricted to the second type of winter robe and the summer style, but medallions on the skirt could not be worn, although this law was flouted during the nineteenth century.

The neck was adorned with the flared collar known as a *pi ling* or shoulder collar (**fig. 3.4**). The *pi ling* is thought to have developed from a hood which had been opened out along the

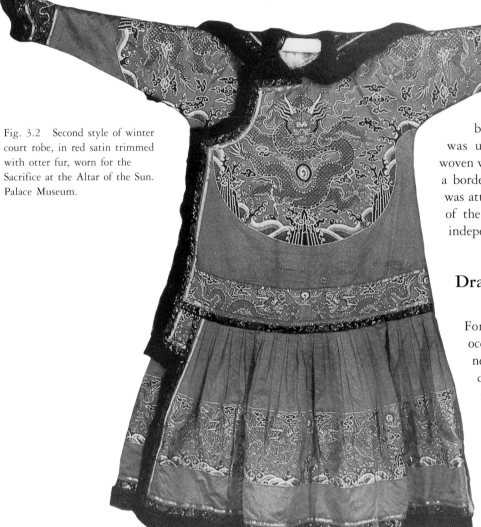

Fig. 3.2   Second style of winter court robe, in red satin trimmed with otter fur, worn for the Sacrifice at the Altar of the Sun. Palace Museum.

top of the crown to extend beyond the shoulders. It was usually embroidered or woven with dragon designs with a border around the edge, and was attached to the top button of the court robe or fastened independently.

Dragon Robes

For less important court occasions and official business, the *ji fu*, or festive dress, otherwise known in the West as a dragon robe, was worn. This was a full-length gown with sleeves and a curved overlapping right front based originally, like the top half of the *chao pao*, on animal skins, with two at the front and one at the back. Like the *chao pao*, it was worn belted, with purses containing daily necessities hanging from the belt. The Manchus later added slits at the front and back hems, in addition to those at the sides, to make it easier to wear when riding.

Circular medallions were used to depict rank for the imperial family and were a continuation of the Ming tradition, with the higher ranks having five-clawed dragons shown front-facing, or *long* or *mang* in profile for lower ranks (**fig. 3.5**). A portrait of the first Qing emperor shows him wearing a yellow

Plate 12 Sleeveless court vest belonging to Empress Dowager Li, mother of the Wanli Emperor, and made for her fiftieth birthday on 7 December 1595. Counted stitch embroidery on silk gauze with couched gold thread dragons and *shou* characters, lined
and wadded with silk floss. 140 cm(L). Asian Art Museum of San Francisco, The Avery Brundage Collection (1990.214).

Plate 13   Wide-sleeved silk blouse embroidered with dragons and 'one hundred boys'. Found in the tomb of Empress Xiaojing, imperial concubine of the Wanli Emperor; lower garment a recent reconstruction. Museum of Dingling.

Plate 14   Imperial princess's insignia back square with ascending and descending phoenix amid lotus, chrysanthemum, and peonies. Embroidered satin stitch on silk gauze. 31 cm(W)(top), 32 cm(W)(bottom) x 32 cm(H), Wanli period. Private collection.

Plate 15   Portrait of Madame Zhu wearing a red *pao* and civil eighth-rank badge depicting the oriole bird. Nanjing Museum.

Plate 16 Portrait of the Kangxi Emperor wearing the summer court robe with dragon medallions along the top of the skirt. Palace Museum.

Plate 17 Court robe belonging to an official. In dark blue satin, edged brocade, with gold couched dragons, satin stitch clouds, Peking knot Buddhist emblems, and six medallions on skirt at front and back. 138 cm(L), mid-19th cent. Private collection.

Plate 18   *Yue bai* ('moon white') brocade dragon robe made to be worn by a nobleman for a ceremony at the Altar of the Moon during the autumn equinox. c.1740. Teresa Coleman Fine Arts.

Plate 19   Emperor's Twelve Symbol dragon robe in *kesi*. 142 cm(L), late 19th cent. Valery Garrett.

Plate 20   Dragon robe in brown satin with edged brocade, indigo satin ribbed sleeves embroidered with clouds and bats, gold couched dragons, and Buddhist emblems in satin stitch. 131 cm(L), late 18th cent. Teresa Coleman Fine Arts.

Plate 21 Insignia back square showing front-facing *mang*, of counted stitch on gauze and worn by an imperial duke. 28.5 cm(W) x 27.5 cm(H), c.1800. Valery Garrett.

Plate 22 Festival procession with civil posturers wearing sashed robes and knee pads. c.1750. Hong Kong Museum of Art.

Chart 3.2

Second Style of Winter and Summer Court Robes		
Rank	*Colour*	*Dragon Placement*
Emperor	yellow (other colours according to occasion)	four front-facing *long* on upper body and four on strip at waist; nine dragon medallions on upper part of skirt at front and back; one front-facing, two profile *long* at front and back on lower skirt; Twelve Symbols
Heir apparent	apricot yellow	as above, but only seven medallions on skirt; no Twelve Symbols
Emperor's sons	golden yellow	four front-facing *long* on upper body; no medallions*; four profile *long* on skirt at front and back
First- and second-rank princes	blue, brown, or colours; golden yellow if bestowed	as above
Third- and fourth-rank princes and imperial dukes	as above	four front-facing *mang* on upper body; four profile *mang* on lower part of skirt at front and back
Chinese dukes and other nobles; first- to fourth-rank civil and military officials; first-rank imperial guardsmen	blue-black	as above
*Some later Qing officials added medallions to their robes, although officially they were not entitled to them.		

Fig. 3.3   Manchu nobleman wearing the summer court robe. Early Qing. Royal Ontario Museum.

robe with eight dragon medallions: at front and back, on each shoulder, plus two on each side of the skirt. The original Ming style, whereon the medallions were in the centre of the skirt, would have been impractical when the skirt of the robe was slit at the front and back seam.

Early robes continued the Ming tradition of the large curling dragons over chest and back with smaller ones at the hem (**fig. 3.6**) but, as the dynasty progressed, the size of the upper dragons became smaller and the lower dragons larger, until all became the same size (**plate 18**). Five-clawed dragons were the prerogative of the emperor and his immediate family, although he could bestow this honour on lesser officials. Such robes were known as *long pao*, while the *mang pao* or four-clawed dragon robes were for princes, noblemen, and officials. Towards the end of the dynasty, however, most robes were of the five-clawed variety and worn by all ranks, as it became unthinkable to be seen wearing the four-clawed dragon.

> The *ch'i-fu* [*ji fu*] is a schematic diagram of the universe. . . . The lower border of diagonal bands and rounded billows represents water; at the four axes of the coat, the cardinal points, rise prism-shaped rocks symbolizing the earth mountain. Above is the cloud-filled firmament against which dragons, the symbols of imperial authority, coil and twist. The symbolism is complete only when the coat is worn. The human body becomes the world axis; the neck opening, the gate of heaven or apex of the universe, separates the material world of the coat from the realm of the spiritual represented by the wearer's head.[2]

Fig. 3.4   *Pi ling* or court collar showing four-clawed dragons embroidered in satin stitch, edged gold brocade. Late Qing. Valery Garrett.

Chart 3.3

Other Types of Court Robes

Rank	Construction
Second-rank imperial guardsmen	as first style of winter court robe, but *pi ling*, side opening, cuffs and lower hem all faced with dark crimped satin; body of robe made of cloud pattern damask satin; strip of dragons at waist; square badges with profile *mang* at chest and back
Third-rank imperial guardsmen	as above, but without the strip of dragons at the waist
Fifth-, sixth-, and seventh-rank officials	as summer court robe, but made of damask satin with cloud pattern, edged with brocade; square badges on chest and back of profile *mang*
Eighth- and ninth-rank officials	as above, but with no badges

Fig. 3.5 Manchu nobleman wearing an eight-medallion robe with profile dragons. Mid-18th cent. Royal Ontario Museum.

Fig. 3.6 Early type of dragon robe, the two large profile dragons embroidered with satin stitch and couched gold thread. c.1675. Royal Ontario Museum.

The Twelve Symbols of Imperial Authority were avoided at first by the Manchus as being associated with the Ming and preceding Chinese dynasties. They were reintroduced by the Qianlong Emperor in 1759, appearing first on the court robes but later extended to the less-formal dragon robes. The first three symbols of sun disc, moon disc, and the constellation of stars, which was now reduced to three from seven, could only be worn by the emperor (**plate 19, fig. 3.7**).

Fig. 3.7   The Twelve Symbols, from top left: the sun disc with the three-legged rooster, the constellation of stars, the moon disc with the hare, the dragon, the mountain, the water weed, the grains of millet, the 'flowery bird' or pheasant, the fire, the sacrificial ax, the sacrificial cups, and the *fu* symbol or Symbol of Discrimination. Bernard Vuilleumier.

Colours for the *long pao* and *mang pao* were in accordance with those for the *chao pao* for all ranks from the emperor to officials. Nine dragons were embroidered on the robes for the emperor and princes: on chest, back, and each shoulder, with two at the front hem, and two at the back hem. The symbolic ninth dragon was hidden on the inside flap of the robe. The number nine, and the fact that it was hidden, had important symbolic connotations in the relationship between farmer and landlord known as the 'well-field' system.[3] Eight dragons were for lower-ranking officials, but towards the end of the dynasty, when weaker emperors imposed fewer constraints, most officials wore the nine dragon robe. The dragons on the upper part were usually front-facing, while those on the lower skirt were in profile (chart 3.4) (plate 20).

Dispersed among these emblems were cloud patterns, and at the hem of the dragon robes were waves and *li shui*, diagonal stripes of the five colours representing deep water. In the early years of the dynasty, the mountains and clouds were

Chart 3.4

Laws for Dragon Robes After 1759			
Rank	*Colour*	*No. of Dragons*	*No. of Slits in Skirt*
Emperor	yellow; others according to occasion	nine *long*	four
Heir apparent	apricot yellow	nine *long*	four
Emperor's sons	golden yellow	nine *long*	four
First- and second-rank princes	blue or brown	nine *long*	four
Third- and fourth-rank princes, imperial dukes, and other nobles	as above	nine *mang*	four
Chinese nobles and first- to third-rank officials	blue	nine *mang*	two (at front and back)
Fourth- to sixth-rank officials	blue	eight *mang*	two
Seventh- to ninth-rank officials*	blue	five *mang*	two
*In practice they did not wear dragon robes.			

towering and bold, but later they became shorter and unnatural, while the *li shui* became much longer and the waves more dominant. By the end of the nineteenth century the decorative elements had weakened, and the robes were cluttered with a multitude of symbols and lucky charms, with the Eight Buddhist Symbols and the Eight Daoist Emblems becoming very popular for use on court and dragon robes alike.

Imperial Surcoats

The circular embroidered form was extended to the *gun fu*, or imperial surcoat, which became part of official court dress after 1759. Here four medallions were placed at chest, back, and shoulders. The Qianlong Emperor, who loved pomp and pageantry, added the first of the Twelve Symbols, the sun and moon, to the shoulder medallions on his *gun fu*, while the medallions at chest and back had the *shou* character, meaning 'long life'. From the middle of the nineteenth century, a constellation of three stars was added to the front medallion, and a mountain to its counterpart at the back (**fig. 3.8**).

Other insignia badges were worn by lower-ranking princes and noblemen on the chest and back of the surcoat. Square rather than circular, they depicted the *long* or *mang* (**chart 3.5**) (**plate 21**).

Fig. 3.8 The Guangxu Emperor (fourth from the left) and members of the imperial family wearing insignia badges on their surcoats. c.1900.

Chart 3.5

Imperial Rank Insignia		
Rank	Insignia	Colour of Surcoat
Emperor	four medallions with front-facing *long*; sun on left shoulder, moon on right; *shou* character on front and back medallions	yellow, or others if desired
Emperor's sons	four medallions showing front-facing *long*	apricot yellow
First-rank princes	four medallions showing front-facing *long* on chest and back with profile dragons on shoulders	golden yellow
Second-rank princes	four medallions showing profile *long*	golden yellow
Third-rank princes	two medallions showing front-facing *mang* at chest and back	blue
Fourth-rank princes	two medallions showing profile *mang*	blue
Imperial dukes	two square badges showing front-facing *mang*	blue
Other non-imperial nobles	as above	blue

Court Attendants' Robes

There were many servants in the employ of the court to carry out varied duties. Eunuchs came to hold great power: they were the emperor's immediate attendants and were responsible for controlling household affairs. They were recruited from poor Chinese families and were the only men, apart from the emperor, allowed to stay overnight within the private areas of the Forbidden City. They wore *chao fu* and *ji fu* according to the imperial status granted.

Officials who attended ceremonies in company with the emperor wore robes for the occasion. For example, those who 'accompanied the plough' in the ceremony at the Temple of Agriculture performed by the emperor—an event which also took place throughout the country each year on Lunar New Year's Day—wore insignia squares on their surcoats which showed the sun among clouds above a triple mountain.

Musicians in the court orchestra wore red robes with square badges on chest and back depicting the yellow oriole. These robes fastened over to the right, with centre-front and back seams. As the badges were woven directly onto the robe, both were bisected by a centre seam.

Civil posturers who performed a slow ritual dance at major ceremonies such as the wedding of an emperor, and sacrificial occasions, wore robes in red, blue, pale blue, or black, according to the occasion. On the side-fastening coat, square embroidered badges with a large golden mallow flower were applied. Military posturers performed a more energetic dance and wore robes in similar colours, but in this case they were embroidered all over with small mallow flowers in couched gold thread. Sashes, not girdles, were worn around the waist. Knee pads tied around the trousers helped to hitch them up, as well as acting as protection when kowtowing. Standard-bearers who accompanied the emperor whenever he left the palace on an official procession wore robes with the *shou* character all over **(plate 22)**.

Accessories

Hats

Hats were an important feature of official dress, and were worn on every public occasion. From the eighth month of the Chinese calendar a winter hat was worn. The style worn with court dress by the emperor and other male members of the imperial family and high officials was called a *chao guan*. It had a turned-up brim of sable or fox fur, and a padded crown covered in red floss silk teased at the edge to stand out **(fig. 3.9)**.

For summer, beginning in the third month of the Chinese calendar, the hat was a conical shape made of finely

Fig. 3.9   Official's winter *chao guan* with double-eyed peacock feather plume. 19th cent. Murray Warner Collection of Oriental Art, University of Oregon Museum of Art.

woven split bamboo covered with silk gauze and edged with a narrow band of brocade. When first introduced in 1646 they had to be cut out of baskets and mats.[4] Those made for use at court were supplied latterly from a cottage industry in villages around Chengdu, the capital of Sichuan province. After two days or more of weaving, a stiff circle of woven rattan covered in red cotton was inserted and tying strings added. Fringes of red floss silk covered the crown from apex to edge (**fig. 3.10**). A *ji guan*, or festive hat, was worn on semi-formal occasions with the *ji fu*, and red silk fringing or dyed red horse or yak hair was used instead of floss silk (**fig. 3.11**).

Fig. 3.10 Summer *chao guan*, with gold and pearl hat insignia, belonging to the Qianlong Emperor. National Palace Museum.

Hat Insignia

Manchu laws relating to the insignia permitted on headwear dating back to 1636 were based on the advantages of a readily visible means of identification of different ranks of officials. For the imperial family the insignia was in the form of a tall gold finial intricately decorated with dragons, Buddhas, and tiers of pearls, the number of tiers dependant on the importance of the wearer. Court musicians wore yellow feather finials, civil posturers a flaming pearl, and the military posturers a trident.

In 1727 the Yongzheng Emperor (r.1723–35) issued an edict introducing a secondary kind of insignia to be worn on less formal occasions. The emperor himself then wore a knot of red silk on his hat on semi-formal and informal occasions (**fig. 3.12**) while

Fig. 3.11 Emperor's *ji guan* with red silk knob. Palace Museum.

Fig. 3.12 The Guangxu
Emperor's informal hat, satin
appliqué with red silk knob and
tassel. Palace Museum.

noblemen and officials wore a simpler form of round hat jewel.[5]

Girdles

The girdle, or *chao dai*,
and the ornamental
plaques on it were an
additional form of rank
identification. A leather
belt with jewelled
plaques had been worn by the
Ming, and the Manchu court adopted the practice
from 1636. However, the Manchu girdle was made of
tightly woven silk with two ribbons or ceremonial kerchiefs echoing those of
the Ming, a pair of purses, a knife case, and other items hanging from it. When
worn with the *chao fu* the kerchiefs were wide and pointed at the end, while
for the *ji fu* they were narrow and straight. Worn bound tightly around court
robes, the colours of the girdles were appropriate to the colour and rank of the
robe and wearer. Four ornamental plaques made of gold set with semi-precious
stones indicated rank **(fig. 3.13)**.

Fig. 3.13 Emperor's formal
court *chao dai* for wearing with
the *ji fu*. Drawstring aromatic
purses with Manchu script
detailed on the outer ones in
seed pearls and gold beads, the
inner one in Peking knot,
together with a knife purse,
compass purse, and toothpick
case. National Palace Museum.

Necklace

The *chao zhu*, sometimes
referred to as a mandarin
chain, developed from a
Buddhist rosary sent in
1643 by the Dalai Lama
to Shunzhi, who became
the first Qing emperor.
The necklace had 108
small beads with four
large beads of contrast-
ing stone known as *fo tou*
and said to represent the
four seasons; these were
placed between groups of
twenty-seven beads.
These necklaces had a
practical purpose too, able
to be used for rapid cal-

culations if no abacus was on hand. On the *fo tou* bead between the counting strings was a long drop extension called a *bei yun* (back cloud) which hung down the back and served as a counterweight as well as an ornament. Three counting strings were also added by the Manchus and were worn with two strings on the left and one on the right. The *chao zhu* worn by the emperor was made of pearls, coral, and jade, while other members of the imperial family were permitted to wear any semi-precious stone other than pearls.

Footwear

Yellow satin boots decorated at the cuff were worn by the emperor, plain black satin ones by the lower ranks. They were knee-high, and made with the leg part a little longer than was necessary so that it lay in folds around the ankle. Leather piping reinforced the front and back seams. Thick soles of 7 centimetres were made of layers of felted paper with a final layer of leather, then whitened around the edges. Inflexible soles originally allowed the Manchu wearer to stand in the stirrups when riding, but the soles were made shorter than the uppers at the toe to make them easier to walk in (**fig. 3.14**).

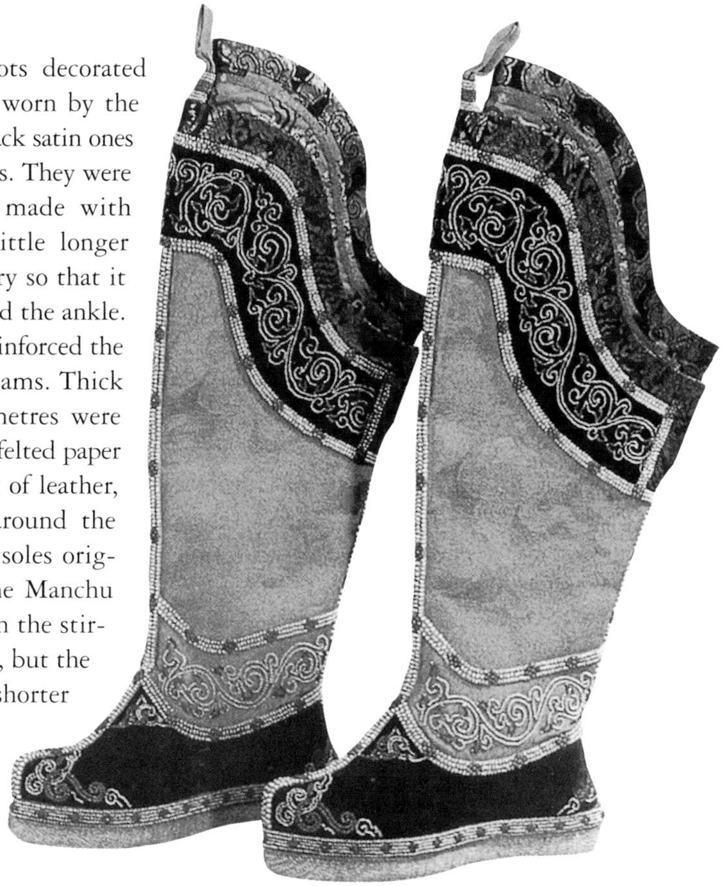

Fig. 3.14 Emperor's yellow satin boots, the tops edged with brocade, decorated with pearls and coral beads. Palace Museum.

Notes

[1] Possible evidence of a two-piece garment stems from the existence of a two-panelled skirt attached to a waistband dating from the mid-eighteenth century in the Victoria and Albert Museum, London. John E. Vollmer, *In the Presence of the Dragon Throne*, Toronto: Royal Ontario Museum, 1977, p. 36; Verity Wilson, *Chinese Dress*, London: Victoria and Albert Museum, 1986, p. 33.

[2] John Vollmer, *In the Presence of the Dragon Throne*, p. 40.

3   'This protecting arrangement referred to the centrally controlled, ideal land division called the *well-field* system. The name, *well-field*, was derived from the character for well—two horizontal lines crossing a pair of verticals. This system marked off nine sections; it symbolized the ideal relationship between farmers who actually worked the fields and the lord who owned the land. Eight farmers were envisioned as working each of the eight fields around the perimeter. All participated in the work necessary to farm the central ninth field. The eight fields protected their ninth by encircling it.' John E. Vollmer, *Five Colours of the Universe*, Edmonton, Alberta: The Edmonton Art Gallery, 1980, p. 22.

4   Verity Wilson, *Chinese Dress*, p. 27.

5   See charts 5.2 and 5.3.

4 Manchu Women's Dress

In order to maintain the 'purity' of the Qing dynasty, the emperors chose their wives from daughters of eminent Manchu families, and although for reasons of political alliance they were sometimes chosen from important Mongol families, wives were not selected from among the Chinese. Qing emperors continued the Ming system of polygamy in order to produce many offspring to ensure the succession; the Kangxi Emperor (r.1662–1722) for example, sired thirty-five sons. In addition to wives, the emperors had many consorts who were recruited every three years, aged between twelve and fifteen, to become Excellent Women. Taken from the important military families of the Eight Banners, their parents could be severely punished if they did not register their daughters' names for selection. If chosen, the girls would spend their time inside the Forbidden City until the age of twenty-five when they were 'retired' and free to leave if they wished. Another group of women in the palace were the daughters of the imperial bond-servants who took care of the personal duties of the emperor and his family. At whim, the emperor could also select a girl from this group to be his concubine or even his next wife.

A Manchu woman's status, like her Chinese counterparts, was determined by that of her husband or father, and women held no official role in the government. However, an empress dowager could act as regent during a ruler's minority, and even held more power than the reigning emperor himself on occasion, due to the importance attached to filial piety.[1] Other women's appearances in public were limited to occasions when they accompanied their husbands, though there were some ceremonial events when women from the imperial family would officiate in their own right. For example, at the Mulberry Leaves Ceremony, the empress and women from her court would ritually pick the first and finest leaves from the sacred grove of mulberry trees to feed silkworms which would then produce silk for state sacrificial dress.

Court Dress

Little is known about early imperial female robes until court and official dress was standardized in 1759. Then, women's clothing—like that for men—was divided into official and non-official, then subdivided according to the degree of formality. Rules for clothing were also in accordance

Chart 4.1

Women's Court Robes After 1759		
Rank	Colour	Pattern
Empress, empress dowager, first-degree consorts	yellow	first winter style: front-facing *long* on chest, back and shoulders; two profile *long* on skirt at front and back; edged in sable
	yellow	second winter style: design as emperor's second winter style, including *long*, edged in otter
	yellow	third winter style: as first winter style but split skirt at back, including *long*, edged in otter
	yellow	first summer style: as second winter style but edged with brocade
	yellow	second summer style: as third winter style but edged with brocade
Heir apparent's consort	apricot yellow	as above
Second- and third-degree consorts	golden yellow	as above
Fourth-degree consorts	*xiang se*	as above
Wives and daughters of first- and second-degree princes	brown, blue	third winter and second summer styles
Wives of other nobles and first- to third-rank officials	blue-black	as above, but with *mang*
Wives of fourth- to seventh-rank officials	blue-black	as above, but with two confronting profile *mang* on front and back

with the season, and changes were made from silk gauze in summer, through to silk and satin, padded or fur-lined, for winter. The seasons for both sexes changed from one to another on a set day on the issuance of an imperial decree.

Official formal dress worn at court, *chao fu*, comprised a full-length garment with a square-cut lapel opening and projecting shoulder epaulets called a *chao pao* (**plate 23**). As with men's robes, the ground colour and arrangement of dragons indicated rank (**chart 4.1**). This garment was worn with a hat, a large flaring collar called a *pi ling* shaped like the man's, and a long, sleeveless vest called a *chao gua*. Beneath the *chao pao* was a skirt made from a single length of silk with eighteen pleats falling from a plain waistband. It was embroidered with small roundels containing the *shou* character, flowers, and dragons around the hem.

There were *chao pao* for winter and summer, the winter ones being subdivided into three types. The first type of winter *chao pao* was a long gown with front-facing and profile dragons displayed over it, with wave motifs at the hem, but without the *li shui* until almost the end of the dynasty. The projecting epaulets on the *chao pao* were thought to be linked to a pre-Qing costume feature which originally protected the arms from bad weather. At the upper part of the long sleeves were bands of coiling dragons inserted above the plain dark-coloured section which ended in horse-hoof cuffs. It was lined with white fur and edged with sable. Colours of the women's robes matched those of their husbands, while a greenish yellow, *xiang se*, was worn by daughters of the emperor and the lower-ranking consorts.

The second variation was very similar to the men's *chao pao*, being made in two sections with a pleated skirt attached to a jacket similar in construction to the first style. A four-lobed yoke pattern of dragons extended over the chest, back, and shoulders, while above the seam of the top and skirt was a band of dragons. A further band of dragons was placed on the lower part of the skirt.

The third style was again similar to the first, but with a centre-back split in the skirt which had black fox fur trim. Unlike the first two styles, this could be worn by women other than those belonging to the imperial family.

Summer *chao pao* were of two types. The first was made of two sections similar to the second type of winter robe (**fig. 4.1**). The second summer style was identical to the third type of winter robe, but made of gauze or satin and edged with brocade (**plate 24**).

Fig. 4.1   First style of summer *chao pao* in yellow, belonging to an empress or empress dowager. Painting on silk from the *Illustrated Precedents for the Ritual Paraphernalia of the Imperial Court*. Victoria and Albert Museum.

Fig. 4.2   Wan Rong, wife of the Xuantong Emperor, wearing the first style of *chao gua*, with the *zai shui*, *chao guan*, and *pi ling*. c.1922.

Worn with the *chao pao* was a full-length sleeveless vest, opening down the centre, called a *chao gua*, or court vest. An antecedent was a sleeveless vest of trapezoidal shape worn by the Ming empress, although the deeply cut arm-holes and sloping shoulder seams appear to be derived from an animal skin construction. A long triangular pendant called a *zai shui* was a ceremonial kerchief which was fastened to a button on the court vest (or dragon robe) to indicate rank.

Again, as with the *chao pao*, there were three styles of *chao gua*, made of dark blue silk edged with brocade. The first had three sections: an upper part, the part from the waist to the knee, and from the knee to the hem. Five horizontal bands of *long* or *mang* and lucky symbols were dispersed around the wearer according to rank (**fig. 4.2**). The second type, similar to the second style of *chao pao* with a sleeveless body part joined to a pleated skirt, is very rare, and like the first style was worn only by members of the imperial family (**fig. 4.3**). The third style with ascending dragons in profile and wave motifs, and later *li shui*, could be worn by all ranks of women (**fig. 4.4**). Lower-ranking noblewomen and officials' wives wore either the third style of winter *chao pao* or the second style of summer *chao pao*. This was worn with the third style of *chao gua* and the *pi ling*.

A further kind of *chao gua* not mentioned in the *Huangchao liqi tushi* is a full-length sleeveless vest with a background colour of yellow, green, white, and possibly other colours as well, with ascending dragons in profile, edged with a velvet band and brass studs. The deep fringe at the hem, which is lined behind, suggests a hybrid garment which has developed from the Chinese women's *xia pei* or ceremonial vest.

Fig. 4.3   Painting on silk depicting the second style of *chao gua* for an imperial consort. Victoria and Albert Museum.

Formal Headwear

The *chao guan*, similar to the winter hat worn by men, incorporated a fur brim, a crown covered with red floss silk tassels, and an inverted gourd-shaped flap of fur at the back. Early in the Qing dynasty, the empresses and women of the imperial family wore a summer as well as a winter hat, but by the reign of the Kangxi Emperor the winter style was worn throughout the year. In summer, the hat brim and neck flap were faced with black satin or velvet (**fig. 4.5**). The hat finial was formed of tiers of golden phoenixes and pearls, and additional gold phoenix ornaments decorated with pearls were placed on top of the red floss silk crown. This creation was then worn with a diadem made of gold, inlaid with semi-precious stones, which encircled the forehead.

Fig. 4.4   An imperial princess wearing the third style of *chao gua. c.1900.*

Court Necklaces

The ladies of the imperial family wore a *chao zhu* or court necklace, similar in style to that worn by their husbands, but two additional necklaces crossing from left shoulder to right underarm, and vice versa, were also worn. Only the empress or empress dowager could wear pearls for the main necklace, the other two being made of coral. Amber and coral were worn by lower-ranking consorts and princesses, while other members of the family were permitted to wear any type of semi-precious stone not restricted to the empress and empress dowager. Imperial ladies would wear a *ling yue,*

Fig. 4.5   Summer hat of a first rank imperial consort. Brim and back flap in black velvet, red floss silk fringing on crown, seven gold phoenixes set with pearls, with one golden pheasant at the back and three phoenixes on the hat finial. National Palace Museum.

a jewelled torque or collar made of gold inlaid with pearls and coral, on the most formal occasions.

Dragon Robes

For semi-formal official dress, *ji fu*, or festive dress, women within the imperial family wore the *long pao*, a side-fastening robe embroidered with five-clawed dragons, with long sleeves ending in horse-hoof cuffs. The only variation from the dragon robes worn by men was the lack of splits at centre-back and front hem, while robes for the empress and high-ranking noblewomen included additional bands of dragons on the sleeves just above the plain area.

Fig. 4.6 Manchu noblewoman wearing the first style *long pao* with the *zai shui*. Early 19th cent. Royal Ontario Museum.

Chart 4.2

| *Women's Dragon Robes* | | |
Rank	Colour	Pattern
empress, empress dowager, first-rank consorts	yellow	nine *long*
heir apparent's consort	apricot yellow	nine *long*
second- and third-rank consorts	golden yellow	nine *long*
other imperial consorts	*xiang se*	nine *long*
wives of first- and second-rank princes	blue, brown*	nine *long*
wives of other nobles and first- to third-rank officials	blue, blue-black	nine *mang*
wives of fourth- to sixth-rank officials	blue, blue-black	eight *mang*
wives of seventh- to ninth-rank officials	blue, blue-black	five *mang*
*golden yellow if conferred on her husband		

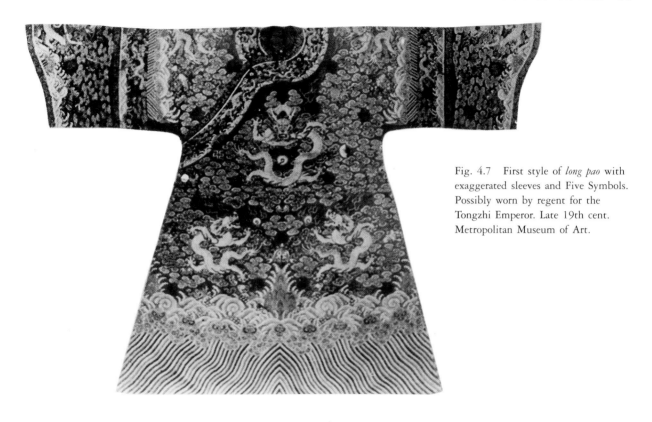

Fig. 4.7   First style of *long pao* with exaggerated sleeves and Five Symbols. Possibly worn by regent for the Tongzhi Emperor. Late 19th cent. Metropolitan Museum of Art.

Again, there were three types: the first, worn by all women, had dragons dispersed over it, the colour and number of dragons indicating rank (**chart 4.2**), and a wave border at the hem (**fig. 4.6**). Later in the nineteenth century, these robes had the exaggeratedly wide horse-hoof cuff sleeves (**fig. 4.7**). Noblewomen and officials' wives wore the *mang pao*, the four-clawed dragon robe in this style. Use of the Twelve Symbols was restricted to the emperor but he could, if he wished, confer the right of use on others, and some women's robes bearing up to twelve symbols are extant, having belonged to an empress or imperial consort (**plate 25**). The second style of *long pao* having eight medallions of dragons with a wave pattern hem was officially restricted for wear by the empresses (**fig. 4.8**). However, some made later in the dynasty with the wide sleeves and wide horse-hoof cuffs popular by this time have this medallion pattern on them and were worn by noblewomen. The third type was also for wear only by the empress and had the eight medallions with no wave pattern (**fig. 4.9**).

For informal occasions, the robes were cut in the same style as the dragon robe with the horse-hoof cuff, but were made of plain-coloured silk damask edged with bands of embroidered dragons at the *tou jin*, or curved opening at the neck, and sleeves (**plate 26**).

Fig. 4.8   Second style of *long pao* with eight dragon medallions embroidered on brown brocade. The robe, bearing the 'hundred cranes', symbols of longevity, is from the tomb of Prince Guo Jinwang (d.1738) and his consorts. 138 cm(L), Yongzheng period. Nelson-Atkins Museum of Art.

Fig. 4.9   Third style of *long pao* with no *li shui,* in yellow silk with eight dragon medallions in *kesi.* 172 cm(L). Victoria and Albert Museum.

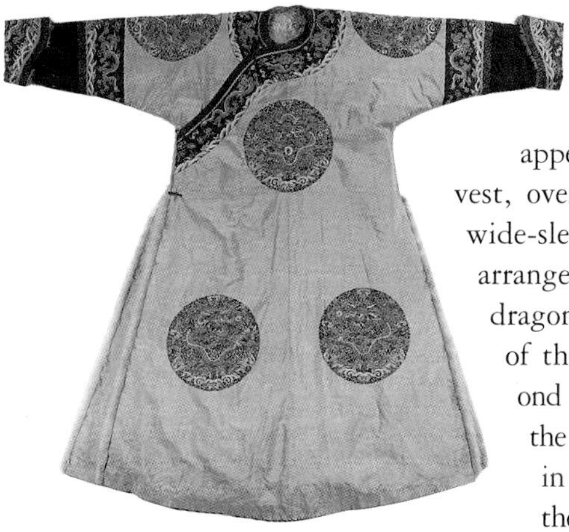

When empresses, high-ranking consorts, and noblewomen appeared in public, they were required to wear the *long gua,* or dragon vest, over the *long pao.* This garment was a full-length, centre-opening, wide-sleeved surcoat in blue-black satin or gauze with dragon medallions arranged over it. There were two types: one had eight medallions of dragons displayed on chest, back, shoulders, and front and back hem of the coat together with the *li shui* pattern, similar to that on the second style of *long pao* (**fig. 4.10**). The other had the medallions without the wave border as in the third style of *long pao.* Several of the empresses in the nineteenth century added the first four of the Twelve Symbols to the upper four medallions.

Imperial princesses were supposed to wear the upper four or two medallions, on a plain surcoat or *pu fu*, corresponding to their husbands' rank, although it seems they preferred to wear the *long gua* with *li shui*. Lower-ranking noblewomen were required to wear the surcoat with eight medallions of flower motifs surrounding the *shou* character and no *li shui*. Wives of officials were also supposed to follow this rule, but in practice they wore the *pu fu* bearing their husbands' badge of rank.[2]

Semi-formal Headwear

The *ji guan*, or festive hat, worn by empresses and imperial consorts resembled that of the emperor's winter hat with the red silk tassels and fur brim, while in summer the brim was faced with satin. It was topped with a pearl if worn by the empresses or those women given the right to wear the pearl. Worn around the forehead, a silk band had a jewel at the centre front and replaced the gold diadem. Lower-ranking noblewomen wore a more elaborate hat, the crown of which was covered with red or blue satin, decorated with semi-precious stones. Small bouquets of flowers were tucked in each side just above the ears. Two wide embroidered streamers hung from the back and it was topped off with a red silk knot on the crown (fig. 4.11). Another style of headdress for festive occasions was made like an inverted basket and was known as a *tian ze*. The framework was made of woven rattan or wire, covered with black gauze or silk net and dressed with many jewelled ornaments (fig. 4.12).

Fig. 4.10 The Guangxu Emperor's consort, Dowager Duan Kang, wearing the first style *long gua* and *long pao*; the headdress is decorated with jewels and artificial flowers.

Fig. 4.11 Noblewomen's *ji guan* with blue satin crown and streamers, decorated with pearls, kingfisher feathers, and precious stones, black sable fur brim, red silk cord knob. National Palace Museum.

Non-official Robes

Non-official formal robes were worn for weddings and for other important family occasions not connected with the court. Toward the end of the nineteenth century formal robes, like the dragon robes of this period, had wide sleeves with horse-hoof cuffs, and a plain band rather than a ribbed one between cuff and upper sleeve. In practice, these robes were the same as those worn for official formal occasions by noblewomen and the wives of officials. Eight medallions with the *shou* character or, later, other motifs were dispersed over the robe with *li shui* or a plain hem (**fig. 4.13, 4.14**). Worn with a surcoat with eight medallions with *shou* or floral patterns, some had the *li shui* pattern at the hem and cuffs, while others did not (**fig. 4.15, 4.16**).

Fig. 4.12 *Tian ze* headdress of wire lattice shaped like an inverted basket, woven with black silk ribbon and decorated with kingfisher feather inlay and gold filigree in the style of the Endless Knot, with butterflies and *shou* character. Palace Museum.

Fig. 4.13 Noblewoman's non-official formal *pao* in golden brown satin with eight medallions embroidered with bats surrounding *shou* characters. From the tomb of Prince Guo Jinwang (d.1738) and his household. 137 cm(L). Metropolitan Museum of Art.

Fig. 4.14 Non-official formal *pao* with eight floral medallions. Qianlong period. Palace Museum.

Fig. 4.15 Noblewoman's robe in green silk *kesi* with medallions containing lanterns surrounded by Buddhist emblems. To be worn at the Lantern Festival. 1875–1900. Murray Warner Collection of Oriental Art, University of Oregon Museum of Art.

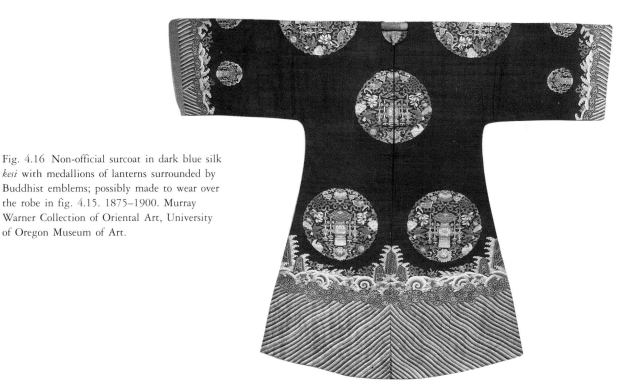

Fig. 4.16 Non-official surcoat in dark blue silk
kesi with medallions of lanterns surrounded by
Buddhist emblems; possibly made to wear over
the robe in fig. 4.15. 1875–1900. Murray
Warner Collection of Oriental Art, University
of Oregon Museum of Art.

Fig. 4.17 Empress Dowager
Cixi wearing non-official semi-
formal robe emblazened with
shou or long-life characters,
headdress, neckband, and nail
extenders. Late 19th cent.

Non-official semi-formal robes were very lavishly embroidered, particularly
those worn by the Empress Dowager Cixi (1835–1908) who preferred to wear
pastel shades of blue and lilac as she felt the
yellow dragon robes were unflattering to her
ageing skin tone (**fig. 4.17, plate 27**). The
contrasting borders on clothing after the
middle of the nineteenth century were based
on Han Chinese styling and indicated an
assimilation of Chinese culture. On the non-
official robes of the late nineteenth century
there often appeared three very wide bands:
the outer made of brocade, the middle a wide
border of embroidery, and the inner a multicoloured woven ribbon (**fig. 4.18**). Semi-formal robes had wide sleeves with turned-back
cuffs which were then lavishly embroidered
on the underside. A separate narrow neckband which crossed over at the side was
embroidered and denoted rank, and was worn
in place of the *zai shui*.

Fig. 4.18 Empress Dowager
Cixi and ladies of her court.
1903.

In addition to the rules governing type of fabric for certain times of the year, each season had its own flower which frequently appeared on semi-formal robes. The flower for winter was plum blossom, for spring the peony, for summer the lotus flower, and for autumn the chrysanthemum. For ladies at court in the late nineteenth century, to wear the wrong flower was to disobey the imperial decree and risk incurring the wrath of the Empress Dowager.[3]

A full-length cape, which was pleated into a neckband and then fell straight to the hem, was often worn by the Empress Dowager when the weather was cooler (**fig. 4.19**).

Informal robes were plainer than the semi-formal ones, with a silk damask body edged with a less elaborate border on straight cuffs, round the neck and down the side, and sometimes without the hem borders of the more formal types (**fig. 4.20**). Inner robes opened at the neck and *tou jin* only. They were worn with a long or short sleeveless waistcoat with a wide decorated border, or a short jacket (**plate 28**).

Fig. 4.19 Empress Dowager
Cixi wearing an embroidered
cape in the garden of the
Summer Palace, with her lady-
in-waiting Princess Der Ling.
c.1905.

Fig. 4.20 Daughters-in-law of Prince Ting in informal dress. c.1910.

Headddress

The headdress worn by Manchu women for unofficial occasions was a very elaborate affair. The bat-wing shapes were made of false hair (**fig. 4.21**) or black satin arranged over a frame. It was said that the hair itself was set and shaped this way originally, but during the nineteenth century it was replaced by black satin as being more practical and easier to keep in order. Large artificial or fresh flowers were placed at each side, silk tas-

Fig. 4.21 Headddress made of false hair worn by a Manchu noblewoman.

sels hung down and the whole creation was embellished with jewelled ornaments. At other times, or when the headdress would be too cumbersome, Manchu women wore a simple centre-parted hairstyle decorated with flowers and hair ornaments.

Footwear

Manchu women did not bind their feet, and those who belonged to the lower ranks wore a flat-soled shoe of embroidered silk or satin. Women from higher-ranking families wore a special shoe which gave the appearance of a small foot.

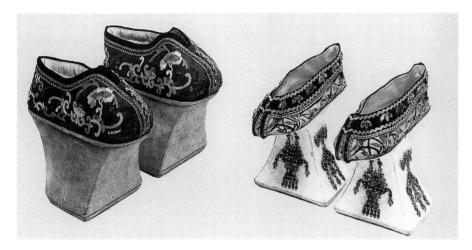

Fig. 4.22 Manchu women's shoes with concave heels, embroidered with jewels. Palace Museum.

This was an exaggeratedly elevated shoe with a concave heel in the centre of the instep. When the shoe was worn only the toe showed, giving the illusion of smallness but without the pain and discomfort associated with bound feet.

> The shoes stand upon a sole of four or six inches [ten to fifteen cm.] in height, or even more. These soles, which consist of a wooden frame upon which white cotton cloth is stretched, are quite thin from the toe and heel to about the centre of the foot, when they curve abruptly downwards, forming a base of two or three inches square [five to eight cm.]. In use they are exceedingly inconvenient, but . . . they show the well-to-do position of the wearer. The Manchus are . . . a taller . . . race than the Chinese, and the artificial increase to the height afforded by these shoes gives them at times almost startling proportions.[4]

The bottom of the shoe was padded with layers of cotton to prevent jarring. The uppers were made of satin embroidered with many designs of flowers, birds, and fruit (**fig. 4.22**). Vertical seams at toe and heel had leather strips inserted to hold the shape.

Notes

[1] The Empress Dowager, Cixi, co-regent for her son and then for her nephew, virtually controlled the government of China between 1860 and 1908.
[2] See chapter 5.
[3] Princess Der Ling, *Imperial Incense*, New York: Dodd, Mead & Co., 1933, p. 49.
[4] Alexander Hosie, *Manchuria, Its People, Resources and Recent History*, London: Methuen & Co., 1904, p. 157.

5 Mandarins and Their Attire

When the Manchu rulers took control of China, it was their intention to follow the system of government already in use by the preceding Ming dynasty, but with checks applied to the weaknesses which had brought about its downfall. Social status was controlled by the imperial government,[1] and it was from a highly-educated group of Manchu and Chinese men that officials known as mandarins were selected.[2] There were two orders: the first, and more highly respected, were the civil mandarins—scholar officials who administered the government of China—while the military officials were responsible for the internal stability and external defence of the country. Within the two orders, civil and military, there were nine ranks, each subdivided into principal and secondary classes.[3]

The Examination System and Graduates' Dress

Civil Examinations

The main route to becoming a civil mandarin was through success in a series of difficult qualifying examinations based on the Chinese classics, which enabled the applicant to become eligible for appointment to office. Selected candidates took an examination in the first of the series which was held annually in the prefectural cities of each province. A pass has been compared by some writers to today's bachelor of arts degree in the West. A successful candidate would become a *sheng yuan*, or government student, colloquially known as *xiu cai*, meaning 'budding talent'. The graduation ceremony was held at the literary chancellor's *yamen* (a walled establishment containing his residency and offices). The graduate wore a long, blue silk gown with horse-hoof cuffs called a *nei tao*, and black satin boots. A red silk scarf was placed diagonally across the chest and tied under the opposite arm at the hip. Two branches of nine leaves made of gold leaf or brass foil were fastened to his winter or summer hat on each side.[4]

The second degree examination was held in the eighth moon of every third year in the provincial capitals (**fig. 5.1**). This was known as the 'deserving promotion' degree (*xiang shi*), and was roughly equivalent to a master of arts. A very small percentage of those taking it achieved success. Strict quotas were imposed nationwide, based in general on the population of the province. Out of some 10,000 to 12,000 entrants in each province, barely 300 would obtain their degree and be known as *ju ren* or 'promoted men'.[5] At the second degree ceremony graduates wore a *pi ling* collar over a long black gown with a wide blue border down the side opening, hem, centre-back and front splits, and cuffs (**fig. 5.2**). These wide contrasting borders resembled those on the robes worn by scholars during the Ming dynasty. Again, a hat with the gold leaves was worn, but on this occasion, a red scarf also crossed the chest twice (**plate 29**).

Fig. 5.1 Examination hall showing individual stalls at Nanjing which would accomodate 30,000 candidates.

In the spring of the year following the passing of the *xiang shi* examinations, graduates were eligible to take a third degree—approximating a doctorate as it is understood today—for which they had to travel to Beijing. Out of 6,000 graduates from all provinces, only about 300 would be selected. This particular examination was known as *hui shi* and a graduate would become a *jin shi* or 'finished scholar'. A final examination took place a few days later in the grounds of the Imperial Palace for admission to the prestigious Hanlin Academy.

Following success in the examination in Beijing, the graduate would be presented in audience with the emperor. For this he wore the *nei tao* in blue with

Fig. 5.2   Ancestor portrait of a *ju ren* graduate. Gary Dickinson.

a wide black border round the side and centre openings, hem, and cuffs. Worn with the *pi ling* and a small plain collar called a *ling tou*, it was sashed around the waist from which were hung many purses. A hat appropriate to the season and black satin boots completed the outfit. Success at third-degree level brought a high position in the government.

Military Examinations

The *wu sheng yuan*, or aspiring military official, was examined by the same officials who invigilated at the civil examinations (**fig. 5.3**). A short essay was required to ascertain candidates' knowledge of military history, and their ability in archery, both standing and on horseback, and in sword play was tested also. Despite the fact that China invented gunpowder, the emphasis on prowess with bow and arrow continued throughout the nineteenth century while other nations developed far more modern firearms. The *wu ju ren* would also go to Beijing to take the third degree. Success there meant immediate employment in the army or navy anywhere in China.

Fig. 5.3   A literary official reviewing troops in western China. c.1900.

Formal examination success was not as important for military office as was the civil degree for civil office. Promotions and appointments could be made on the basis of service to the court, or even on family connections, or for financial considerations, and as a reward for bravery in war. Those with some military education could purchase the *jian sheng* title as a short cut to military office, and for many Chinese commoners it was a means of gaining social mobility.[6] The majority of officers in the Chinese Green Standard army, for example, rose up through the ranks without a degree.

Because military examinations were largely based upon physical feats, rather than literary ability, a military degree was never held in high esteem by the intellectual elite. Lower military ranks were considered less prestigious than the equivalent civil ones, though higher up the ladder both categories of official were on more equal terms.

Official Clothing

Both orders of mandarins wore Manchu style robes for formal occasions such as government business, celebrations, and festivals, though the Chinese were allowed to wear their own Han Chinese style robes for informal occasions. As with the dress of the imperial family and their courtiers, clothing was divided into official and non-official attire and subdivided into formal, semi-formal, and informal.

Fig. 5.4   Liu Changyu, governor-general of Guangdong and Guangxi provinces, wearing official formal court attire of summer hat, *pu fu* with civil rank badge, court necklace, *pi ling*, and *chao pao*. 1863.

Formal

Official formal clothing consisted of the *chao fu* worn by high-ranking mandarins for all important occasions and court attendances (**fig. 5.4**). First- to third-rank civil, and first- and second-rank military mandarins were permitted to wear the first style winter *chao pao* in blue-black, with four profile *mang* on the upper body and two *mang* on front and back of the skirt. The second style of winter and summer *chao pao* was also in blue-black and worn by the first four ranks of both mandarins. Here the upper part had four front-facing *mang*, while the lower part of the skirt had four profile *mang* at front and back. No medallions like those worn by the emperor and heir apparent were allowed on the skirt, although they did make an appearance towards the end of the dynasty. At this time too—as an economy, and because traditions were breaking down—some men wore only the skirt part of the *chao pao* under the surcoat.

Mandarins of fifth- to seventh-ranks wore plain blue silk damask *chao pao* with gold and black brocade edging (**fig. 5.5**). On the chest and back were profile *mang* squares, while the eighth and ninth ranks wore plain *chao pao* with no squares. Robes of this type belonging to lower-ranking officials are quite rare today as it was usual for a man to be buried in his *chao fu*, and such plain items were not deemed sufficiently valuable or interesting by collectors.

Fig. 5.5   Summer *chao pao* edged in brocade for fifth- to seventh-rank officials. 19th cent. Metropolitan Museum of Art.

Semi-formal

For less important court occasions and official or government business, semi-formal official clothing was worn. Colloquially known as 'full dress' this *ji fu* comprised a dragon robe worn with the *pi ling* and a surcoat bearing badges of rank, known to the West as 'mandarin squares'. First-, second- and third-rank mandarins could wear nine embroidered *mang* on the robe. Dragons were placed one each at chest and back, one at each shoulder, and two at front and back hem. A symbolic ninth dragon was hidden under the front inside flap of the robe. Fourth- to sixth-rank civil and military officials wore eight four-clawed dragons. *Long*, normally a symbol of the emperor, were also worn by lower ranks if they had been awarded the privilege and, towards the end of the dynasty, many were worn with or without permission.

Lower officials of the seventh to ninth ranks, and unclassified officials, were said to have been assigned to wear five *mang*, but this did not seem to have been put into practice, and low-ranking officials would anyway seldom have needed to wear dragon robes. Those who had a low income could not have afforded one, and those who were richer would have used their wealth or influence to gain a higher rank. At the end of the dynasty even the lowest

Fig. 5.6   A mandarin, with his retainers, about to step out of his sedan chair.

Plate 23   Empress Wen, mother of the Shunzhi Emperor, in full court dress: *chao pao*, *chao gua*, and *zai shui*; hat, diadem, torque necklace, and three mandarin chains. Palace Museum.

Plate 24   Second style of summer *chao pao* with *pi ling*. 18th cent. Palace Museum.

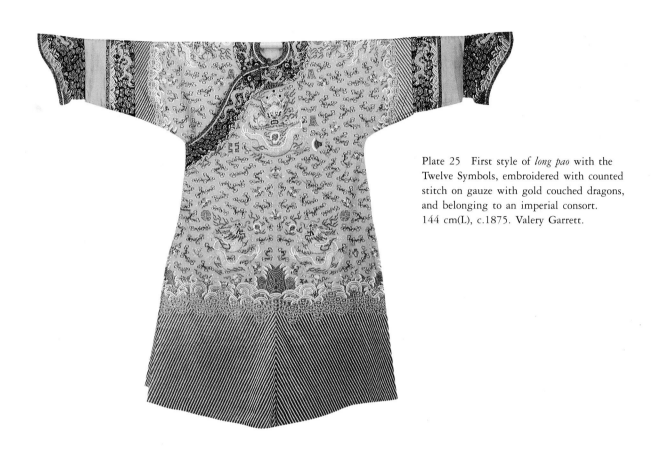

Plate 25 First style of *long pao* with the
Twelve Symbols, embroidered with counted
stitch on gauze with gold couched dragons,
and belonging to an imperial consort.
144 cm(L), c.1875. Valery Garrett.

Plate 26 Official informal *pao* with
embroidered facings and damask weave
medallions in turquoise green. *Imperial
Wardrobe*, 1990.

Plate 27   Lilac *kesi* robe with *shou* character, chrysanthemums, and bats, and with more *shou* characters and chrysanthemums inside sleeves; an outer robe said to have belonged to Empress Dowager Cixi. 138 cm(L). Private collection.

Plate 28   Empress Dowager Cixi's short jacket embroidered with narcissi and *shou* characters on wine twill silk and made for spring. c.1900. Royal Ontario Museum.

Plate 29 Graduate of the second degree wearing crossed scarf and hat decorations. As depicted in a painting by Tinqua. c.1854. Private collection.

Plate 30 First-rank civil badge in *kesi* with crane standing on a rock between plum blossom and peaches, the border of *mang* and *shou* characters. 31.5 cm(W) x 31 cm(H), Qianlong period. Private Collection.

Plate 31   Third-rank civil badge, showing peacock, of couched gold thread and peacock feathers. Kangxi period. Teresa Coleman Fine Arts.

Plate 32   Fifth-rank civil badge, showing silver pheasant, gold couched tendrils and satin stitch. 29.5 cm(H) x 31 cm(W), early 19th cent. Valery Garrett.

Plate 33   First-rank military badge, showing *qilin*, of brocade. 25 cm(W) x 26 cm(H), Qianlong period. Private collection.

Plate 34   Third-rank military badge, showing leopard, of gold brocade; with no sun disc. 23 cm(H)(cut away at top and bottom) x 27 cm(W), Yongzheng period. Private collection.

Plate 35 Sedan chair bearers and their customers. Guangzhou, 1807. Hong Kong Museum of Art.

Plate 36 Set of purses: a spectacle case, a fan case, a *da lian* type, and two drawstring purses in beige and blue silk brocade. Private collection.

officials could have openly worn an eight-dragon robe if the occasion warranted it.

A calf-length centre-fastening surcoat was mandatory for formal occasions after 1759, and all who appeared at court were required to wear it, regardless of background or income. Called a *pu fu*, or 'garment with a patch', when a badge of rank was applied; or *wai tao*, meaning 'outer covering', without the badge, it was made from blue or purple-black satin. For winter it was often lined or edged with white fur (sable fur was reserved for mandarins of third rank and above), for spring and autumn the lining was cotton, and the garment itself was made of silk gauze with no lining for the summer (**fig. 5.6**). A roundel design was frequently incorporated into the weave.

This surcoat was loose-fitting, made of two lengths of cloth folded at the shoulders and opening down the centre-front, with side and back vents. The three-quarter length sleeves and the fact that the coat reached mid-calf enabled the wearer to show off the sleeves and embroidered hem of the *chao pao* or dragon robe underneath. In addition, the simple shape of the coat meant it made an ideal background for the badges of rank fixed to front and back. A fur surcoat called *duan zhao* of the same style was worn for extra warmth with the winter dragon robes (**fig. 5.7**). However, its use was restricted to the imperial family, imperial guardsmen, and the first three ranks of mandarins.

Fig. 5.7   Mandarins wearing the *duan zhao* and winter hat with peacock feather. 1906.

Informal

Official informal clothing was worn for other events which were not connected with major ceremonies or government matters. It was considered bad taste to wear formal robes on private occasions, at home, or when visiting friends. Ordinary dress, *chang fu*, consisting of a *nei tao* or plain long gown of silk, usually reddish brown, grey, or blue and cut in the same style as the dragon robe, was worn under the *pu fu*. Low-ranking officials would generally also wear the *nei tao* under a *pu fu* on semi-formal occasions. This *nei tao* was a Manchu garment, originally designed for travelling by horse. It had long sleeves and narrow horse-hoof cuffs to protect the hands, and centre splits at front and back as well as the sides. On some there was a detachable section at the lower right side above the hem for removal when riding on horseback, and this was often worn by military mandarins who were not supposed to ride in sedan chairs. For formal wear the cuffs would be worn down to cover the hands as it was considered impolite to show them, but for informal occasions the cuffs could be turned back and the sleeves pushed up.

Fig. 5.8   A fourth-rank civil
mandarin in official informal
dress of *pu fu* and *ling tou*, with
nei tao underneath. c.1900.
Valery Garrett.

During the second half of the nineteenth
century, it became fashionable to wear a
small plain stiffened collar called a *ling tou*
which fitted over the *pu fu*. Made of silk,
velvet, or fur according to the season, it was
worn sometimes with the *pi ling*, or alone,
on informal occasions (**fig. 5.8, 5.9**).

Non-official Clothing

The second group of regulations for non-
official occasions was also subdivided into
three categories. In practice, however, the
non-official formal group, which was worn
when the mandarin was on public view for
celebrations, festivals, birthdays, and family gatherings, was the same as the official
semi-formal clothing, except that the *ling
tou* was worn over the *nei tao* and *pu fu*, in
place of the *pi ling*.

Fig. 5.9   *Ling tou*, the collar of
blue silk with cream silk body.
Valery Garrett.

Non-official semi-formal wear and informal wear were called 'half dress' which
indicated that the mandarin did not need to wear his badge of rank. Semi-formal attire consisted of the *nei tao* worn with the *wai tao* and *ling tou*. For informal wear at home and out of the public eye the *nei tao* was worn on its own,
sometimes combined with a short, sleeveless waistcoat, or more often with a
short jacket known as a *ma gua*, literally 'riding dress'.

At first the *ma gua* fastened over to the right, but later down the centre-
front with five loops and brass buttons. It had a small stand collar and slits at
side seams and centre-back. The fabric was black satin lined with blue silk;
later emblems of bats, *fu*, a homonym for happiness and good fortune, *shou*
characters, and other auspicious designs were incorporated into the fabric weave
in set formation. The side-fastening waistcoat was based on the construction of
the Manchu robe, and the sloping shoulder seams and fastening down the right
point to a garment which had developed from animal skins, where one skin
made up the back and two overlapped at the front for warmth and extra protection. A variation of this style, whose origins were based on a two-skin development, was a plastron style which fastened across the top front and sides to
an extended back piece. A centre-opening sleeveless style with sloping shoulder seams also developed later. These formal waistcoats were made of silk damask
edged in plain satin or velvet.

Below the nine ranks of mandarins, there was a large body of men employed within the government as clerks or in other comparable work. Those men waiting to be promoted to the ninth and lowest rank on the ladder of promotion would have worn their graduation robes for their daily business.

Badges of Rank

Although the Manchus, on taking power, made a break with Chinese tradition and retained their own national costume, they brought in the Ming custom of indicating rank by insignia squares in 1652. With slight modifications, they continued the system of having the nine ranks of civil officials depicted by birds and the military mandarins by animals (**chart 5.1**). The ability of birds to fly high to heaven indicated the superiority of the civil mandarins over the military mandarins whose animals were earth-bound.

Chart 5.1

Qing Insignia Squares			
	Civil Officials	*Military Officials*	
Rank		*Early Qing*	*Late Qing*
First	crane	lion	*qilin* (after 1662)
Second	golden pheasant	lion	lion
Third	peacock	tiger	leopard (after 1664)
Fourth	wild goose	leopard	tiger (after 1664)
Fifth	silver pheasant	bear	bear
Sixth	egret	panther	panther
Seventh	mandarin duck	panther	rhinoceros (after 1759)
Eighth	quail	rhinoceros	rhinoceros
Ninth	paradise flycatcher	sea-horse	sea-horse
Unclassed officials	paradise flycatcher		

Source: Schuyler Cammann, *China's Dragon Robes*, New York: Ronald Press, 1952.

The single bird on most of the late Ming squares was retained by the Qing, but was depicted in a stiff, unrealistic way. The badges of the early Kangxi period were also smaller than those of the Ming. The sun disc made its appearance on civil squares towards the end of the seventeenth century, although it appeared much later on military squares. For a civil official, the bird's head faced to the wearer's right, and for his wife the bird faced to her left and looked up to the sun, symbolizing the official looking up to his emperor.[7] For a military official, the animal's head faced the wearer's left, and for his wife it faced right. Often the bird or animal faced backward over its shoulder, possibly to produce a more compact pictorial composition (**plates 30, 31, 32, 33, 34**).

Although it had always been possible for a man to purchase a degree and consequently a rank, this trend increased rapidly towards the end of the dynasty as the Qing government began selling ranks as a means of generating revenue. Ranks without office began to be sold, even to merchants and tradesmen. This led to the practice of wearing appliquéd birds and animals instead of those embroidered into the square, as the speed with which the officials rose through the ranks meant that the base could be retained and just the bird changed.

Other Badges

There were also badges worn which related more to occasion than to rank. Four Character squares, for instance, were bestowed on elderly men who had continually tried to pass the examinations and failed, and who held no official rank.

Fig. 5.10 Four-character presentation square with characters and bats in couched gold thread on satin background. Royal Ontario Museum.

Such squares were of similar size to mandarin squares, but in place of an animal or bird, there were four characters on the front squre, *huang en qin zi*, or similar, implying they were 'conferred by imperial grace', while on the back square was a large *shou* character (**fig. 5.10**). Birthday squares, made as presents for elderly parents, featured a chrysanthemum or peony instead of a bird or animal.

Accessories

Hats

A mandarin was seldom seen without his hat, and then only in the private quarters of his home. Hats were worn irrespective of the degree of official formality. From the eighth month of the Chinese calendar the head was covered by a hat with a turned-up brim of black satin, mink, sealskin, or velvet, and a padded crown covered in red silk fringing. For summer, beginning in the third month of the Chinese calendar, the hat was conical and made of woven straw for the lower ranks, and split bamboo for higher officials (**fig. 5.11**). Fringes of red silk cord or dyed horse or goat hair covered the crown from apex to edge.

Fig. 5.11 A cap maker trimming a summer hat. From a painting by Pu Qua. 1799. Valery Garrett.

Hat Insignia

The use of cap finials and spheres meant that the rank of the mandarin could be easily identified at a glance. They were more conspicuous than the rank badges, especially as the badges were only worn on 'full dress' occasions.

Chart 5.2

Hat Insignia for Officials' Chao Guan					
Rank	1636	1645		1730–1911	
	Jewel	Jewel	Smaller setting	Jewel	Smaller setting
First	ruby	ruby	pearl	ruby	pearl
Second	ruby	ruby	red	coral	red
Third	ruby	ruby	blue	sapphire	blue
Fouth	sapphire	sapphire	blue	lapis lazuli	blue
Fifth	crystal	crystal	blue	crystal	blue
Sixth	crystal	crystal	—	white jade	crystal
Seventh	gold	chased gold	—	plain gold	crystal
Eighth	gold	chased gold	—	chased gold	—
Ninth	—	chased silver	—	chased silver	—

Source: Gary Dickinson, and Linda Wrigglesworth, *Imperial Wardrobe*, Hong Kong: Oxford University Press, 1990.

Worn for ceremonial occasions and a simpler version of those worn by the imperial family, the finials were fixed to the apex of the crown by a long metal screw passed through a hole in the hat (**chart 5.2**). Above the ornamental base was a spherical shape with a small setting of transparent stone or glass, then above that the tall jewel depicting rank. Colours of the jewels were based on the Manchu banners, the military divisions whose flags were red, blue, yellow, and white. These laws were laid down in 1636 when the Manchu court in Shenyang split the civil and military officials into four ranks. After the conquest of China, with the consequent take-over of the Ming system of nine ranks, the small settings were added to depict the principal and the subordinate ranks. Later, in 1730, the Yongzheng Emperor decreed the introduction of opaque stones to the transparent ones already in use, to denote the subordinate ranks.

Hat spheres, often called 'mandarin buttons' in the West, were introduced in 1727 by the Yongzheng Emperor to be worn on less formal occasions to avoid confusion of rank when the insignia squares were not worn, or when the belt plaques were covered (**chart 5.3**). In 1730, a new set of regulations stipulated that glass could be used instead of semi-precious stones to minimize expense, but also because glass itself was highly prized.

Graduates of the provincial examinations wore a hat ornament with a gold bird on top, instead of a jewel; for graduates of the first degree leading to the *ju ren* status, the bird was silver (**fig. 5.12**). The *jin shi*, or metropolitan graduate, wore a gold ornament with a branch of nine leaves at the top.

Chart 5.3

Hat Insignia for Officials' Ji Guan		
Rank	*1727–30*	*1730–1911*
First	coral (or ruby if permitted)	coral or opaque red glass
Second	coral with engraved *shou* character	coral or opaque red glass with engraved *shou* character
Third	as above	sapphire or clear blue glass
Fourth	lapis lazuli	lapis lazuli or opaque blue glass
Fifth	as above	crystal or clear glass
Sixth	crystal	moonstone or opaque white glass
Seventh	gold	plain gold or gilt
Eighth	gold	gold or gilt with an engraved *shou* character
Ninth	gold	silver until 1800, then gold or gilt with an embossed *shou* character

For the fifth rank and above, peacock feathers, *hua yu*, would be attached to the cap button through a jade tube. These were worn on public occasions and seen as a sign of great honour accorded by the emperor for services rendered. One, two, or three overlapping peacock feathers were sometimes worn—the more eyes, the greater

Fig. 5.12 From the top centre, clockwise: gold hat finial with crystal and small blue stone setting; hat finial in gilt topped with a bird for a provincial graduate; plain gilt hat knob denoting seventh rank; blue glass hat knob for third rank. Valery Garrett.

the honour. However, towards the end of the dynasty, these were openly for sale, with one example in the Victoria and Albert Museum in London still bearing the label from the Wan Sheng Yong Feather Shop in the main street in Beijing.[8] Officials and military officers of the sixth rank and below used dark blue quills, *lan yu*, from the crow's tail (**fig. 5.13**).

Mandarin Chains

Chao zhu, the necklace of 108 semi-precious stones worn by the emperor and his court, was also worn by the mandarin. Civil officials of the fifth rank and above, and military officials of fourth rank and above, were required to wear the chain, which could use any semi-precious stones other than pearls (**fig. 5.14**).

Fig. 5.13 From the left: crow's feather plume in a wooden box; double-eyed peacock feather plume, and a lacquer box inscribed and dated 1876. Valery Garrett.

Girdles

A coarsely woven girdle, in blue or blue-black silk, tightly belted the gown and was part of the Manchu traditional costume. The belt buckle and three similarly

designed plaques were a further means of denoting rank (**chart 5.4**). As there were no pockets in the robes, the side plaques, which had oval metal rings at the bottom, were used to carry all the essentials of daily life: the fan case, tobacco pouch, a pair of chopsticks in a case with a knife, an archer's ring, and a watch—a most valued possession in later times.

Footwear

Black satin boots, *ma xue*, similar to those worn by men at court, were an indication that the wearer never left his home on foot. They were an important but expensive part of the regalia, said to cost as much as a servant's wage for one year[9] (**fig. 5.15**). In fact, they were such a symbol of superiority that a proverb of the time stated 'A man in boots will not speak to a man in shoes'.[10]

Fig. 5.14 Mandarin chain of amber, lapis lazuli, and jade. Valery Garrett.

Chart 5.4

Girdle Clasp Fittings 1645–1911	
Rank	*Clasp Style*
First	Four rectangular jade plaques mounted in gold, each set with one ruby or red stone
Second	Four circular engraved gold plaques, each set with one ruby or red stone
Third	Four circular engraved gold plaques
Fourth	Four circular engraved gold plaques set in silver
Fifth	Four circular plain gold plaques set in silver
Sixth	Four circular tortoiseshell plaques set in gold
Seventh	Four circular silver plaques
Eighth	Four circular clear ram's horn plaques set in silver
Ninth	Four circular black horn plaques set in silver

Fig. 5.15 Black satin boots with thick white soles inscribed on the lining as being made for a military official. Valery Garrett.

Notes

1 This was done through the examination system and the sale of ranks and appointments.

2 The word mandarin (*guan* in Chinese) is derived from the Portuguese word *mandar* meaning 'to command'.

3 Thus, for example, a governor of a province was of second rank, secondary class 2b; a provincial judge was of third rank, principal class 3a.

4 This tradition of crossed red scarf and foil decoration is still worn today by some Cantonese and Hakka bridegrooms in the New Territories of Hong Kong. Headmen in some villages there also wear the decoration in their hats at important festivals such as the Daoist ceremony *Da jiao* (held every ten years to pacify the dragon).

5 W. F. Mayers, *The Chinese Government: A Manual of Chinese Titles*, 3rd ed., revised by G. M. H. Playfair, Shanghai: Kelly and Walsh, 1896, p. 78.

6 Robert M. Marsh, *The Mandarins: The Circulation of Elites in China, 1600–1900*, Glencoe, Illinois: The Free Press of Glencoe, 1961. Many wealthy Chinese merchants also took this route, and are portrayed wearing military squares.

7 Also a kind of rebus, 'Point at the sun and rise high' (*zhi ri sheng rao*). Schuyler Cammann, *Chinese Mandarin Squares: Brief Catalogue of the Letcher Collection*, Philadelphia: University of Pennsylvania, 1953, p. 11.

8 Verity Wilson, *Chinese Dress*, London: Victoria and Albert Museum, 1986, p. 28.

9 Verity Wilson, *Chinese Dress*, p. 29.

10 H. S. Sirr, *China and the Chinese*, London: W. S. Orr & Co., 1849, Vol. 1, p. 309.

6 Dress for Han Chinese Men

According to Qing dynastic laws, all Chinese men who had reached positions of authority in the government were required to wear the Manchu dress of *chao fu*, *ji fu*, or *chang fu* on all official occasions. However, when out of the public eye, at ceremonies within the family, village, or city ward, or for informal wear—and for those who were not entitled to wear mandarin's attire, such as merchants and clerks—clothing of Han Chinese style was worn (**plate 35**).

Chang Shan

The voluminous Ming dynasty robes had been slimmed down during the Qing by the Han Chinese, and the side-fastening *chang shan*, or ordinary

Fig. 6.1 Chinese scholar wearing a long gown, holding a folding paper fan and a pipe. Late 19th cent.

Fig. 6.2 A group of Chinese mathematicians. Beijing, c.1870.

gown, incorporated some features from Manchu garments. These were the curved front opening which echoed animal-skin origins, and the fastening of loops and toggles, again of nomadic derivation. The Chinese gown was made to suit a more sedentary way of life than the *nei tao*, with the centre-back and front slits being closed, and the sleeves long and tapering (**fig. 6.1, 6.2**). Over the *chang shan* would be worn the *ma gua*, a hip-length jacket with long sleeves, or for less formal occasions, a sleeveless jacket (**fig. 6.3, 6.4, 6.5**).

Silk was used, often gauze for summer and wadded for winter, or cotton for the lower classes. To add greater protection in cold weather, gowns were fur-lined: cat and dog fur was used, as well as goatskin and sheepskin. The fur-lined gowns would pass from father to son as part of his inheritance, this being possible because styles changed little over the years. It was also the custom for rich and poor alike to pawn their fur-lined garments during the summer months as they would be better stored. Wearing another's clothes was a common habit, as this description of the celebrations to mark the start of the New Year gives evidence:

> Everyone will appear, if possible, in long robes and jackets of silk and satin, with their red-buttoned and tasselled skull caps on. ...These fine clothes can be hired, the price being gradually lowered as the hours of the first six days pass by. We complained once of the very late arrival of a caller, who should

Fig. 6.3   Chinese men wearing the extended-sleeve gown.

Fig. 6.4   Rust silk damask waistcoat with endless knot design. Mid-19th cent. Valery Garrett.

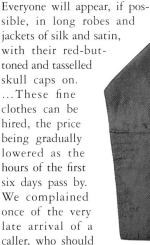

Fig. 6.5   Dark cream silk damask padded jacket with long tapering sleeves and *shou* characters surrounded by emblems of the Eight Immortals. c.1870. Valery Garrett.

have been among the first to salute us. He replied that money was scarce and he was obliged to wait for the cheapest day to secure a fine robe already donned and doffed by a dozen others.[1]

Shan Ku

A long gown was not a practical garment for the lower classes. It restricted movement, deliberately indicating that the wearer had the sedentary occupation of scholar and gentleman. The stonecutters, farmers, fishermen, servants, or common labourers known as coolies (from the word *ku li*, literally 'bitter strength') wore the cotton *shan ku*[2] dyed indigo blue. This thigh-length version of the long gown, worn with a pair of loose-fitting trousers, was a plain, functional outfit well-suited to the Chinese climate and the lifestyle of working people (**fig. 6.6**).

The majority of Han Chinese were farmers who among their crops grew cotton and hemp and cultivated silkworms, all of which they would subsequently spin and weave into yarn to make fabric. Hemp had been used as a fabric since the eleventh century BC, and was popular as it was cool and hard-wearing. The most common fabric, however, was cotton produced locally, or during the nine-

Fig. 6.6 Chinese barber and his customers wearing the gown or *shan ku*.

teenth century from the main cotton producing and manufacturing areas of China such as Shanghai and the Yangzi River Delta.

Before the advent of mass-produced fabrics, construction of the *shan ku*, and of the long gown, was based on lengths of cloth woven by hand within the family on a narrow backstrap loom. The most manageable width was 36 to 40 centimetres, and this necessitated several seams in the garment. Because the production of cloth was a fairly slow and laborious process, the cutting of the garments had to be made in the most economical way possible. One width of cloth formed one-half of the front and back of the *shan*, with a folded edge at the shoulder. Another width made the opposite side, while sleeves were made from strips of cloth attached to the edges. As well as being economical in cut, it made for a style of garment which was easy to store folded flat in camphor wood chests.

Towards the end of the nineteenth century the outer flap was removed from the garment, and men began wearing the centre-front-opening jacket. This was fastened with odd-numbered loops and buttons. Five were popular during the last century, followed by seven, nine, or even eleven for the man-about-town, but finally seven became the established number of fastenings.

Like the *shan*, the style of the *ku* also originated from the Manchus, who wore animal skins wrapped around their legs to prevent them from chafing while on horseback. Ties at the ankles and waist were added to keep the leggings in place when they were made of cloth; finally, tubes of cloth attached to a waistband became the forerunner of the *ku*. *Ku* were cut in the same woven tradition as the *shan*, with full and half widths of cloth utilized economically. A wide waistband enabled the *ku* to be stepped into easily; it was then folded across the body, secured with a belt or cord, and the surplus cloth tucked in. The loose trouser legs were often fastened round the ankle with a strip of cloth.

Underwear

Special clothing for sleeping or for wearing under the outer garments was, with a few exceptions, not common in China, and underwear or nightwear was often an older or thinner version of the top garment.

Dating back to the Ming dynasty was the bamboo vest or jacket, which was worn in the hot weather up to the beginning of this century. 'Bamboo clothing is made from the finest branches of the tree, worn in summer next to the skin to keep the light cotton shirt or inner jacket from irritating the skin when moist from perspiration'.[3] Made like a large jacket with a centre-front opening, it was constructed from tiny pieces of hollow bamboo sewn together in a diagonal pattern. A decorative pattern of bamboo was placed about ten centimetres up from

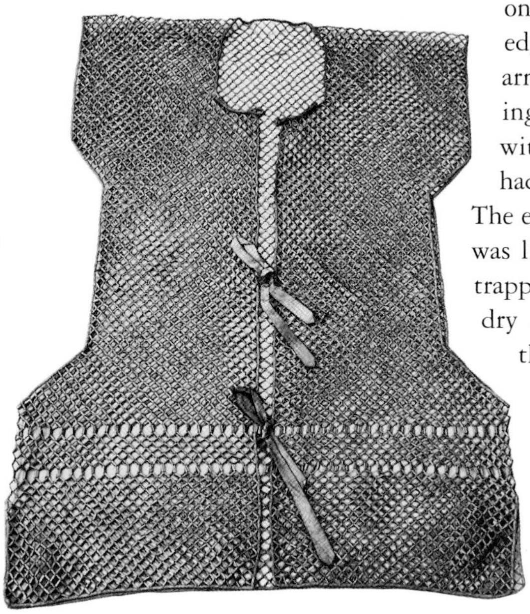

Fig. 6.7 Bamboo vest edged with cotton binding. 19th cent. Valery Garrett.

the edge of the sleeve and from the hem by omitting one row of bamboo pieces. Around the edges at the neck, sleeves, and under-arms was cotton binding; the fastening at the neck was a button and loop, with ties at the waist. Some garments had sleeves and others were sleeveless. The effect of this open-work construction was like that of a modern string vest: it trapped the air, kept the wearer cool and dry in the hot weather, and protected the outer clothing (**fig. 6.7**).

An unshaped loincloth covered the crotch and was held in place by a belt round the waist. Worn over the loincloth were separate leggings which were attached to the belt and tapered towards the ankles.

Accessories

There were no pockets in gowns or jackets, and often small items were tucked into sleeves: 'sleeve editions' (small books concealed by candidates in the examinations), and even 'sleeve dogs' (Pekinese or lap dogs) were carried there. Generally, however, daily necessities were suspended from a girdle around the waist (**plate 36**). The 'Official Nine' set of purses consisted of the *da lian*, which had two flaps, one of which hung over the girdle, a spectacle case, a fan case, a thumb ring box holding an archer's ring, a tobacco pouch, a watch case, two drawstring scent purses, and a box for carrying visiting cards.[4]

Fans

Fans had been an important accessory for thousands of years. Those made of pheasant feathers were recorded during the Shang dynasty, and rigid round or oval fans of bamboo or ivory with silk stretched across the frame were popular in the Tang dynasty. During the Song period the folding fan made of horn, bone, ivory, and sandalwood was introduced into China from Japan via Korea, and by the early fifteenth century had become very fashionable for its convenience in carrying. The number of ribs varied from around ten to thirty with fewer used for a man's fan than for a woman's.

A fan was carried not just to cool the air but also to gesticulate and make a point. They were also used as a means of artistic expression and were often inscribed with calligraphy and paintings. A wealthy man would carry his fan in a case attached to his girdle or tucked into the top of his boots, while a coolie would keep it in his stocking top, or at the back of the neck of his jacket. Folding fans were used throughout the year, but palm leaf and feather fans were used mostly in the summer, and silk ones in early autumn. Indeed, a well-known saying referred to a deserted wife as being 'an autumn fan', put aside when no longer needed.

Hairstyles and Headwear

As a sign of subjugation, all Chinese males had to shave the front of their head and wear their hair in a single plait in the style of the ruling Manchus. Resented at first, it was later accepted and became most respectable. Coolies wore the queue coiled round the head when working, but it had to hang free in the presence of a superior. As a punishment the queue could be cut off, and to be called 'tailless', *wu bian*, was a great insult.

The head, except for a circle of hair in the middle at the back, was shaved by itinerant barbers about once every ten days. The remaining hair was allowed to grow and was then plaited into a queue which would be as long and as thick as possible, and was lengthened by using false hair when necessary. Towards the end of the nineteenth century when men began to travel abroad to further their education they would cut off the queue, but on returning to China it was frequently necessary to wear a hat with a false queue attached to maintain respectability. After 1912 the queue was forbidden, and gradually it died out.

Fig. 6.8   Farmer pushing a cart with a sail hoisted to improve velocity. He is wearing the *shan ku*, his queue wound round the skullcap, and ear covers.

For those not entitled to wear the mandarin's hat, or for informal dress, a black satin skullcap with a red or black knotted silk cord knob (in blue if the wearer was in mourning) was worn.[5] Black heart-shaped embroidered ear covers were frequently worn in winter (**fig. 6.8**).

Fig. 6.9   A pair of red and black silk shoes appliquéd in black velvet and silk, and a pair of black silk shoes with a padded lining, both with thick white soles. Valery Garrett.

Footwear

Black cloth shoes were worn. Like the boot, the shoes had a stiff sole of between 3 and 7 centimetres thick, made of layers of paper (said to be from a high proportion of the Bibles distributed in China), or old cotton rags among poorer people. There were two main styles for men: one with a pointed toe curving back round to the sole, and the other with a wide toe the same width as the heel. As the sole was quite flat and inelastic, it was made shorter than the upper to give sufficient spring for walking. Shoes of both styles could fit either foot.

The uppers on mens' shoes were normally of black satin, cotton, or velvet, plain or appliquéd, but in summer the shapes were repeated in woven palm leaves for the uppers, and embroidered straw soles with padded cotton or leather. Leather was used only for trimming or binding (**fig. 6.9**). Sandals worn by coolies were made from rice straw, wheat straw, or rushes, and were provided as part of their pay, especially during wet weather, to prevent the wearer from slipping in the mud.

Blue or white cotton socks were worn with boots and shoes. These had reinforcing stitching at the soles and heels. Kneelength stockings which opened down the back, but often had no soles, were made of cotton or linen, lined and padded with rows of stitching (**fig. 6.10**).

Fig. 6.10 White cotton socks and blue silk socks, both with stitched cotton soles. 19th cent. Valery Garrett.

Notes

1   Venerable Arthur Evans Moule, *The Chinese People: A Handbook on China*, London: SPCK, 1914, p. 201.
2   Also known as *sam fu* in Cantonese.
3   John Dudgeon, *Diet, Dress and Dwellings of the Chinese in Relation to Health*, published for the International Health Exhibition, 1884.
4   Wang Yarong, *Chinese Folk Embroidery*, London: Thames and Hudson, 1987, p. 21.
5   This hat continues to be worn for special ceremonies in the New Territories of Hong Kong.

7 Han Chinese Women's Clothing

As persons of little consequence within the Manchu regime, Han Chinese women, except for those whose husbands or fathers were connected with the court in Beijing, were not required to wear any official attire. Most Chinese women were keen to show their national identity as pure Chinese and took care not to wear Manchu-style clothing. At the beginning of the dynasty wives of Chinese officials were expected to continue to wear Ming costume, but gradually Ming conventions were forgotten and aberrations crept in.

Quasi-official Dress

The dynastic laws did not refer to dress worn by Han Chinese women, but it appears from written accounts of the period that there was an accepted code according to class and occasion. High-ranking officials' or Chinese noblemens' wives would wear quasi-official formal dress on ceremonial occasions when their husbands wore the *chao fu*. This consisted of a *mang ao* or dragon jacket, *xia pei* or vest, skirt, and coronet (**fig.** 7.1).

The *mang ao* was a loose-fitting jacket with bell sleeves, a plain round neck, and

Fig. 7.1   Wife of Huang Cantang, governor of Guangdong, wearing a *xia pei, mang ao,* skirt, and phoenix crown. c.1862.

a side opening from neck to underarm similar to that of the Ming robes, and sometimes with the *bai* side extensions. It was usually made in red, the dynastic colour of the Ming and therefore considered auspicious, although occasionally it was made in blue. Originally, the jacket was undecorated, but at some point around the eighteenth century it began to be embroidered with four to ten *mang* according to status (**plate 37**). The *mang ao* was also worn by lower-ranking officials' wives as part of their bridal dress. Over the *mang ao* was worn the *jiao dai*, a rigid hooped belt made of bamboo and covered with red silk with ornamental plaques akin to those worn by men in the Ming dynasty to denote rank.

Towards the end of the Qing dynasty the *mang ao* became shorter and narrower, and the *li shui* pattern which had been used at the hem was seldom seen. The *xia pei*, first worn on the wedding day and later at events of special importance connected with a husband's status, was worn over the *mang ao*. It had developed from the Ming stole into a wider, sleeveless tabard which fastened with ties at the sides, reaching to below the knee and finishing with a fringe at the pointed hem. The *xia pei* was decorated with profile dragons and *li shui*, and on the front and back a space for a badge of rank corresponding to that of the husband was provided (**plate 38**). A four-pointed collar, *yun jian* or cloud collar—with the four lobes at chest, back, and over each shoulder—was incorporated into the *xia pei*, or else worn separately over the upper garment.

The *mang ao* was worn over a panelled and pleated brightly coloured skirt, often in red or green silk, called a *mang chu* or dragon skirt. With dragons and phoenixes depicted on the front and back panels, it was first worn at the time of marriage. Wearing a skirt was seen as a symbol of maturity, and it was only worn by married women on formal occasions, but was never worn alone, always over trousers, leggings, or leg wrappings. The Qing garment was very similar in style to those found in tombs dating back to the second century BC, as well as finds from Song dynasty tombs discovered in Fujian. The skirt comprised a pair of pleated or gored aprons with panels back and front. Wrapping around the body, they were attached to a wide waistband which was secured with ties or loops and buttons. The waistband was made of cotton or hemp to prevent the skirt from slipping, while the skirt was of silk. Because the skirt was worn together with a knee-length jacket, the panels were only embroidered up to the meeting point of the jacket and skirt. Back and front panels were identical and edged in braid. Many narrow pleats caught down in a honeycomb or fish-scale pattern, or godets to the left side of the panels widening towards the hem, gave ease of movement.

Headdresses

For formal occasions a coronet, modelled on those worn by empresses in previous dynasties, was worn. This had a lattice base placed on top of the wearer's hair to which were attached kingfisher feathers and jewelled hairpins. Hairpins were made of gold, enamel, silver, or semi-precious stones such as jade or coral, and would be fashioned into the shapes of insects, birds, or butterflies. In particular, hairpins made of kingfisher feathers were very popular, a fashion dating back to the Tang dynasty. Wedding headdresses, haircombs, pins, and earrings were also made from these irridescent blue feathers. Great quantities were produced for the domestic market, and many pieces exported to Europe; the last major consignment was produced as recently as the 1930s in a Guangzhou factory.

Formal Dress

Fig. 7.2   Black silk damask surcoat with couched gold and silver embroidery on blue satin sleevebands, with streamers representing a form of *zai shui*; sixth-rank civil badge. c.1900. Valery Garrett.

When accompanying their husbands on occasions when the officials wore the *ji fu*, wives wore the formal dress of the surcoat and highly decorated skirt. Although the surcoat was cut like the man's, it became more detailed and was made with wide bands of embroidered satin at the deep cuffs towards the end of the dynasty. It opened down the front, and the badge of rank would be attached to front and back for 'full dress' occasions. Two short lappets hung down each side at the centre-front, echoing the *zai shui* worn by Manchu women but with less adornment (fig. 7.2, 7.3).

Fig. 7.3   Wives of high officials wearing the surcoat with rank badge, ornamented headband, and elaborate skirt with streamers. Late 19th cent.

With the surcoat, and the more formal *xia pei*, would be worn a *chao zhu* or mandarin chain similar to that of the wearer's husband, but with the position of the three counting strings reversed. In place of the coronet a silk headband decorated with semi-precious stones was worn across the forehead.

Semi-formal Dress

For semi-formal occasions in public, the surcoat was worn without the rank badge, corresponding to the 'half dress' worn by the husband. For other more private functions a wife wore the *ao*, an upper garment which was cut like a man's but elaborately decorated, made from self-patterned silk damask with wide plain and/or embroidered bands at sleeves, neck, hem, and curved opening, or *tou jin*. The curved front overlap of the *ao*, fastening with toggles on the right, was based on a Manchu tradition of skins which did not need reinforcing, but after the mid-eighteenth cen-

Fig. 7.4   Three ladies and a servant. Late 19th cent.

tury contrasting bias-cut borders outlined the edges to neaten and strengthen, and later to decorate. From the middle to the end of the nineteenth century, the woman's *ao* was cut very large, reaching to the calf, with wide sleeves. Bulky garments, like those worn by men in the Ming dynasty, were a sign of wealth and dignity.[1] Large quantities of fabric, which took a long time to produce, reflected the status of the wearer. At this time, wide, elaborate borders of contrasting colours edged with braid, and sometimes lace following a fashion influence from the West, outlined the curved edge, sleeves, and hem (**plate 39, fig. 7.4**).

The *ao* was worn with a skirt, *gun*, which could be very colourful and decorative (**plate 40**). Certain colours indicated marital status: black was worn by older women for example, while white was only worn by widows. 'Marrying the wearer of a white skirt' meant marrying a widow.[2]

Informal Dress

The *ao* worn everyday had narrower, plainer borders at the neck and curved opening, and was often made of cotton (**fig. 7.5, 7.6**). For warmth, a sleeveless side-fastening waist-coat edged with braid could be worn over it. Unlike men, women did not wear a waist girdle, so accessories such as scented purses to sweeten the air were often hung from the top button at the side of the *ao*. Smoking became fashionable and gourd-shaped tobacco pouches were suspended from the stem of a long pipe.

Fig. 7.5   Women in northern China sitting on the *kang* while working in the kitchen. They are wearing the bulky style *ao*.

Fig. 7.6   Semi-formal *ao* and trousers worn by girls at a grad-uation class. c.1900.

Unmarried women wore *ku* or trousers with the *ao*. These were cut as straight tubes of fabric, with gussets to form the crotch part, and were attached to a cotton waistband. The hems of the trousers were decorated with bands of silk or embroidery which sometimes, but not always, matched the *ao* worn with them (**plate** 41). Leggings were also worn under the skirt in place of trousers (**fig.** 7.7). These were separate for each leg and fastened with a button or ties to a band round the waist. Lower-class women tied the leggings or trousers tightly round the ankle to cover the bindings of the bound feet, while the trousers of upper-class women were wide and loose.

Underwear

Tapering trousers were worn as underwear, along with a small triangular apron to cover the breasts and stomach. Known as a *dou dou*, it had developed from the bodice worn in the Ming dynasty, and continued to be worn by women and children up to the early years of the twentieth century. The apron was narrower at the neck with a wider

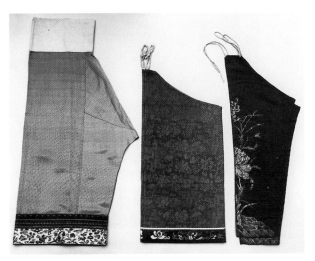

Fig. 7.7   From the left: lilac silk trousers with embroidered band and braid at hem, 99 cm(L); blue silk jacquard leggings with san lan, 'three blues', embroidery at hem, 74 cm(L); blue satin leggings tapering to the ankle with couched gold and silver thread design of chrysanthemums, 80 cm(L). Valery Garrett.

curved base and was held to the body by a silver chain or tape around the neck and waist. At the base of the apron there would often be a pocket stretching across the full width of the garment. Made of cotton or silk, these little aprons were richly embroidered with auspicious symbols. Another type, sometimes called a money belt, was a shallow embroidered pouch for daily necessities worn around the waist and over the stomach to fasten with tapes at the back (**plate 42**). Bamboo jackets, vests, and aprons were also worn in hot weather to aid air circulation, and to prevent outer garments from being soiled with perspiration.

Accessories

Cosmetics and Hairstyles

Apart from the lowest classes, no Chinese (or Manchu) woman would consider herself dressed without a liberal application of cosmetics. White powder was used to make a dark skin appear fair. 'This powder for the face, which is dusted lightly on the skin, is a mixture of rice powder and lead. The rice used is a mixture of fresh white rice and "old rice", or rice that has been treated in such a fashion that it has become slightly browned. A very little lead is used to prevent the powder from flaking.'[3] Rouge was made from a dye made from safflowers and french chalk. Mixed with water it was applied with the fingers to the cheeks and the centre of the lower lip. Eyebrows were plucked into a high arch and drawn in with charcoal.

Unmarried women wore their hair in a long single plait with a fringe over the forehead. Young girls spent many hours dressing their hair in the fashion of their time and re-gion. Chiang Yee, author of *A Chinese Childhood*, describes how his sister would 'make freshly the jelly-like liquid with

Fig. 7.8   Portrait of an official's wife wearing typical hairstyle for a Chinese woman. Early 19th cent. Sotheby's.

which she polished her hair. For this she used very thin shavings of a wood called *wu-mo* or *pau-hua-mo*, which, after being steeped in water for a short time, formed a jelly-like liquid. After combing her hair out straight, my sister would brush it with this liquid and comb it again. She then dressed her hair according to the fashion of the time'[4] (**fig. 7.8, 7.9**).

On marriage, the hairs on the woman's forehead were removed with two red threads to give a more open-faced look, the process being known as *kai mian*, literally 'opening the face'. The hair was coiled into a bun and dressed with many ornaments or artificial flowers, depending on the style

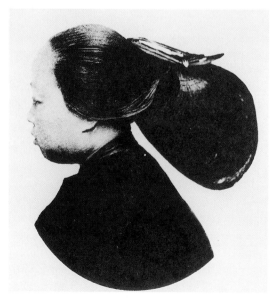

Fig. 7.9   A hairstyle worn by some women in Ningbo. 1870.

Fig. 7.10 From the top: head-band decorated with kingfisher feathers, enamel, and semi-precious stones and worn on formal occasions; black satin open-crown hat, padded, with back flap, and gold embroidered *mang* at front; headband of black satin embroidered with Pekinese stitch of flowers, gourds, coins, etc.; headband of black cut velvet with reverse appliqué design of orchid and endless knot. Valery Garrett.

of the region. Beijing and Xiamen were the centres for these flowers, and those made from rice paper took the shape particularly well. As the hairline tended to recede with this hairstyle, in middle age a woman would wear a shaped and embroidered band across her forehead to add warmth. Some of these also had an extended flap to keep the neck warm (**fig. 7.10**).

Jewellery

A Chinese woman would wear many rings, bracelets, anklets, nail extenders, and other jewellery made of jade, gold, silver, gilded silver, or enamel. Elaborately carved silver chatelaines, comprising needlecases and tongue scrapers, as well as a toothpick, earpick, nail cleaner and tweezers (which were also used for making fabric ball buttons), were fastened to the top button on the *ao*. Much of the jewellery worn by the less well-to-do was made of an alloy known as *bai tong*, or white copper, which was copper containing a small amount of zinc and nickel, but resembling silver.

Footwear

Han Chinese women continued the fashion of having small feet, although the Manchus, on taking power, tried to ban the custom of foot-binding. It

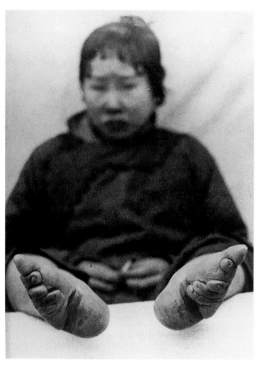

Fig. 7.11 Girl with small feet deformed by binding.

was a style not adopted by Hakka women, many domestic servants, or the poorest women who worked in the fields or on a boat, but most mothers did bow to pressure and bind their daughters' feet (**fig. 7.11**). If not, the girl would be considered unmarriageable. Foot-binding was extremely painful, and usually began any time between the ages of three and twelve. A binding cloth of finely woven cotton or silk, in black or white and about 180 centimetres long and 7 centimetres wide, was wrapped around the foot, starting at the toes and finishing at the heel. The feet were usually bound to a length of 13 centimetres (5 inches); the '3-inch lotus' was quite rare, and only for those women who did no work and had servants to support them while walking.

Over the binding cloths fine cotton or silk socks were worn, with soles and heels reinforced with stitching. The socks, whose tops flared out so they could be pulled over the foot, were held in place with ribbons. Over these would be separate ankle covers of silk, richly embroidered, or else the shoe would have an extension at the ankle to cover the binding (**fig. 7.12**).

As part of her dowry a woman would make between four and sixteen pairs of shoes, proof of her needlework ability as well as her small feet.[5] The uppers were of silk or cotton, often embroidered, while the soles were usually of densely layered and stitched white cotton. After the wedding each of the main female in-laws were given a pair. Black was a popular colour for shoes, but green and red were worn on special occasions, and especially at weddings. The shoes had high or low heels, the former being slightly easier to walk in. Sleeping shoes of red satin were worn in bed, some with bells inside the toes to fuel the erotic associations linked to the foot-binding custom (**plates 43, 44**).

There were some regional differences in the shoes. In general, those from the north, especially Beijing, had a 'bow' shape, an exaggerated curved sole and heel in one piece, often with leather reinforcements at toe and heel. In the late nineteenth century, fashion-conscious women from Shanghai liked a multiple heel, while those shoes from the southern provinces such as Guangdong were often made of black cotton or silk, with a fairly flat heel. Some shoes had a heel tongue and loops at the sides to enable them to be pulled onto the foot more easily. Iron or wooden studs were added in some cases to raise and protect the embroidered silk shoes from the dirt of the streets, while another type was the studded overshoe, into which the bound-foot shoe fitted.

It was not until the end of the nineteenth century that foot-binding started to decline due to Western influences. Various anti-foot-binding societies were formed to promote its demise; it was banned by the new Republic in 1912, and gradually died out amid resistance throughout much of the country for some decades.[6]

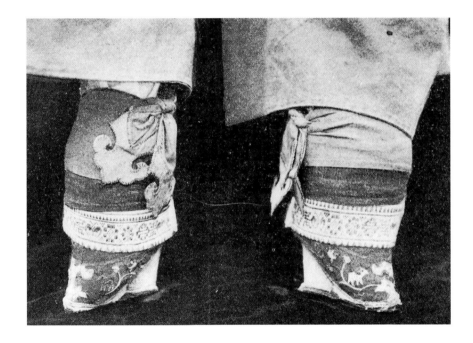

Fig. 7.12 Woman wearing small shoes and ankle covers.

Notes

1   Other aspects of male dress from the Ming period have been adopted by women. The patron saint of fisherpeople in southern China, Tin Hau, wears the flat-topped headdress worn by the Ming emperors for ceremonial wear; when not having the full status of a goddess, she wears the ridged coronet known as *pi bian*.

2   Rev. Justus Doolittle, *Social Life of the Chinese*, New York: Harper & Bros., 1895, vol. 1, p. 100.

3   Princess Der Ling, *Imperial Incense*, New York: Dodd, Mead & Co., 1933, p. 230.

4   Chiang Yee, *A Chinese Childhood*, London: Methuen & Co., 1940, p. 52. This *pao hua* gel is still used today by Chinese opera actresses in Hong Kong to shape the hair for performances.

5 The Chinese characters for 'shoe' and 'together' are pronounced *xie*, a punning reference and wish that the couple will stay together for many years. Wang Yarong, *Chinese Folk Embroidery*, London: Thames and Hudson, 1987, p. 18.
6 Harry A. Franck, *Roving Through Southern China*, New York: The Century Co., 1925, p. 418.

Part III
The Twentieth Century (After 1912)

8 Urban Men's Clothing

Qing dynasty China was ruled by lesser men following the death of the Qianlong Emperor in 1795. A close control on foreign trade had been maintained for centuries, but the strength of Western interests was brought to a head in the Opium War of 1840–42, the result of Chinese attempts to suppress trade in opium in which the British, in particular, had been long involved. China was forced to make numerous concessions following her defeat; one of these was the opening, in addition to Guangzhou, of the four ports of Shanghai, Ningbo, Fuzhou, and Xiamen to trade from the West. Also as a result of the Treaty of Nanjing of 1842, the island of Hong Kong was ceded to Britain in perpetuity. By the end of the century further encroachment by Western powers had resulted in territorial leases at fifteen Treaty Ports, most notably in Shanghai, but also at Wei Hai Wei and Qingdao in Shandong province, and the New Territories adjacent to Hong Kong.

The Xianfeng Emperor died in 1861. Cixi, the Empress Dowager, and mother of the Tongzhi Emperor, a minor, became co-regent and, in effect, ruled the country for the next fifty years. Following her son's death in 1874, the succession went to Cixi's nephew, whom she had adopted. The Empress Dowager was suspicious both of modernization and foreign influence, and the Guangxu Emperor fell from her favour because of his support for reform. In 1898 he announced a series of decrees aimed at the modernization of all aspects of government, including the civil service examinations.[1] This short-lived period, known as the Hundred Days of Reform, ended when the Empress Dowager executed some of the reformers and imprisoned the Emperor. Belated reforms of her own were attempted in an effort to hold the empire together, but time ran out for the 'Old Buddha' and she died in November 1908, less than a day after her nephew.

Although Dr Sun Yatsen was the leader of the *Tung Men Hui*, the Revolutionary Alliance Party which eventually brought about the fall of the Qing dynasty and its last emperor, the infant Puyi, the Republic of China established in 1912 was led by the northern general, Yuan Shikai, whose ambition was to continue the empire under his own rule. In 1914 he revived an important ceremony, the

Sacrifice at the Temple of Heaven, which had only been carried out by emperors, and proclaimed the beginning of a new dynasty. Yuan died in mid-1916, however, and dispute over the control of Beijing intensified.

'Republican' Ceremonial Robes

A robe and hat designed for Yuan Shikai to wear at the Temple of Heaven was based on the regalia worn by the Han and Ming emperors at sacrificial ceremonies. The robe, with a border of gold brocade and made of black satin fastened over to the right, had twelve medallions, each containing the full Twelve Symbols (**fig. 8.1**).

Fig. 8.1 A member of Yuan Shikai's government wearing a hat and black satin robe edged with blue brocade and modelled on the old Chinese ceremonial attire, the robe having seven medallions containing seven of the Twelve Symbols. These are placed one on each shoulder, one on each lower sleeve, one on the lower front and back skirt, and one on the upper back.

Fig. 8.2 Medallion of black satin from the Republican robes, containing five of the Twelve Symbols embroidered in blue and white. Diameter 21 cm. Valery Garrett.

Officials who participated in the ceremony wore gowns of black satin edged with bands of blue brocade. The first rank wore nine medallions with nine symbols; the second rank had seven with seven symbols; the third, five with five symbols; the fourth, three with three symbols; the lowest-ranking officials wore a robe with no border or medallions (**fig. 8.2**).

Around the waist was a belt of matching brocade with a separate bow and long ties; the gown was worn over an apron skirt of red satin edged with blue brocade. A flat hat made of black satin with couched gold thread embroidery was worn; some had strings of pearls hanging over the face, similar to the style of the earlier emperors.

Plate 37 *Mang ao* in red satin lined with natural hemp, with ten dragons, including one on the back of each sleeve. Embroidery of satin stitch and Peking knot peonies. Inscription on inside back reads '...ordered 11th year of Daoguang, 8th month [1832], one *long pao* and one *lu gun* [green skirt]'. 120 cm(L). Hong Kong Museum of Art.

Plate 38 *Xia pei* in dark blue silk, with embroidered gold couched dragons, satin stitch clouds and bats, Peking knot birds of first, third, and fourth ranks on front, fifth, seventh, and ninth on back; fourth-rank civil badge of gold couched thread. 110 cm(L, incl. fringe). Valery Garrett.

Plate 39 Turquoise silk leno *ao* with wide three-type border of plain bias-cut silk in pale pink, braid, and black lace; 'coins' and 'butterflies' at fastening. 87 cm(L), late 19th cent. Valery Garrett.

Plate 40 Lilac silk leno skirt densely embroidered with peonies and butterflies in *san lan*, 'three blues', a type of embroidery worn by older women; blue cotton waistband. 94 cm(L). Valery Garrett.

Plate 41   Cream silk *ao* and trousers set, edged with pink bias-cut satin and braid, 'coins' and 'bats' outlined with piping for fastening of bird and flowers; hemp waistband. *Ao* 85 cm(L); trousers 105 cm(L). Valery Garrett.

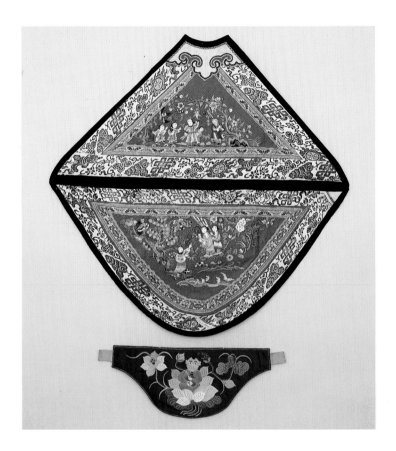

Plate 42   At the top: lady's *dou dou*, with embroidery showing figures in a garden, the edges trimmed with braid depicting the eight Buddhist emblems; money belt with embroidery of a child wearing a *dou dou* sitting in a lotus flower. 19th cent. Valery Garrett.

Plate 43   From the top, clockwise: red satin bound feet shoes with leather sole and heel reinforcements, Beijing style; red silk embroidered shoes with undulating sole, Shanghai style; pink embroidered shoes with flat heel, southern China style; red satin embroidered sleeping shoes with bells inside the toes. Shanghai. Valery Garrett.

Plate 44 From the top, clockwise: supports for bound feet shoes; apricot silk embroidered and padded socks to be worn inside bound feet shoes; blue silk couched gold and silver embroidered ankle covers for bound feet; blue silk embroidered socks with cutaway heels for wearing with bound feet. Valery Garrett.

Plate 45 'Zhongshan' style uniform which belonged to Dr Sun Yat Sen.

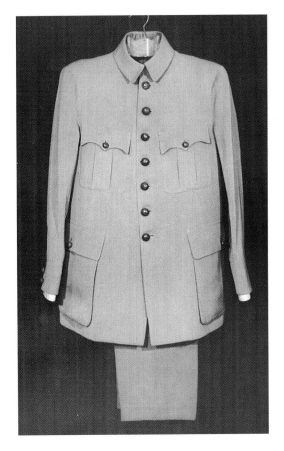

Plate 46   Cream silk *ao* and skirt set, embroidered with floral sprays, hem edged with sequins and beads, and
with an elastic tunnel waist. Shanghai. *Ao* 50 cm(L); skirt 78 cm(L); c.1920. Valery Garrett.

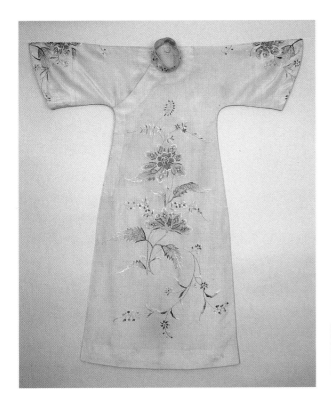

Plate 47   The earliest style of *qi pao,* with a straight cut *tou jin*, round stiff collar, and side seams falling straight. Yellow silk embroidered with floral sprays. 103 cm(L), c.1925. Valery Garrett.

Plate 48   Calendar, advertising Two Girls brand of cosmetics, depicting knee-length *qi pao*. 1930. Kwong Sang Hong.

Plate 49 A poster
from Shanghai advert-
ising soap, showing two
women wearing the
long *qi pao*. c.1935.
Valery Garrett.

Western Influences

With the collapse of imperial rule, and after attempts to restore the monarchy had failed, dragon robes and the attendant regalia were gradually phased out, although Puyi, the deposed Xuantong Emperor, continued to live in the northern section of the Forbidden City until November 1924. From the establishment of the Republic in 1912, government ministers and people in public life were required to wear Western-style dress. Regulations published in government gazettes laid down the correct attire, together with drawings illustrating clothing and even headwear: at first top hats and bowlers, later trilby hats and straw boaters (**fig. 8.3**). However, it was stipulated that the various forms of male and female dress were to be made from Chinese (or 'national' as opposed to foreign) materials. It is clear that, despite its foreign origins and appearance, the new dress, designated for all ceremonial occasions great and small, was to be utilized as an instrument of the newly re-established national pride in China and being Chinese.

Nevertheless, by the end of the nineteenth century, Western influences had even begun to affect clothing traditions for men involved in commerce and industry. Foreign businesses began to pour into the country, and a mixture of Western and Chinese dress began to be worn, particularly in the main ports and cities. People began to travel and work overseas and their 'home remittances' affected the lifestyle of those left behind, while many returning students adopted Western dress.

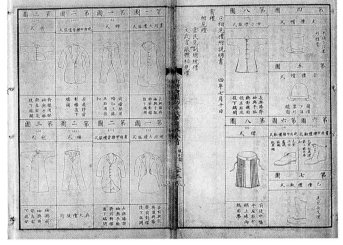

Fig. 8.3   Pages from a compendium guide first published in 1920 showing formal wear, a mixture of Chinese and Western dress, for men and women. Shanghai. Reprinted (70th impression) 1929.

Chang Shan Ma Qua

With the capital moved south to Nanjing in 1927, formal wear was established for men consisting of the *ma qua* worn with the *chang shan*. This was official dress for important ceremonial occasions such as weddings, and for worshipping in temples and ancestral halls.[2] When worn with the *ma qua* as formal wear, the long gown was usually blue, but when worn alone it could be grey,

Fig. 8.4   Four generations aged between 13 and 85 years; the seated men are wearing the *ma qua* with the long gown, the young boy a *bei xin* with the gown. 1913. Public Records Office, Hong Kong.

Fig. 8.5   Three men in a park wearing *chang shan, ma qua,* and trilby hat or skullcap. 1920s. Valery Garrett.

Fig. 8.6   Jacket and under-jacket in polyester and cotton. Hong Kong, 1979. Valery Garrett.

brown, or black. A stand collar had replaced the narrow collar binding at the beginning of the century (**fig. 8.4**). For less formal occasions a sleeveless, centre- or side-fastening waistcoat would be worn over the gown.

The *chang shan ma qua* was worn with the black skullcap seen since the Ming, or else a Western-style felt trilby hat (**fig. 8.5**). Since the over-throw of the Manchus, Han Chinese men were no longer required to wear the queue, but many continued to shave their heads, often completely. To keep out the winter cold in the north, a black satin hat, lined with fur, was worn with ear flaps and a back flap. The high black satin boots were replaced by black cloth shoes, often made of felt with thin leather soles, and white cotton socks.

By the 1940s a two-piece outfit of centre-opening jacket and *ku* was worn by all classes for more informal occasions. The jacket was cut like the gown, minus the inside flap at the right-hand side. The sleeves were longer and wider; the cuffs of the under-garment might be turned over the top jacket or coat. For an added touch of elegance, detachable white cuffs were worn (**fig. 8.6**).

The centre-front fastened with seven buttons, and patch pockets were added. The jacket and *ku* were often in matching fabrics of different types of silk or wool mixtures.

Communist Influence on Dress

Increased domination by the Japanese, who had commercial and political interests in Manchuria, led to full-scale aggression and war with China between 1937 and 1945. The struggle between Nationalists and Communists intensified following Japan's defeat in World War II and continued until the Communists finally gained control and proclaimed the People's Republic of China in October 1949. The establishment of the People's Republic was to have a more marked effect on national dress than any previous event in the country's history, as it affected everyone regardless of sex, age, or class.

The *chang shan* was considered unpatriotic and disappeared. It was replaced by a utilitarian outfit produced to emphasize the fact that society was now taking its lead from workers, peasants, and soldiers rather than from the gentry and scholar officials as tradition dictated. A jacket developed from one introduced by Dr Sun Yatsen as military uniform (**plate 45**) was reintroduced and worn by Mao Zedong to unify the proletariat (**fig. 8.7**). Mass-produced and loose-fitting, with the centre-front always closely buttoned to the neck, it was worn with Western-style trousers, a soft flat cloth cap with a red star at centre-front, and cloth shoes. Civilians, factory workers, and peasants wore the 'uniform' in shades of deep blue cotton, but party cadres might wear the outfit made of grey barathea. In winter in the north, padded cotton coats helped to keep out the cold. In some parts of the country this outfit is still worn, but during the 1980s there were increasing signs in major cities, such as Beijing and Shanghai in particular, that greater variation and colour were permitted, including many Western styles.

Fig. 8.7 Mao Zedong in the style of jacket which was to become commonplace throughout China. 1936.

Notes

1 One such reform included the recommendation that Chinese clothing be abandoned in favour of Western dress, a change which would have had disastrous effects on the Chinese silk industry.
2 The *ma gua* and *chang shan* continue to be worn at important clan rituals in the New Territories of Hong Kong in the early 1990s.

9 Urban Women's Dress

The atmosphere of change in the late Qing period, the demise of Manchu rule, and the formation of the Republic in 1912 brought wide-sweeping reforms for women, including women's clothing. Foot-binding was legally abolished, and girls were granted a formal place in the educational system, with some daughters of wealthy families being sent overseas to study. Many educated women, especially those in the Treaty Ports, adopted Western fashions, a trend which had begun at the end of the nineteenth century when a number of Chinese women in the public eye wore Western dress. Some may have been influenced by missionaries, or other Western women with whom they came into contact, or by foreign magazines and newspapers which were increasingly available. But the tightly corseted dresses, large hats, gloves, and parasols of the Victorian era looked costume-like on the diminutive Chinese lady, just as the *ao gun* and phoenix crown might have done on Western women, and the trend was short-lived.

Ao Gun, 1912–1925

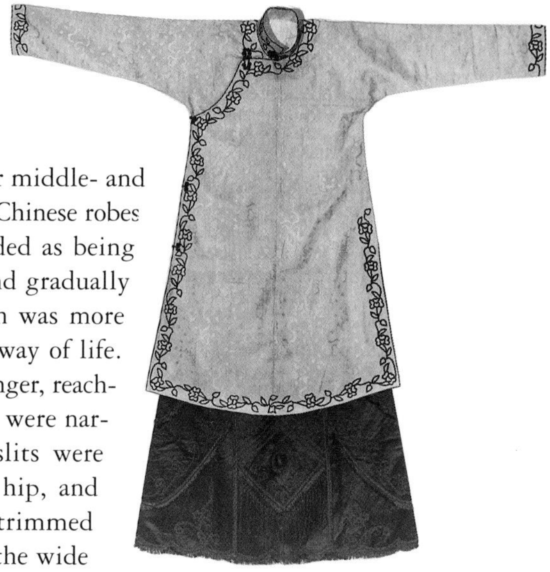

Fig. 9.1 Pale green silk leno *ao* with appliquéd black piping decoration around edges, 96 cm(L); black satin skirt with elaborate fringing and piping decoration, 99 cm(L). c.1915. Valery Garrett.

With greater emancipation for middle- and upper-class women, the bulky Chinese robes worn in the past were discarded as being outdated and cumbersome, and gradually a style of dress evolved which was more in keeping with the Chinese way of life. The *ao* became slimmer and longer, reaching to below the knee; sleeves were narrow to the wrists; the side slits were short, reaching to the lower hip, and all the edges of the *ao* were trimmed with narrow braid, instead of the wide bands of embroidery which had been popular in the past (**fig. 9.1**). The collar was high, as high as it would ever be, and sometimes had the corners turned down. Some exaggerated collars reached up to the ears to meet the wide headband, accentuating the wearer's oval face (**fig. 9.2**).

Fig. 9.2 Shanghai 'sing song' girls wearing headbands and the fashionable, exaggeratedly high collars on the *ao*. c.1915.

Fig. 9.3 Miss Chia Yu-Wen, a Tianjin courtesan noted for her small feet. c.1912.

The *ao* was worn over an ankle-length skirt, usually black, which had now become a one-piece garment with panels at front and back attached to pleats and godets at the sides. Where the *ao* was worn with trousers or leggings by the unmarried, the trousers were narrower and the colour softer, often pastel, and usually the garments matched (**fig. 9.3**).

By the early 1920s the upper garment had become more fitted, and finished at the top hip with the hem rounded. The sleeves were three-quarter length— with wide rounded cuffs worn by the very fashionable woman—and the collar was reduced to a more comfortable width (**fig. 9.4, 9.5**). An alternative style was a sleeveless tunic with a square neck worn over a plain blouse, cut like the *ao* (**fig. 9.6**).

With the shortening of the upper garments at the beginning of the 1920s, the skirt became plainer and hem lengths rose gradually. The skirt was now a simple flared style finishing at mid-calf, very often of black silk damask and worn by married and unmarried

Fig. 9.4 'Sing song' girls from Hangzhou.

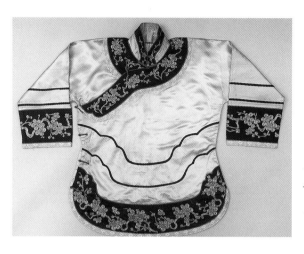

Fig. 9.5   Pale green satin *ao*, displaying wide black satin bands with couched gold embroidery of plum blossoms. Shanghai. 64 cm(L), 1920s. Valery Garrett.

women alike. By this time the wide waistband had been replaced by a narrow tunnel through which a cord or elastic was threaded (**plate 46**). By 1925 the top, blouse, and skirt had combined to create a one-piece garment called a *qi pao*, literally 'banner gown', as it resembled the style worn by Manchu women in the past.[1] At the time it was considered a very daring style, revealing the lines of the figure as never before. The *qi pao* was never adopted by women in rural areas, as it was considered far too restricting. The *ao ku* also continued to be worn by unmarried women and those who enjoyed the freedom of movement that trousers gave.

Fig. 9.6   A group of prominent women from Guangzhou wearing the two- and three-piece top and skirt.

Development of the *Qi Pao*, 1925–1950

Styles of clothing for formal wear for women were also stipulated when Nanjing became the capital of the Republic of China in 1927. The first was a black jacket and blue skirt cut as earlier outfits, with the jacket reaching to the top of the hips, a straight band collar, a fastening down the right-hand side with buttons and loops, and three-quarter length sleeves.

The second style was the *qi pao,* and this garment soon became the fashionable choice for most women **(plate 47, fig. 9.7)**. The garment fell straight from the shoulders in an A-line to the hem, which was just below the knee, corresponding to the shorter length skirts worn in the West. The collar was a narrow band opening at the *tou jin,* which was cut in a straight line with the garment fastening to the hip on the right side with press-studs. The sleeves were shortened to the elbow and widened with a curved edge. The decoration was of embroidered sprays of flowers scattered over the dress, or edging with wide bands of embroidery attached to hem and cuffs **(plate 48)**.

During the 1930s hemlines dropped to the ankle; by the middle of the decade the dress, in some cases, was long enough to cover the feet **(plate 49)**. Gradually, the garment became quite fitted, while some worn by very fashion-conscious women had side slits reaching right up to the thigh, emphasized by legs clad in silk stockings (a recent innovation) and high heels. Sleeves were slimmer, finishing above the elbow, or the garment might have cap sleeves or be sleeveless. Towards the end of the decade the hem rose to lower mid-calf, sleeves lengthened to the wrist in some cases, and all edges were outlined with narrow piping. There was a loosening of the garment with the waist and hips more exaggerated; the hem was even indented to accentuate the curve.

The influence on fashion from Shanghai, where the *qi pao* first appeared, was very strong throughout the country at this time, and the city remains a centre of style in China. Often called the 'Paris of the East', Shanghai was glittering and sophisticated while Hong Kong at this period was considered a quiet colonial backwater. The film industry in Shanghai was big business: its sixty theatres, catering for some three million inhabitants, accounted for more than 20 per cent of the cinemas in China. Movie stars, both male and female, were treated grandly and their tastes in fashion were detailed in magazines eagerly devoured by their admirers. The permanent wave, especially, was copied by all women with style.

Fig. 9.7   *Qi pao* with contrast sleeves. c.1925. Valery Garrett.

Fig. 9.8   A group of women wearing the cap-sleeved *qi pao*. Hong Kong, c.1940. Hong Kong Museum of History.

During the 1940s the *qi pao* was long to the ankle and, for more conservative women, had long sleeves often fur-lined or wadded with silk. For the younger, more fashion-conscious woman, the garment was still slim-fitting, the sleeves shortened to small cap sleeves, or a sleeveless version, and the *tou jin* was often extended to the left side, though this did not always open (**fig. 9.8**). The collar was outlined at top and bottom edges with piping which matched that at the hem and sleeves. Decorative frog buttons were placed on the *tou jin* and collar.

Post-war, 1950–1990

Following the end of World War II hemlines rose gradually to reach mid-calf by the 1950s. Shoulder seams were introduced to give a sloping shoulder effect, and the collar, which had piped edges, was rounded for a softer effect. By the end of the decade the garment had become very fitted with a high-waisted look created by the use of bust and waist darts. The dress had set-in sleeves, either cap or long and narrow, was fastened with press-studs at the *tou jin*, and with a zipper, used for the first time, down the side (**fig. 9.9**). The piping then disappeared, and the indented hem accentuated the curvaceous look. In the 1960s, the style popularized by Nancy Kwan in the British-made film *The World of Suzie Wong* caught world attention, and was even worn by a member of the British royal family visiting Hong Kong.

Clothing traditions were swept aside in post-1949 China, and during the ten years of the Cultural Revolution the *qi pao* was outlawed as being decadent.

Fig. 9.9 Celebrating the six-teenth anniversary of the victory of the Chinese Communists, the last time the *qi pao* would be tolerated until very recently. 1965. Valery Garrett.

Skirts were also banned, and women then wore a female standard-issue version of the so-called Mao suit of dark blue or grey cotton jacket and trousers. This outfit had a centre button-fastening jacket with a peter pan collar, two or four patch pockets and baggy trousers; it was a puritanical, distinctly unflattering mode of dress. The permanent wave was forbidden until the early 1980s; unmarried women frequently wore two long plaits, while others wore their hair cropped short in the style of early revolutionary women.

In Taiwan and Hong Kong there was a gradual discarding of traditional styles in the late 1960s and 1970s, and an increased adoption by the younger generation of Western styles, especially fashions from Italy and France which entered via Japan. In mainland China the death of Mao Zedong in 1976 led to a slow loosening of rules relating to dress and social constraints (fig. 9.10). By the 1980s younger women in the major cities had begun to integrate Western styles, starting with trousers and denim jeans, and more recently, dresses and skirts. This trend crept through China gradually, the influence coming from Hong Kong via Guangdong province: a neat reversal of the 1920s and 1930s era, when fashion originated in Shanghai and filtered down via Guangzhou to Hong Kong.

Over the years, the *qi pao*, in silk or rayon brocade, with or without a matching jacket, was worn less and less in Hong Kong and Taiwan except by the older, more traditional women, and its use was reserved for special occasions. However, in China itself, in very recent times, there have been a few indications that it may make a comeback.

Fig. 9.10 Women in regulation jacket and trousers. 1980.

Note

1 In Cantonese, *cheung sam*, which literally means 'long gown'.

10   Rural Clothing

China has always been primarily an agricultural nation with the majority of the population living and working on the land. As a result, in traditional China agriculture was considered an honourable profession next in importance to serving the emperor as an official.[1] Men were proud to be farmers; a merchant or trader had far less status. Fishing was another important occupation for country people, especially in southern and central China, around the long coastline, and along the numerous rivers and waterways.

Everyday rural clothing was made of hard-wearing fabrics in sombre colours reflecting the difficulty and uncertainty of rural life. An often harsh working life was enhanced in many ways through the festivals and rituals which occurred each year, marking the development of the individual, as well as the farming calendar and the worshipping of local gods. At these times women brightened their dark clothing by adding ornaments to their hats and hair, and children wore specially made decorative clothing. Senior male members of the clan or village elders dressed in the style of the scholar officials of the Qing dynasty.

Shan Ku

Peasant farmers or fishermen wore a simple *shan ku*, a garment which is still worn today in some rural areas. The two-piece outfit was made of hard-wearing fabrics (**fig. 10.1**). Hemp was popular as it was cool to wear; it was grown in some villages up to the 1920s. Cotton was very common, either produced locally or in the main cotton-producing areas of Shanghai and the Yangzi River Delta. It was usually dyed

Fig. 10.1 Hakka woman with her child by a rice winnowing machine. 1909.

blue or black, and ox blood used to overdye black to give a purplish tint was very popular for a while. Egg whites were used in
some regions to give a glossy look; this could also be obtained by
calendering, achieved by rolling a heavy stone over the fabric. Some
regional fabric treatments were developed, such as black gummed
silk, *hei jiao chou*, from the district of Shunde in Guangdong province,
which was favoured by all strata of society in Hong Kong and the
Pearl River Delta, especially during the 1920s and 1930s. It was
utilized particularly by boat people as it was easy to wash, and was
waterproof as well as being cool to wear.

Mass-produced fabrics became widespread after the Sino-Japanese
War and *shan ku* were either made-to-measure by local tailors or
bought from market stalls and hawkers. In the past, however, many
women would make *shan ku* by hand as part of their wedding
dowry, then for their families. Paste made from 'thirty parts of
wheat flour to one part of cooked rice',[2] mixed with water, was
used to hold the seams together rather than basting with thread;
seams were then ironed in place and machined. Paste was also used
to stiffen the collar, but was later replaced by nylon net.

In tune with the prevailing fashions of the time, the nineteenth-
century *shan ku* was a large, long garment with wide trousers, particularly so in the type worn by the Hakka (Kejia) women, but
during the twentieth century it gradually became shorter and more fitted, with
a narrow neckband. When the fabric was mass-produced and wider after the
Sino-Japanese War, the centre seams were omitted.

Fabrics for the *ku* were similar to those used for the *shan*, although the two
garments were not always made as a set. The main part was usually black, blue,
or grey, but the waistband, which was always of a lighter quality, was generally
blue, or natural white. In Guangdong province a white waistband was referred
to as *bai tou dao lao*, literally 'white head, old age'—a fanciful way of referring
to the white waistband, as well as a wish for a long and happy marriage.

In the late nineteenth century the *shan* was discarded by men in favour of
the centre-opening jacket (**fig. 10.2**). Patch pockets were then added to the
front, as many as three or four on the outside, and often two or three inside as
well. Inside pockets were called *dai kou*, literally 'pocket mouths', implying that
the wearer had many mouths at home to feed.

Fig. 10.2 Village coolie wearing layered jackets and skullcap. c.1937. Osgood, 1963.

Underwear

In general, no special type of underwear was worn by rural people. Old *shan
ku* were worn as underwear, as well as for sleeping.[3] In the past, a special type

of under-garment worn by farmers and coolies was the knotted string jacket. Closely resembling today's string vest, it opened down the front and was made of rice straw twisted into string joined together in an open weave design. A decorative row of weaving was placed a few centimetres above the hem and sleeve edges; the neck and waist fastened with loops and ball buttons. The shoulder and top back were made of indigo-dyed or natural cotton, or hemp, in a double layer to prevent soreness when carrying a heavy load.

Headwear

Straw Hats

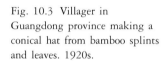

Fig. 10.3 Villager in Guangdong province making a conical hat from bamboo splints and leaves. 1920s.

The conical hat made of bamboo splints and leaves was a common sight, particularly in the warmer provinces south of the Yangzi, and it is still worn by farmers as protection against the sun and rain (fig. 10.3). An unusual variation, the *liang mao* or 'cool hat', is still worn by Hakka women, a group who migrated from northern China and settled in Fujian, Guangdong, and Hong Kong. A flat circular shape of woven straw and bamboo with a hole in the centre and a black cotton fringe around the edge, it is worn when working out of doors to give protection from both flies and the weather (fig. 10.4).

Coolies and boat people wore a hat of bamboo with a domed crown and turned-down brim, and this is still worn in the fishing communities of southern China. Along the south coast of Guangdong, women now often have the crown of their hats decorated with coloured plastic cord in the form of an elaborately woven star covering the whole of the crown, and sometimes extending to the brim. Even today, it is said to bring safety and luck to the wearer (plate 50).

Headcloths

When not working in the fields, especially during the cooler months, women in rural areas wore a headband high on the forehead similar to those worn by

Fig. 10.4 Hakka woman wearing headcloth, woven band, apron, and wrist covers, holding the *liang mao*. Hong Kong, 1940s. Public Records Office, Hong Kong.

women in the Qing dynasty. Only married women could wear them, and they were made or purchased as part of the dowry (**plate 51**). Some were elaborately embroidered with pearls, beads and sequins with a jade or gold ornament at the centre, while others were covered completely with small Peking glass beads in a floral design. In winter, older women still wear a black velvet hat with a crown pleated into the shaped headband.

Headcloths were worn around the home, and by older women in other ethnic groups. Still seen today is the black *bao tou* worn at home by Hakka women in southern China and Hong Kong. Made of black cotton or gummed silk, it is a rectangle with one-third folded back over the head, and held in place by a woven patterned band. Han peasant women in Yunnan province wear a blue cotton headcloth, which is often embroidered with a white cross-stitch pattern at the centre.

The Tanka (Daan ga) boatwomen in Guangdong, and especially in Hong Kong and Macau, also wore a headscarf in cooler weather. This was a large black cotton folded square with an embroidered border, in red, orange, or purple in an irregular zig-zag pattern (**plate 52**). Into the folded edge of the triangle was placed a metal or bamboo bar which was flexible and framed the face to protect the eyes from the sun. Younger women wore scarves of brightly checked cotton with the same embroidery design in multi-colours at the edges.[4]

A blue and white patterned scarf is worn by the Hui'an women in Fujian province. Over this large headscarf, secured with many plastic flowers and ornaments, is worn a straw hat with a pointed crown and a flat brim (**plate 53**).

Straw Raincoats

As well as wearing straw headwear as a protection from the elements, farmers, boat people, and coolies wore clothing made of rice straw or palm fibre (**fig. 10.5**). The straw raincoat, *suo yi*, had been worn for centuries:

> Watermen, peasantry, and others employed in the open air, are generally provided with a coat made of straw, from which the rain runs off . . . in addition to this they sometimes wear a cloak, formed of the stalks of *kow-liang* [*kao liang*] (millet), which completely covers the shoulders; and a broad hat,

Fig. 10.5 Farmer wearing the straw raincoat and straw apron. c.1890. Hong Kong Museum of History.

composed of straw and split bamboo, which defends them both from sun and rain. A Chinese thus equipped . . . may certainly defy the heaviest showers.[5]

Dried leaves from palm trees or rice straw were used, depending on the region, and layers of the leaves or straw were folded and stitched to the layer above with string made from rice straw. The layers were made wider at the top to form a cape. In some cases 'the stalks of the stubble are sewed to a clumsy weft of the same substance, the meshes of which are very wide'.[6] A similar method of construction applied to palm fibre capes worn in Shantou (Swatow) which were made by stripping pieces of fibre from the bark and flattening and sewing them together to make a cloak 75 centimetres square, held round the neck by sewing the edge to a length of rope.[7] These are still seen occasionally in some areas of western China.

Straw aprons were also worn by men and women, especially the latter, when threshing rice. Constructed in similar fashion to the raincoat, they were made of four layers of rice straw or palm leaves reaching from chest to knee, and were hung round the neck by a long string of rice straw. Wrist covers of plaited straw and cotton mittens protected the hands when cutting rice or grass.

Accessories

Aprons

Aprons were worn by farming women as part of their everyday attire, irrespective of the task at hand. Hakka women wore two types, referred to as summer and winter aprons, but this definition related more to the age of the woman than to the season of the year. Summer aprons were of blue or black cotton decorated across the top with ric-rac braid and decorative stitching. They were held in place with a silver chain which had silver coins at each end for threading through the apron loops. A woven patterned band went across the back waist. Winter aprons utilized the top part of a summer apron, a length of striped or patterned cotton formed the waistband, and the apron skirt was made of brown glazed cotton. They were fastened across the back with a long cotton or silk patterned band.

Cantonese women also wore a summer apron made of black cotton, trimmed at the upper sides with narrow blue or green piping. The decoration across the top was of folded coloured cotton, sometimes with two fabric rosettes and loops to hold the silver neck chain. A woven silk and patterned band held it in place at the waist (plate 54). A blue cotton apron with an embroidered flap at the front is still worn by Han peasant women in Yunnan (plate 55).

Patterned Bands

Woven patterned bands, *hua dai*, were used in some areas as apron strings at the waist as well as to anchor hats. Made of cotton and silk, they were a Hakka tradition which was adopted by Cantonese women. Measuring about 1 centimetre wide and between 33 and 110 centimetres long, those worn by the Hakka were made of either white cotton with the pattern in coloured silk or else all in silk, while the Cantonese wore only those in multi-coloured silk. The pattern woven through the centre of the band was said to indicate the woman's marital status, in addition to the individual patterns being good luck symbols.[8]

Individual bands made of small beads threaded on to nylon fishing line were worn by Hoklo and Tanka boatwomen as cotton or silk would get wet and be uncomfortable to wear. Made by the wearer, these sometimes depicted the characters of the owner's name.

Jewellery

As well as being a means of dressing up otherwise often sombre apparel, jewellery made in gold was a convenient way of saving. The pure metal was stamped with a jeweller's mark, thus binding him by guild law to buy back the article at any time by weight. Silver was not as prized and was often gilded to look like gold. Even so, articles in an alloy known as *bai tong* (white copper) were frequently purchased by peasants as it resembled silver but was cheaper. Jade, thought to have long life properties, is still widely worn today.

Women in rural areas dressed their hair with many colourful and elaborate hair ornaments, especially on festive occasions. The Hoklo boatwomen in Fujian and Guangdong were particularly fond of this form of decoration (**fig. 10.6**). Into large, and sometimes false, hairbuns were pushed jade and gilt butterfly pins, gilt and diamanté stars, and pink wool flowers. Silver and gold hairpins hung over the right ear attached by chains to the rest of the ornaments. Cantonese women also wore bright pink wool decorations,

Fig. 10.6 Hoklo hair bun studded with many gilt hair ornaments. Guangdong province, c.1950. Valery Garrett.

together with a flat gold hair-pin with oval ends, pushed into the bun. Hairbuns made of twisted silk fabric and decorated with red or pink wool are favoured by Han peasant women in Yunnan.

Apron chains made of many silver coins were popular, as were carved silver bangles worn around the wrist, or in pairs around the ankles of a bride (**fig. 10.7**). Jade bangles are still popular and worn by all ages: . . . 'a married woman sometimes wears two, one on behalf of her husband. If the bangle is broken by a blow, it is considered that the jade absorbed the shock which would otherwise have broken the wrist'.[9]

Fig. 10.7 Hakka apron chain made up of link chain and silver coins from the reigns of Queen Victoria and Edward VII. Macau. Valery Garrett.

Pendants of gold or jade charms were worn as protection against evil. Most popular were carved jade Buddhas, coins with a hole in the centre surrounded by lucky symbols, and the Eight Trigrams (an ancient system of divination). Earrings worn by the different ethnic groups were made of gold and/or jade.

Fans

A fan had a variety of uses—to cool the air, to gesticulate—and no man considered himself properly dressed without one. Xin Hui in Guangdong was the centre of an important industry making palm leaf fans dating back many centuries. Made from *pu kui* (*Livistonia chinensis*) one tree would produce between five and fifteen fans per year for over a hundred years. The ends trimmed off the leaves utilized for straw raincoats were used for the cheapest fans, while the finest quality palm leaves were used for fans with bound edges. Folding paper fans and black feather fans were also carried.

Footwear

Many peasants wore no shoes at all, except in the coldest weather when black cloth shoes or straw sandals were worn. Wooden clogs, crudely hewn from a block of wood, about five centimetres thick, with an upper foot strap made of rubber, were worn by some villagers, especially those working in fish markets. An earlier version worn by villagers and labourers, dating back to the last century, was a kind of backless shoe with a wooden sole and leather upper made from buffalo hide.

Notes

1 Charles O. Hucker, *The Traditional Chinese State in Ming Times (1368–1644)*, Tucson: The University of Arizona Press, 1972, p. 30.

2 C. Osgood, *The Chinese: A Study of a Hong Kong Community*, vol. I–III, Tucson: The University of Arizona Press, 1975, vol. 2, p. 568.

3 In recent years under-*shan* have begun to be made in the same style as outer-*shan*, but in lighter fabrics such as polyester and cotton. There are normally pockets on the under-*shan*, which are always missing on the outer-*shan*, and the sleeves are short, or it is sleeveless.

4 These scarves can be seen in the mid-nineteenth century paintings by George Chinnery and his student Lamqua of the boatwomen in Macau.

5 William Alexander, 'A Group of Chinese, Habited for Rainy Weather', in *The Costume of China*, London, 1805.

6 M. Breton, *China: Its Costume, Arts, Manufacturing, Etc.*, London, 1812, vol. IV, p. 35.

7 C. Osgood, *Village Life in Old China*, New York: Ronald Press, 1963, p. 174.

8 See E. I. Johnson, 'Patterned Bands in the New Territories of Hong Kong', *Journal of the Hong Kong Branch of the Royal Asiatic Society*, 16 (1976): 81–91.

9 V. R. Burkhardt, *Chinese Creeds and Customs*, Hong Kong: South China Morning Post, 1955–9, vol. 1, p. 180.

Part IV
Military Uniforms and Dress for Special Occasions

11 Military Uniforms

China's rulers often attempted to pacify potential aggressors with titles and sumptuous robes, but incursions and warfare ensued when such tactics failed. In times of peace, ceremonial armour was worn by the emperors and high officials on occasion as a display of might and magnificence. Such splendour contrasted greatly with the non-standard and disparate style of the uniforms of lower-ranking soldiers.

Ming Dynasty Uniforms

Two types of military uniform were stipulated for the emperor, but these were worn in non-combat situations and there was nothing protective about the clothing.[1] The Jiajing Emperor is depicted wearing true military uniform in paintings of his procession to the imperial tombs at the time of his mother's death. The scholar Hu Ching, describing these scrolls in the Qing dynasty, notes 'Being in mourning, the emperor wore a military uniform to visit the imperial tombs'[2] **(plate 56)**. In the painting showing his departure, the emperor is wearing a military officer's uniform, not the 'regular military attire' of the emperor. He is wearing a suit of grey chain-mail encrusted with profile gold dragons on the chest. Dragons are embroidered on the inner side of the purple sleeves, while the outsides have gold overlapping scales of armour. A border of dragons runs down the centre-front opening and round the hem which is finished with a coloured fringe. His helmet is decorated with phoenixes and a tall red plume. The vizard, pennants, and armour on the horse also distinguish the rider from the other officials and guards, who are wearing armour of the same style but without the dragons on chest and sleeves. Foot soldiers wear padded red jackets reaching to the knees, with narrow sleeves.

The 'spirit road' to the tombs outside Beijing where thirteen of the Ming emperors are buried is lined with twelve pairs of stone animals and six pairs of stone officials; two of these are pairs of warriors wearing the more cumbersome court uniform of Ming generals. They are wearing a long robe of several layers made of cloth embroidered with lotus flowers or galloping horses amid waves and clouds. Armour covers the upper arms, the chest and back, and some parts of the skirt. Incorporated into the back of the upper sleeves are prominent folds. Elaborately knotted thongs fasten parts of the garment, and the belt clasp is held in the mouth of a fierce animal. A shoulder-length helmet, which would have been made of metal, painted gold and edged with gold or bronze, has a large knob at the top and large ear covers (**fig. 11.1**). Heavy decorated boots complete the outfit, with the first pair of generals each holding a baton, a symbol of military command.

Fig. 11.1 Statue of a general on the Sacred Way to the Ming tomb, Nanjing.

Qing Dynasty Uniforms

The Manchus, with their history of successful military conquests, placed great emphasis on military training. There were two main armies, the Manchu *Ba Qi* or Eight Banners, and the Chinese *Lu Ying*, or Green Standard Army.

Eight Banners

Originally this was an exclusively Manchu army, instrumental in the overthrow of the Ming empire. By 1601, Nurhachi, the leader of the Nuzhen tribe, had organized all Manchu troops into companies comprising 300 soldiers, with five companies forming a battalion, and had established a military organization known as the Eight Banners. The tribes would move around in battalions while hunting, and the system served as a defence, as well as a means of organizing taxes and land distribution for the whole Manchu population.

Each of the battalions followed a banner of yellow, white (actually a buff shade), blue, and red. These colours were based on 'a mystic system whereby the yellow is made to represent the centre; the red the south; and the white, the west; the north should have been black, but for this, as of bad omen, was substituted the blue; and to the east . . . was assigned . . . the green, which the native troops were directed to assume as their standard.'[3] In 1615, when most of northern China came under Nurhachi's rule and the army was reformed, four more banners were added by trimming the first three with red, and the red one with white. The Eight Banners were divided into Three Upper Banners, whose identifying ensigns were 'Bordered Yellow', 'Plain Yellow', and 'Plain White', and Five Lower Banners, which carried ensigns of 'Plain Red', 'Bordered Red', 'Plain Blue', 'Bordered Blue', and 'Bordered White'. These 'flame' bordered banners were not square in uniformity with the plain banners but were pointed at the right side. They were all embroidered with a dragon chasing a flaming pearl.

Although the Manchu system of military organization continued to be collectively called the Eight Banners, from the start of the Qing period it actually comprised twenty-four banners or units, made up of eight banners of Manchu soldiers, plus eight of Chinese soldiers, and eight of Mongolian soldiers who were direct descendants of those who had assisted in the conquest of China. Every adult Manchu was entitled to belong to one of the Eight Banners and share in the benefits thereof. All banner garrisons were commanded by Manchu generals, of which more than half were in Beijing; the rest were located in China's major cities, theoretically to control the local Chinese. Within the metropolitan areas there were eight ranks of commissioned officers, both principal and subordinate, and in the provinces six ranks, plus the lower-ranking non-commissioned officers and soldiers.

Ceremonial Uniform

During the first half of the dynasty, the Qing emperors held a triennial review of troops at which they inspected the armies to assess their strength. During the parade, demonstrations of cavalry, archery, and combat techniques took place. On these occasions, the emperor would wear a suit of ceremonial armour. Whilst these inspections did not take place regularly after the reign of the Qianlong Emperor, ceremonial suits of armour were still part of the imperial wardrobe and continued to be made, if never worn.

The armour was made of bands of copper gilt plates alternating with brocade and copper studs. The jacket and skirt were made up of loose sections, held together with loops and toggles. Shoulder flaps and a centre flap at the lower edge of the jacket were covered in studs. Each section was heavily padded and lined with blue silk. Earlier armour was even more elaborate, as is seen in that worn by the Qianlong Emperor when reviewing his troops. Here the upper garment was made of yellow silk embroidered with dragons and studded all over, with more dragons around the borders at the skirt hem. The emperor wore a helmet made of iron with a silver gilt inlay design of tassels and dragons. At the top was a tall spike with silk fringing finishing with a large pearl (**plate 57**).

Fig. 11.2 Manchu general's ceremonial uniform in satin covered with metal studs, embroidered with dragon roundels over which are placed metal plates. Early 19th cent. Museo Oriental de Valladolid.

Ceremonial armour for noblemen and high-ranking officials was similar in style to that worn by the emperor, but made of satin padded with cotton, trimmed and lined with blue silk. They were covered with gilt studs, and the separate sections of bodice, skirt, sleeves, shoulder capes, armpit gussets, and groin apron were fastened together with loops and buttons (**fig. 11.2**). The helmet was made of animal hide, lacquered, decorated with copper gilt, and topped with a silk plume and worn over a black silk padded under-hat. Thousands of sets were made in the imperial workshops in Hangzhou, and when not worn were stored at the Western Gate of the Forbidden City.

Ceremonial armour for the bannermen was in plain silk in the colour of their banner. Imperial guardsmen, whose job it was to guard the Forbidden City, wore white satin tunics, while cavalry brigade banner troops wore dark blue satin.

Regular Soldiers' Uniform

The regular uniform was made in the colour of the banner to which the soldier belonged. A short, loose, sleeveless jacket was in either the plain or bordered colour of the banner. It was worn over a white tunic, with stockings the same colour as the jacket, and black cloth boots. Large banners were carried indicating the division, while smaller flags were placed in flag holders strapped to the soldiers' backs. Soldiers on active service wore the sable tail *diao wei*, originally part of the uniform worn on imperial hunting expeditions. Two fur tails were arranged in a V shape and were fixed to the crown of the winter hat, sticking out at the back. They were worn subsequently by all military ranks from general to private (**fig. 11.3**).

Fig. 11.3 Manchu bannermen stationed in Guangzhou where they formed the guard for the British Consul. c.1870.

Green Standard Army

The second of the two regular armies within the Qing administration was entirely Chinese and was known as the Green Standard Army, or *Lu Ying*, because of the large triangular standard carried, made of green satin with a scalloped red satin border representing flames. A gold dragon was embroidered in the centre. The Green Standard Army, established by the Manchus as a form of provincial constabulary, was divided into an army and a navy, and was responsible for the defence and internal security of the country. It was made up of two kinds of soldiers, those permanently employed, and those, named *yung* or 'braves', who were called up to fight when required.

Military Officials

Manchu officers shared the responsibility for the Green Standard Army units with Chinese officers. This regular army was organized by province with a commander-in-chief known as a *ti du* who was stationed in the provincial capital or prefectural city. Below the *ti du* came the brigadier-generals, colonels, majors and captains, lieutenants, sergeants, and corporals who were stationed in the smaller cities and towns, and who cooperated with the civil mandarins and village headmen in maintaining order.

There were nine ranks of military officials, both principal and subordinate. The lower ranks of military mandarins did not have the same status as the equivalent civil ranks and were supposed to ride on horseback rather than in a sedan chair, though this was not always honoured toward the end of the Qing dynasty (**fig. 11.4, 11.5**). Those from *ti du* down to warrant officer wore similar hats and robes to those designated for civil mandarins, but were distinguished by the animal on the rank badge.[4] Two kinds of *ma qua* were

Fig. 11.4 A military mandarin at home with his uniform and weapons in the background.

Fig. 11.5 Lower-ranking officers wearing the military version of the *nei tao*.

worn with the long gown. The first type fastened over to the right with the lower part cut away from the right hand corner in the same way as the second type of *nei tao*. The other kind fastened down the front, and was eventually worn by both military and civil officials up to the twentieth century.

Tigers of War

Any formation of archers, musketeers, pikemen, cavalry, or artillery men on the battlefield was led by shield-bearers known as *ten nai*, or tiger men. With their brightly coloured and ferocious-looking dress, they were assigned to break up enemy cavalry charges with their sabres and grappling hooks. Their uniform was a long-sleeved jacket with yellow and black stripes imitating a tiger skin, worn with matching leggings and boots. The cloth helmet with ears was made to resemble a tiger's face. They carried woven rattan shields on which was painted a monster in grotesque style with the character for 'king' (the tiger was referred to as the king of beasts) at the top, put there to further frighten the enemy (**fig. 11.6**).

Fig. 11.6 Tiger of War. As depicted by William Alexander, the artist officially attached to the 1792 embassy, led by Lord Macartney, to the Emperor of China. 1797. Valery Garrett.

Regular Soldiers' Uniform

When dressed for battle, a soldier wore a long coat of quilted nankeen cotton or a thickly wadded jacket made of 'thirty to sixty layers of tough bark-pulp paper',[5] covered with thin plates of metal surrounded by brass studs (**fig. 11.7**). A breastplate was inscribed with characters denoting the corps to which he belonged. Round the waist would be a girdle to which was attached a knife and chopsticks in a case, and a purse for tobacco. A box carried in front would hold arrow heads, bowstrings, and such. A conical helmet made of leather and iron was topped with a spear and a tassel of dyed horse hair. Weapons used were bows and arrows, pikes, sabres, matchlocks, and muskets, and a rattan shield was also carried.[6]

Away from the battlefield, an ordinary soldier wore a short nankeen cotton jacket in black, blue, red, brown, or yellow with a border of another colour. Circular plaques at front and back with black characters denoted his company and corps. Jackets were worn over the civilian long blue gown or *shan ku* with the loose blue trousers pushed into black cloth boots with thick paper soles for the higher ranks, or stockings of quilted cotton and shoes. Paired aprons matching the upper garment were also worn, plus a rattan helmet or a turban (**fig. 11.8, 11.9**).

Fig. 11.7 An archer in full dress wearing padded jacket and skirt with metal plates and studs. c.1800. British Library.

Fig. 11.8 Chinese infantry soldiers wearing bamboo helmets and holding rattan shields, the character for *ting*, or 'patrol', on their tunics. Late 19th cent.

Fig. 11.9 The governor of Shanxi's bodyguard.

Braves

In the nineteenth century, the Manchu rulers were forced to recruit Chinese volunteer forces to assist in dealing with both foreign invasions and internal revolt. With official permission, many Chinese landowners raised units to fight the Taiping and other rebels. Known as 'braves' or *yung*, by the character written in the circular badge on the front or back of the jacket, they wore jackets bordered with another colour. A rattan conical hat was also worn. These 'braves' received double the pay of the regular soldiers when enlisted for combat duty (**fig. 11.10**).

As these uniforms and weaponry were used infrequently, they might be pawned by the commanding officer, also a not uncommon practice for special civilian dress among the general population. An indicative incident occured when the defeated military leader Li Hong-Zhang arrived in Shanghai after the Sino-Japanese war of 1894–95. The guard of honour was made up of two battalions of braves, carrying weapons more at home in an armourer's museum. Attached to each was a pawnbroker's ticket![7] The traveller and writer Isabella Bird remarks similarly on seeing Chinese troops on their way to the same war:

> The uniform is easy, but unfit for hard wear, and very stagey—a short, loose, sleeved red cloak, bordered with black velvet, loose blue, black, or apricot trousers, and long boots of black cotton cloth with thick soles of quilted rag. The discipline may be inferred from the fact that some regiments of fine physique straggled through Mukden for the seat of war carrying rusty muskets in one hand, and in the other poles with perches, on which singing birds were loosely tethered![8]

Fig. 11.10 An escort in undress. Public Records Office, Hong Kong.

Bravery Awards

As a distinction for public service or bravery in battle, the emperor could bestow the honour of wearing the single, double, or treble-eyed overlapping peacock feather plumes. A lesser award was the *lan yu* or blue plume, made of horsehair and crow's feathers, conferred as a reward for services on officials below the sixth rank, and was also worn by the imperial guards as part of their uniform.

A *ma gua* of the colour of the banner to which the man belonged was a distinction highly coveted, and was worn when accompanying the emperor on his travels. However, the highest military honour bestowed by the emperor was the riding jacket, *huang ma gua*, in imperial yellow. This was also exceptionally awarded to two foreigners: to M. Giquel for military services and the establishment of the arsenal at Fuzhou, and in 1863 to General Gordon for his role in ending the Taiping Rebellion.

Uniforms of the Taiping Rebels

In 1838 a Hakka village schoolmaster in Guangdong province, Hong Xiuquan, who had gleaned a little knowledge of Christianity from missionary pamphlets, fell ill and suffered hallucinations. He believed he was a nineteenth-century younger brother of Jesus Christ whose calling was to establish the Kingdom of God on earth and to liberate China from the rule of the Manchus. Attracting fellow Hakkas and members of other anti-Manchu secret societies, an open rebellion began in earnest in 1850. By 1851 Hong had announced the coming of the 'Heavenly Kingdom of Great Peace', the *Taiping Tian Guo*, and been proclaimed 'Heavenly King'. Nanjing was seized in 1853 and became the capital of the Taiping kingdom.

In the course of occupying Nanjing, the rebels gained control of the factories where brocade and satin were woven for the imperial robes. Instead of rejecting Manchu dress as part of their anti-Manchu stance, and adopting simple robes more in keeping with their newly acquired faith, Hong and his followers instituted a style of dress based on the dragon robes worn by the imperial family. Under the Heavenly King were four princes representing the four points of the compass. Yellow was used for robes worn by Hong Xiuquan, and blue, red, white, and black were worn by the Eastern, Southern, Western, and Northern Princes respectively. Dragon robes which were Chinese in style, without the horse-hoof cuffs and centre-hem splits, were embroidered with dragons, from nine down to four according to rank. Over the robe a yellow *ma qua* was worn with dragon medallions, in defiance of the Manchu laws. Lower-ranking officials wore yellow or red jackets with peony medallions, or red jackets with no embroidery. The jackets had the wearer's rank or title inscribed in the centre medallion to distinguish them from Manchu insignia.

Guards and military units belonging to the king and four princes wore uniforms in corresponding colours, with insignia squares with characters for 'peace' at the front and 'holy fighter' at the back. Bamboo helmets were worn during battles, and turbans at other times. As a further defiance, the followers cut off their Manchu-imposed queues, and from the habit of letting their hair grow long they became known as the 'Long-haired Rebels'.[9]

Twentieth-century Uniforms

The Qing dynasty finally crumbled in 1911, and during the first half of the twentieth century, military uniform underwent great change, becoming more Westernized while borrowing from many nations, in particular the United States and Russia. A jacket with a high rounded collar which buttoned down the centre, worn with trousers pushed into knee-high boots and a hard flat peaked cap, was the style adopted by the new Republic for its officers. By the early 1920s four gussetted patch pockets were placed on the front of the jacket, and Dr Sun Yatsen had adopted the outfit which became known as the 'Zhongshan' style, a name referring to his birthplace in Guangdong.

President of the Republic Yuan Shikai died in 1916 and there followed another turbulent period in China's history: warlordism, war with Japan, natural disasters, and civil war. After Sun Yatsen's death from cancer in 1925, Chiang Kaishek became commander-in-chief of the Nationalist armies of the Guomindang. In 1928 the Communist leader Mao Zedong founded the Red Army to fight against the Nationalist government. The Red Army was made up of young peasants and workers from all provinces who became commanders and fighters rather than officers and soldiers, and received no salary. The Communists, who gained control of the whole country in 1949, were proud of their egalitarian approach to rank and sex. All troops wore a loose jacket buttoning down the front with a high rounded collar, Western-style trousers, a soft peaked cap with a red star at the front, puttees, and cloth shoes or sandals.

People's Liberation Army

At the beginning of the three-year civil war which began in 1946 the Red Army was renamed the People's Liberation Army, but its uniforms remained basically unchanged. Made in a yellow-green cotton, this was a khaki colour originating from the dyeing facilities available at Yan'an in Shaanxi province where the Communists had their headquarters for a number of years.[10] For winter, the jacket was wadded with layers of cotton, and a fur-lined balaclava hat was worn. Rank was only depicted by the number of pockets, normally two breast pockets on the jacket, but party members with seniority were allowed

additional patch pockets below the belt (**fig. 11.11**). Red flashes at the collar of the jacket bore no stars of rank or other identifying marks until the mid-1980s.

Red neck-scarves were worn by those children who merited joining the Young Pioneer Corps of the Communist Party.[11] Red Guards, young people who left their schools and universities to serve as a huge vigilante force during the Cultural Revolution from 1966 to 1976, reported on and disrupted the lives of former landlords and many suspect intellectuals. The Red Guards wore old army uniforms fastened around the waist with leather belts and red armbands with slogans avowing their resolve to fight capitalism and Western decadence for the good of the proletariat (**fig. 11.12**).

Fig. 11.11 Chairman Mao Zedong greeting People's Liberation Army soldiers.

Fig. 11.12 Members of the China Ballet Troupe in a performance of the *Red Detachment of Women*, a revolutionary ballet popular during the Cultural Revolution.

Notes

1 See Chapter 1.

2 Hu Ching, *Studies of Paintings at Nan-shun Tien,* as described in *The Emperor's Procession,* Taipei: National Palace Museum, 1970, p. 129.

3 Thomas Wade, *The Army of the Chinese Empire,* Canton: The Chinese Repository, 1851, vol. XX, reprint, Tokyo: Maruzen Co. Ltd., pp. 252–415.

4 See Chapter 5.

5 C. A. S. Williams, *Outlines of Chinese Symbolism and Art Motives,* Peking: Customs College Press, 1931, p. 94.

6 Rattan shields continue to be used by villagers when threatened by rival factions, and are used occasionally in Hong Kong today by the riot police.

7 Alfred Cunningham, *The Chinese Soldier,* 1902, p. 75.

8 Isabella Bird Bishop, *Korea and Her Neighbours* (1898), reprint, Seoul: Yonsei University Press.

9 Both Manchu and Taiping leaders used Western military experts. One of the best-known was General Gordon, otherwise known as 'Chinese' Gordon, who commanded the 'Ever Victorious Army' of Chinese led by European officers to victory, subsequently helping to end the rebellion in 1864. Gordon received the rank of Provincial Commander-in-Chief, or *tidu*; Hong Xiuquan committed suicide.

10 A. C. Scott, *Chinese Costume in Transition,* Singapore: Donald Moore, 1958, p. 94.

11 A movement which continues its activities.

Plate 50 Tanka boat girl wearing straw hat with woven star. Hong Kong, 1980s. Keith Macgregor.

Plate 51 Jewelled headband worn by Cantonese woman. Hong Kong, 1979. Valery Garrett.

Plate 52 Tanka boatwoman wearing black cotton headscarf. Hong Kong, 1988. Valery Garrett/Hong Kong Museum of History.

Plate 53 Hui'an girls in Fujian province wearing the patterned headscarf, secured with plastic decorations, and the short *shan* with curved hem and embroidered cuffs. 1990. China Tourism.

Plate 54 Cantonese apron with woven silk patterned band. Hong Kong, 1979. Valery Garrett.

Plate 55 Han woman wearing blue cotton headcloth and flowered embroidered apron. Kunming, 1990. Valery Garrett.

Plate 56 The Jiajing Emperor on horseback wearing military armour and plumed helmet. As depicted in the scroll painting *Ch'u-ching T'u* (the departure from the palace). National Palace Museum.

Plate 57   Qianlong Emperor in ceremonial armour riding to the Grand Review. As depicted in a painting by
Castiglione. Palace Museum.

Plate 58　Manchu bride's red robe in *kesi*, with Buddhist emblems in the eight medallions, deep *li shui* at the hem, and fur-trimmed cuffs. 148 cm(L), mid-19th cent. Private collection.

Plate 59　Over-skirt with red pointed panels at front and back, fringing and multicoloured streamers, embroidered Peking knot phoenixes standing and descending, and dragons. 95 cm(L, incl. fringe), mid-19th cent. Valery Garrett.

Plate 60 Chinese bride and
groom being serenaded by a
group of musicians wearing
flower badges. In a painting by
Youqua. c.1850. Valery Garrett.

Plate 61 Black satin jacket and
red satin skirt heavily couched
with gold and silver thread in
dragon and phoenix design, with
lotus flowers and mandarin
ducks, symbols of purity and
marital fidelity. Jacket 64 cm(L);
skirt 94 cm(L); mid-20th cent.
Valery Garrett.

Plate 62 Puff-ball crown with strings of imitation pearls and tassels, with red satin fringed collar decorated with sequins and fur and depicting double happiness characters and phoenixes. Rented out to brides in the New Territories of Hong Kong, mid-20th cent. Valery Garrett.

Plate 63 Rural wedding: Hakka bride stepping into a rattan sieve on her way to the bridegroom's home. Hong Kong, 1979. Valery Garrett.

12 Wedding Clothes and Customs

A marriage ceremony in traditional China was a matter of utmost importance, not only for the bride and groom, but also for their immediate families and for the community in which they lived. The union was seen as a means of maintaining good ties and of establishing a firm bond between another family or village. The marriage was always an arranged one with a matchmaker being called upon to consult horoscopes in an effort to find a son a suitable mate, and it was likely that the pair had not even seen each other before the actual wedding day. This custom continued in many rural areas well into the twentieth century.

Qing Dynasty Marriage Customs

The ceremony was the subject of elaborate preparations. An auspicious day was chosen according to the Chinese almanac, and the question of dowry and other gifts settled. The day before the wedding, the bride would undergo the custom known as *kai mian* to give a more open-faced look; this procedure was performed by an old woman with many sons.[1] Her hair was then styled in the manner of the married women of her class.

A custom in some areas entailed the bridegroom's family sending to the bride 'a girdle, a headdress, a silken covering for the head and face, and several articles of ready-made clothing, which are usually borrowed or rented for the occasion. These are to be worn by the bride on entering the bridal sedan to be carried to the home of her husband on the morning of her marriage'.[2] The wearing of a wedding veil to conceal the features of the bride is known to have taken place as early as the Song dynasty (960–1279). On the appointed day, the bride left her home in a richly decorated sedan chair, closed and hidden

Fig. 12.1 Bride being carried in a sedan chair, the bearers having the character for 'double happiness' on their jackets. Valery Garrett.

from view (**fig. 12.1**). When the wedding procession arrived at the groom's home, he would knock on the door of the chair with his fan; the bride then stepped out and the groom raised the red veil over the bride's head. Even so, her face remained partially obscured by her headdress. Firecrackers were set off, and the bride was carried over a charcoal fire on the back of a female servant, this to purify the bride from any contamination she may have encountered on the journey. An umbrella was also often held over her by an older woman to prevent bad luck from falling upon her, a custom which still continues in parts of Hong Kong and mainland China.

After prostrating themselves before the ancestral altar, the couple were escorted to the bridal chamber where they were given refreshments, usually tea and cakes.

> The bride tries hard at this time to get a piece of her husband's dress under her when she sits down, for, if she does, it will ensure her having the upper hand of him, while he tries to prevent her and to do the same himself with her dress. The strings of pearls on her coronet are now drawn aside by the maids in attendance, in order that the bridegroom may have an opportunity of seeing the features of his bride . . . .³

The bride then kowtowed to her new in-laws and offered them a cup of tea. Following a feast, friends and relatives made personal remarks at the bride's expense, often late into the night. On the third day the ancestors were worshipped again, and the couple would pay a visit to the bride's parents. After this there would be little communication between the bride and her family, as she was considered now to belong to her husband's family.

The Dress of the Bride

Female members of the Manchu imperial family wore the dragon robe which often had the double happiness character *shuang xi* included with other symbols. A Manchu bride of an official wore a non-official formal robe with horse-hoof cuffs and eight roundels on the body. Later in the dynasty these garments were predominantly in red, reflecting the influence of this auspicious 'Chinese' colour (**plate 58**). Over this robe a dark blue surcoat was worn, and a phoenix headdress completed the outfit (**fig. 12.2**).

Fig. 12.2 Manchu bride, with her maid, wearing eight-medallion robe with no *li shui*. c.1870.

The Chinese bride would be dressed in the red embroidered jacket known as a *mang ao*, together with the *jiao dai* or hooped belt. Not every bride wore the *mang ao*; some Cantonese brides, and those who were less wealthy, wore a plain red silk or cotton *ao* (**fig. 12.3**). The jacket was worn over a dragon skirt, or *mang chu*, a pleated skirt with panels at front and back decorated with dragons and phoenixes (**fig. 12.4, 12.5**). The symbolism of dragon and phoenix, which represented the emperor and empress of China, was meant to emphasize the relationship between the imperial family and their subjects, and indicated that the couple were 'emperor and empress' for the day. The colours of the skirt varied according to personal choice, although red or green were the most common. In order to raise the status of the skirt, it often had stream-

Fig. 12.3 Cantonese bride wearing plain *ao* with *jiao dai* and phoenix crown; the groom wears the surcoat with rank badge and red sash. c.1870.

ers attached to the pleated parts. In some instances an over-skirt was worn, consisting of two elongated pointed embroidered panels at front and back, and loose streamers at the sides attached to a cotton waistband. This ensured that the skirt itself could be worn on other less-important occasions after the wedding (**plate 59**).

If the couple were of sufficiently high rank, the bride wore the *xia pei* over this outfit, with a sleeveless vest or stole with a fringe at the pointed hem which reached to the bottom of the jacket. After the wedding day, this would be worn on formal occasions. Richly decorated with dragons and *li shui*, a badge

Fig. 12.4 Red satin dragon jacket with gold couched dragons and *li shui*. 106 cm(L), c.1875. Private collection.

Fig. 12.5 Green *mang chu* in *kesi* with dragon on front and back panels, and standing and descending phoenixes on the godets. 97 cm(L), mid-19th cent. Private collection.

Fig. 12.6 *Yun jian* or cloud collar of red satin embroidered in Peking knot with auspicious symbols. 19th cent. Valery Garrett.

depicting the rank of the bride's husband was attached to front and back.

To compensate for the plain neck of the *mang ao* and *xia pei*, a detachable four-pointed collar known as a cloud collar, or *yun jian,* was worn, with the four lobes at chest, back, and over each shoulder, often in three descending layers. These lobes indicated the cardinal points, with the wearer's head the cosmic centre **(fig. 12.6)**. Other multi-lobed collars had many petals radiating from the neckband over the shoulder. Highly decorated, some even had the addition of many elaborate tassels.

The number of clothes worn by the bride and groom was important and conformed to the *yin* and *yang* principle, with an even number (*yin*) of garments for the female and an odd number (*yang*) for the male. Over the cotton under-jacket and trousers, a bamboo jacket or vest was worn. This garment, made of tiny pieces of hollow bamboo sewn together in a diagonal pattern, protected the heavily embroidered outer jacket from perspiration stains in hot weather.

The bride would wear an ornate headdress, imitating the phoenix crown of Ming empresses, made of gilded silver inlaid with kingfisher feathers, and embellished with pearls **(fig. 12.7)**. These strings of pearls hid the face of the bride from the groom until the last minute. Finally, a large red veil was placed over the headdress to obscure her features totally **(fig. 12.8)**.

The Groom's Attire

The groom's wedding attire was based on Manchu official dress. The centre-opening surcoat with badges of rank fixed to front and back was worn over the dragon robe if the man was an official. A plain surcoat and blue long gown were worn if he was not. A long red sash or two, symbols of a graduate of the civil service examinations, were draped over the shoulder and tied at the waist. A winter or summer hat was worn with the insignia showing his rank as a mandarin if he had such status. Fixed at each side were the two gilt sprays of leaves which were also part of graduation dress (**plate 60**).

Twentieth-century Marriage Customs

In a well-to-do family at the beginning of this century, there was much work for a bride during the months before her wedding. Chiang Yee describes the preparations made by his sister for her forthcoming wedding:

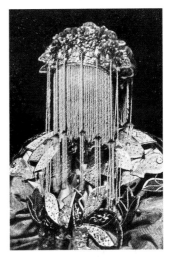

Fig. 12.7 Bride wearing crown decorated with artificial flowers, with strings of pearls covering the face. 19th cent.

For the bed alone she had to embroider a sheet, two pillowcases, the cover of the eiderdown, and two narrow curtains, one for the top and the other for the bottom. She also had to embroider the door curtains, window curtains, cushion and mirror covers, and all her own clothes and shoes. Besides these big items, she had to embroider a number of silk handkerchiefs, powder puffs, little cases for visiting-cards, silk bookmarks and small flower baskets for distribution to the relatives and intimate friends of the bridegroom after the wedding. The designs for these embroideries were common subjects such as 'a pair of mandarin ducks with lotus flowers', 'a pair of swallows flying round willows', 'phoenix and peony', 'peacock and roses', 'a pair of butterflies gathering honey from flowers', . . . and so on, all of which stood for love, happiness and joy.

Fig. 12.8 Chinese bride, her head covered with a red cloth, and groom with a servant. 1905. Library of Congress.

Only the cooler weather was suitable for such work and it had to be started a full two years before the wedding date.[4]

Dress of the Bride and Groom

Up to the middle of this century there were few changes in the actual cere-mony, but after the founding of the Republic in 1912 brides began to wear a slimmer, more fitted black satin jacket which opened down the front. This was partnered with a red or pink satin skirt which, by this time, had the panels at front and back attached to the side gores (**plate 61**). Both garments were dec-orated with auspicious flowers and birds as well as, and sometimes instead of, the dragon and phoenix, and a semblance of the *li shui* pattern of couched gold and silver thread all added up to a very ornate and glittering style. Three sets of jacket and skirt were made for the bride, each set being slightly different in embroidery treatment. After the wedding, the outfits would be worn at special events, including the Lunar New Year. By the mid-twentieth century, the jacket was also made in red to match the skirt, and the outfit was then called a *hong gua* (**fig. 12.9**). The dragon and phoenix predominated in the design, often with the metal couched threads covering the whole of the satin. The elaborate head-dress was still worn, but in place of red bound-feet shoes the bride wore flat slippers embroidered with the dragon and phoenix. It then became far more usual to hire these expensive outfits.

Fig. 12.9 Family celebration with wives, daughters, and daughters-in-law wearing the *hong gua*. 1956. Valery Garrett.

The fashion of wearing Western styles was adopted in cities such as Shanghai—and latterly Hong Kong—by some middle- and upper-class brides who began to wear white wedding dresses. But the traditional *hong gua* was still worn for kowtowing to the ancestors and both sets of parents, and for the banquet in the evening.

Make-up, applied by a specialist in wedding make-up, has always been an important part of the marriage ritual. The bride would have her face made up twice: once before the ceremony and again before the banquet at night. The cosmetics were quite heavily applied, by normal standards, in order to complement both the elaborate decoration on the clothes, and the gold jewellery worn in the form of large ornate necklaces and bangles with long life and double happiness characters and dragon and phoenix symbols on them.

In place of the surcoat, it became usual for the groom to wear the *ma qua* which was the designated male formal attire after the founding of the Republic of China. This was worn with the long gown of blue silk, but with addition of a Western trilby hat. From the 1960s, in keeping with many brides' decision to wear Western dress, Hong Kong grooms began to wear Western formal evening wear of dinner jacket, white dress shirt, and black bow tie.

In post-1949 China, many traditions relating to the marriage ceremony were considered to be decadent. There has been a softening of attitude in recent years, however, and some of the traditions such as *kai mian*, the plucking of the hairline, and dowry baskets containing offerings, have reappeared. Red accessories such as the diagonal cloth draped over the groom's shoulder, a headcover for the bride, and even a newly constructed sedan chair to carry the bride in procession, have all made occasional recent reappearances. Nevertheless, there is official discouragement of the often burdensome cost surrounding wedding celebrations.

Rural Wedding Attire

The traditional bridal outfit for a woman living and working in rural areas was quite simple, and the *shan ku* and matching skirt would have been made by the bride. Fabrics were homespun hemp, cotton, usually in blue or black, or a type of silk known as *hei jiao chou*, or black gummed silk. The wedding ceremony might be the only time the bride would wear a skirt, as it was not a practical garment for country life. Even after the end of the dynasty these skirts resembled those of Qing cut and style, but they were always bereft of decoration with just a narrow braid edging on the panels and hem.

In the middle of the twentieth century in Hong Kong, Macau, and Taiwan, the *hong gua* was worn with a richly decorated collar and an ornate headdress, all of which were usually hired for the occasion (**plate 62**). The headdress was made of a kind of plaster of Paris or cloth-covered card, on top of which were beads and sequinned motifs in the form of butterflies, flowers, and the phoenix. Colourful puff balls quivered on wires, pink or red tassels hung at each side, and rows of pearls hung over the front to cover the face, while at the back was a flap with more sequinned decorations and tassels.

Around each ankle was a heavy silver bangle. One superstition for some brides, especially from the Hakka people in the rural areas of the New Territories of Hong Kong, was the wearing of a small convex metal disk, highly-polished to resemble a mirror, around the neck in order to frighten away bad spirits. A bride might also wear a red bag round her neck in which to put the *li shi* money packets traditionally given to newlyweds.

A pink feather fan was carried, and red shoes or painted wooden sandals completed the bride's outfit. Custom dictated she should change her shoes after worshipping the ancestors to signify a new start in life (**plate 63, fig. 12.10**).

Dress for men in the rural areas of Hong Kong and Taiwan continued to be the traditional blue gown with the red sash worn diagonally, and the gilt hat sprays placed on each side of a trilby hat or skullcap.

Fig. 12.10 Hoklo fishing people's wedding procession with 'dragon boat' women 'rowing' the couple to their new home. Hong Kong, 1988. South China Morning Post.

Notes

[1] Still performed in the early 1990s, this practice dates back to the Shang dynasty.

[2] Rev. Justus Doolittle, *Social Life of the Chinese*, New York: Harper & Bros., 1895, vol. 1, p. 72.

[3] J. Dyer Ball, *Things Chinese*, 5th edn., Shanghai: Kelly and Walsh, 1925; reprint, Hong Kong: Oxford University Press, 1982, p. 370.

[4] Chiang Yee, *A Chinese Childhood*, London: Methuen & Co., 1940, p. 134.

13 Funeral Rites and Clothing

Spiritual solace for the vast majority of Chinese people has stemmed from Buddhism and Daoism, and both religions play a major role in the rituals of a traditional funeral ceremony. But even more deep-rooted in their lives, and dating back to pre-historic times, is ancestor worship.[1]

Fig. 13.1 Dingling, the Wanli Emperor's tomb near Beijing. Museum of Dingling.

Because of the importance of the continuity of the lineage and the relationship between living members of the family and their ancestors, preparation for the afterlife was, and still is, of great consequence to the Chinese. During the Ming dynasty and earlier centuries, the tombs of the imperial family and high officials were filled with a splendid array of objects and textiles to be used by the incumbents in the next world. The 1950s discovery of the entrance to the Dingling tomb of the Wanli Emperor near Beijing, and its subsequent excavation, provided testament to this belief. The tomb contained over 400 garments and fragments of dress, together with more than 600 specimens of silk cloth, jewellery, and many artefacts, all placed there to accompany Wanli, his wife, and the mother of his son to the next world. Its discovery was of immeasurable value to the understanding of Ming court costume (**fig. 13.1**).

Qing Dynasty Burial Customs

The Qing court and wealthy families continued the tradition of lavish funeral processions, and of being buried in great finery with many treasures (fig. 13.2, 13.3). Those men who had held a position of power and authority wished to arrive in the next world with ample proof of their status. Funeral customs varied slightly between Manchu and Chinese and from province to province, but there were many similarities.

Preparations for burial would start when a person reached his or her sixtieth birthday, particularly with regard to the outfit in which they would be buried.[2] Burial clothing for the wealthy was either made-to-measure or purchased ready-made from specialist shops. Ready-made clothes for poorer people were often pasted together of the cheapest satin or even paper; richer people had most of their outfits made from silk with only the final items, purchased at the last minute by relatives, speedily made by the pasting method.

Fig. 13.2 Funeral procession of the Empress Dowager Cixi. 1908. Public Records Office, Hong Kong.

Fig. 13.3 Chinese catafalque being carried by professional mourners. Early 20th cent. Valery Garrett.

There were certain superstitions attached to the choice of clothing. Brass buttons were never used for fastening as they would weight the body to the earth and, in general, buttons were avoided as the Chinese phrase for buttoning a gown is similar to that meaning to detain somebody against their will, *kou niu*. No fur was used on the clothing in case the deceased be reborn into the body of an animal. As it is considered more fortuitous, burial clothing is called *shou yi* (long-life garment) rather than a more literal expression.

Burial Dress

As at a wedding, the number of pieces of clothing worn was very important:

> It is an established custom that, if three garments are put on the lower part of the person, five must be put on the upper part. The rule is *that there must be two more upon the upper than upon the lower part of the corpse*. Oftentimes there are nine upon the upper and seven upon the lower. Sometimes rich families provide as high as twenty-one pieces for the upper part of the corpse, and nineteen for the lower part.[3]

For women, as a rule, there were six pieces on the upper part and four on the lower. Layers of clothing would be first put on to the chief mourner who sat on a chair within a large rattan frame. When all were ready, the layers were sewn together with a few large stitches. They were then removed and placed on the corpse.

Next to the skin would be a bleached cotton or ramie under-*shan* and under-*ku* which would have been first worn for marriage, then put aside for burial. Two or three *shan* were placed over these garments, then the finest attire worn in life. High officials would wear the *chao pao* (lower ranks wore the *nei tao* fastened around the waist with a sash), a surcoat, a winter hat, and satin boots. Fixed to the surcoat were the badges of rank. Summer official dress was never worn, as winter apparel was considered to be more in keeping with death. Men without official rank wore the black *ma gua*, the blue gown worn for ancestor worship or made for the occasion, plus skullcap, shoes, and stockings. The lower classes and coolies wore the *shan ku*.

Wives of mandarins wore for burial their bridal clothes which had also been their official dress. These would consist of a red silk embroidered *mang ao*, the *xia pei*, the *jiao dai*, and a green *mang chu*. Placed on the bound feet would be boots of red silk, on the head, the phoenix crown. She also would wear many hairpins, rings, and bangles decorated with deer, tortoise, peach, and crane—all symbols of longevity, good fortune, and happiness. If lower-ranking wives and rural brides were fortunate enough to own their bridal attire, these would then be carefully stored in a dowry chest after the wedding ceremony and saved to be worn at the next very important milestone—that of the sixtieth birthday—and subsequent occasions, until finally the owner was buried in them.

Shen Yi

Another type of clothing made for burial for those wealthy people without official rank was the *shen yi*, or 'deep garment'.⁴ It was made of dark blue silk, edged with an 8 centimetre band of bright blue or white, and tied at the underarm. This large, enveloping garment with bell-shaped sleeves, similar to Ming robes, fastened over to the right or down the centre-front, and had a long history dating back to the Zhou dynasty. It was worn with a long cowl hood and black satin boots.

Fig. 13.4 *Bai shou yi* jacket in black satin with gold couched *shou* characters; sixth-rank badge at front and back. 101 cm(L), 19th cent. Hong Kong Museum of Art.

A different type of *shen yi* was the longevity gown or *bai shou yi*, literally 'one hundred longevity character garment'. This was made from deep blue or black silk edged with bright blue or white, and had *shou* characters embroidered all over in gold which were thought to have the power to extend the wearer's life. It fastened over to the right like the 'deep' garment, or with a centre-front opening. Only used by the wealthy, it was prepared in advance, sometimes being given to the parent by affectionate offspring. As those men who had had power and authority preferred to be buried in their official clothes, it was usually the women who would be presented with the longevity garment which would be worn with a pleated skirt also decorated with many *shou* characters **(fig. 13.4, 13.5)**.

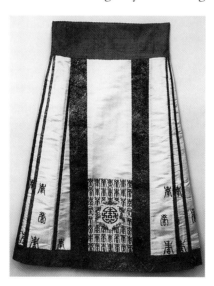

Fig. 13.5 *Bai shou yi* skirt in white satin with *shou* character embroidered in blue. 19th cent. Valery Garrett.

Mourning Customs

The death of an emperor had repercussions which affected everybody in the land. No man was allowed to shave his head for a hundred days thereafter, while mandarins had to wear plain black clothes, over which was worn a long white coat extending to the ankles, and fastened round the waist with a white cotton girdle. The red fringing and the button of rank had to be removed from their hats and the latter replaced with a plain conical one. The silk cord often used in the queue to make it longer was taken out at this time. Women were not allowed to wear flowers or ornaments in their hair.

The rituals surrounding death and mourning were strict. A man was required to wear mourning dress for those superior, or equal, in status to himself, and this naturally excluded his wife and children whose funeral he did not attend, although some affectionate husbands adopted a modified version of mourning dress to honour their deceased wives. Relatives older than the deceased observed no obligatory mourning period, but a father would mourn his eldest son.

There were five grades of mourning costume, known as *wu fu*. The first, and most important, was for parents or husband. A dress of undyed, unhemmed coarse hemp was worn, together with a headdress of hemp, grass sandals, and a mourning staff. This grade of mourning lasted twenty-seven months. The wearing of hemp in this unfinished state symbolized the greatest manifestation of poverty by the son, and represented the traditional idea of giving all one's possessions to the deceased to ensure a comfortable life in the next world; this sacrifice was demonstrated by the dead person's rich finery as well. The second grade was for grandparents and great-grandparents, for whom the mourning period was one year. They were accorded a dress of undyed, hemmed coarse hemp with a hemp headdress, shoes, and bamboo mourning staff. The third grade was for brothers, sisters, and other close relatives, and a dress of coarse hemp was worn during the nine months of mourning. A fourth grade of mourning, lasting for five months, was for aunts and uncles and consisted of a dress of medium coarse hemp. The final grade was for distant relatives and lasted for three months; here finished hemp was worn.

Men in mourning for their parents had to relinquish public office for a period of time and funeral rites were performed every seventh day after the death for forty-nine days. After the third period of seven days, hemp was replaced by white clothes, shoes, cap button, and cord in the queue for deep mourning, and after that blue clothes, shoes, silk knob, and blue cord in the queue. Towards the end of mourning silk could be worn.

Ancestor portraits were painted after the death of the subject, and hung in the ancestral temple or altar room for veneration at the Lunar New Year, other important anniversaries, and at weddings. They would be painted by artists who would often offer a selection of features from which the relatives would choose the closest. The most important part of the portrait was the badge of rank, and often the *pu fu* with the rank badge would be handed over to the painter so that the detail would be exact. After the advent of the camera, a man and his wife would usually be photographed wearing their official robes during their lifetime; the photograph would then be hung in the altar room or temple for future worship by their descendants.

Twentieth-century Customs

Burial Dress

In the mid-twentieth century, burial clothing for a wealthy man in Hong Kong or Taiwan would be the *ma qua* worn over a gown and trousers which were padded; with these he would wear a felt hat or black skull-cap, white silk socks, and black satin shoes. Buried with him would be a handkerchief, a white paper folding fan, a walking stick, and a silver coin placed in the mouth to pay the spirits in the next world. Alternatively, men could wear

Fig. 13.6 Replica of mandarin's winter hat with a wooden hat knob, worn as burial dress. 1979. Valery Garrett.

a copy of a mandarin's hat with red fringing and a wooden centre ornament (**fig. 13.6**). If a man had held an important position in life, he would have stitched to the front and back of his robe an embroidered square usually representing the ninth civil rank, the paradise flycatcher (**fig. 13.7**). Squares made in more recent years were often crudely embroidered and the birds depicted symbolized no particular rank.

Fig. 13.7 Crude imitation of a ninth-rank mandarin square worn on the back of a jacket for festivals, major birthdays, and subsequently as burial attire. 25 cm square. Hong Kong, 1979. Valery Garrett.

A woman would be buried in a *shan*, *ku*, and skirt. Two kinds of burial clothing for women were still on sale in the New Territories of Hong Kong in recent times. The first set comprised a shiny black rayon jacquard jacket with a 'mandarin square' on front and back. This was worn over a dull black figured rayon *shan* worn over a white cotton *shan*. A skirt in fabric to match the jacket was worn over a cotton *ku*. The alternative set of garments was an embroidered jacket and skirt cut like the formal jacket, and a pleated and panelled skirt from the Qing style (**plate 64**). On the deceased woman's head would be the headdress she wore at her wedding, or a cardboard replica, and on her feet would be embroidered shoes and white socks. A mirror, comb, handkerchief, patterned fan, and silver coin would also accompany her to the heavenly world.

Mourning Customs

As the century advanced, the period of conspicuous mourning became much shorter, and in recent years only two grades of mourning clothes remain: undyed coarse hemp for close relatives in deepest mourning, and fine cream hemp for others, although latterly this has been replaced by unbleached calico. Mourning attire was not cut and sewn into an actual garment, rather it was generally just torn and folded into shape. A man wore a long wide band tied around the head with the ends hanging down the back. In the centre was stitched a small piece of red cloth to bring good luck to the wearer. A woman wore a piece of cloth folded and sewn down one side to make a half-open bag which was placed over the head so that the wearer's face was covered, and she could only look down at her feet (**fig. 13.8, plate 65**).

Fig. 13.8 Group of mourners wearing undyed hemp and unbleached calico 'garments' at a ceremony to mark the end of mourning. Hong Kong, 1960s. Hugh D. R. Baker.

After a funeral ceremony in Hong Kong, up to recent times, wool flowers were worn in the hair by the female mourners: white for parents or husband, blue for grandparents, and green for great-grandparents. After a hundred days a pink wool flower was worn for the last three days to show that mourning was nearly over. Men wore a small piece of black ribbon fastened to an upper garment, and their period of mourning was six weeks. The wearing of the wool flowers and black ribbon is known as *dai xiao*, literally, 'wearing filial piety'.

Qing Ming, a solar ceremony held on 5 or 6 April, and Chong Yang, held on the ninth day of the ninth month of the lunar calendar, are two occasions in the year when a family will make a pilgrimage to the graves of earlier generations to leave offerings. Clans, which now are only acknowledged in Hong Kong and Taiwan, accord great importance to these ceremonies, as indeed do all Chinese in these territories. Paper offerings of folded, coloured Qing-style official dress can be burnt while the name of the recipient is spoken; the smoke thus transports the gifts to heaven. As well as clothing, more elaborate offerings of bamboo splints covered with paper are made by specialists. Today they might include apartment blocks, expensive cars complete with uniformed chauffeurs, computers, portable telephones, and even television satellite dishes!

Notes

[1] 'Ancestor worship insists that the soul continues to exist after the body has ceased to function, and that that soul is able to bring blessings to its living descendants if it is properly worshipped by them. It is equally capable of taking unpleasant revenge on descendants who fail to worship it properly.' Hugh D. R. Baker, *More Ancestral Images*, Hong Kong: South China Morning Post, 1980, p. 5.

[2] Inevitably, elderly men's birthdays were celebrated more grandly than those of elderly women. The most splendid celebrations marked a new decade, i.e., the sixtieth, seventieth birthday and so on. This date was according to the Chinese system of numbering years in which a baby is one year old at the moment of birth.

[3] Rev. Justus Doolittle, *Social Life of the Chinese*, New York: Harper & Bros., 1895, vol. 1, p. 175.

[4] According to J.J.M. De Groot, writing in volume one of *The Religious System of China*, (Leyden: E. J. Brill, 1892–1910), it was so called as 'it deeply concealed the body'. It closely resembled the full-length robe worn in the Ming dynasty; see Chapter 1.

Plate 64   Black satin embroidered jacket and skirt worn by women for burial. Hong Kong, 1988. Hong Kong Museum of History.

Plate 65   Coffin being transported across a lake by family mourners in Hebei province. c.1990. China Tourism.

Plate 66 Set of cotton clothing presented to a baby
by its grandmother at the first-month celebration.
1950s. Valery Garrett.

Plate 67 Child's *dou dou*: the outer ones of embroidered satin, the centre one of cotton appliqué
showing two fierce animals. Valery Garrett.

Plate 68 Silk patchwork gown or 'hundred families coat', the style based on the habit of a bonze or Buddhist monk who begs for alms. 19th cent. Valery Garrett.

Plate 69   Red satin *shan* fastening across to the right in the Ming style and leggings embroidered with gold couched thread; green satin divided trousers embroidered with phoenix and flowers. Shanghai, early 20th cent. Valery Garrett.

Plate 70   Red satin dress embroidered with Shou Xing, symbolizing long life, and the Heavenly Twins, symbolizing harmony. Early 20th cent. Valery Garrett.

Plate 71   Hoklo child wearing an embroidered collar and sash for the Dai Wong Yeh Festival; grand-mother holds the crown. Hong Kong, 1979. Valery Garrett.

Plate 72   From left: Hoklo child's black cotton open-crown hat embellished with sequins, embroidery, and tassels, with padded birds and butterflies, 1970s; 'rice bowl' hat of red satin embroidered with pomegran-ates (many seeds indicates a hope for many more sons) and the *shou* character for long life, early 20th cent; red satin 'dog's head' cap, trimmed with fur at the 'ears' and with amulets of the Eight Immortals and Shou Xing across front, Late 19th cent. Valery Garrett.

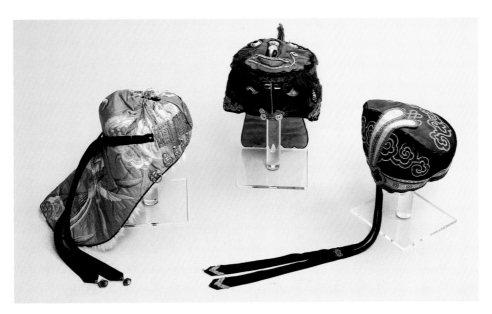

Plate 73   From left: pink satin hood embroidered with cranes and amulets across front; animal hat with back flap for extra warmth, showing a lion riding on the back of a dog for double protection; scholar's hat, black satin with blue crown, yellow 'feathers', and black streamers imitating those worn by officials during the Ming dynasty. Late 19th cent. Valery Garrett.

Plate 74   Hoklo fisherwoman and child in an appliquéd carrier decorated with sequins and with lattice head support. Hong Kong, 1970s. Valery Garrett.

Plate 75 Baby carrier cover made of printed cotton and showing the rising sun, sunflowers (a symbol for Mao Zedong during the Cultural Revolution), and the Chinese characters for 'Long life to Chairman Mao'. Guangdong province, c.1967. Valery Garrett.

Plate 76 From the top, clockwise: red satin bootees embroidered with a dragon with a 'pearl' in its mouth; woven straw shoes; orange and blue 'tiger' shoes; girl's red satin bound feet shoes; boy's shoes in black satin embroidered at the toes. Late 19th to early 20th cent. Valery Garrett.

Part V
Children's Wear

14 Children's Clothing

The birth of many sons has been the traditional desire of Chinese couples. In poorer families, boys were needed to help with agricultural labour, while for others more fortunate, success by their male offspring in the imperial civil service examinations brought wealth and distinction to the clan. Furthermore, sons were needed to ensure the continuation of the clan, as well as to perform the very necessary ritual ceremonies of ancestor worship. But China has always been predominantly an agricultural society where a lack of good medical care, coupled with a poor awareness of basic hygiene, meant—until the second half of the twentieth century—that large numbers of babies did not survive to their first birthday. However, with improved living standards in the late twentieth century, China has had to impose a 'one child' policy on Han Chinese families to limit the pace of population growth.

Symbolism and superstition play an important part in the folklore of many societies, with certain objects or species being endowed with auspicious or protective properties. The Chinese language is homophonic and many things are symbolic because their name sounds the same as something which is thought to be lucky. Consequently, for many centuries, a child's clothing was embroidered with flowers, fruit, animals, and insects, each endowed with protective properties to ward off evil, as well as to bring the child great success in the future. Fierce animals such as the tiger, dog, lion, and dragon were frequently depicted on children's clothing as protection. Also, the five evil creatures, or five poisons, consisting of the snake, three-legged toad, scorpion, spider, and centipede were often shown together as a talisman. Cats would be embroidered on to clothing because of their ability to see in the dark and thus see evil lurking.

Another animal often depicted was the deer. The word for deer, *lu*, and for a high salary are the same. It was an emblem for good fortune and often shown with the god of longevity. The three most popular mythological figures: *fu*, *lu*, and *shou*, denoting good fortune, an abundance of good things, and long life, respectively, were also depicted on many articles of children's dress. Cotton was used for everyday wear, with silk and satin for special occasions. Colours were bright, and reds and pinks were frequently used because these hues were considered to be auspicious.

Babies' Clothing

When a child was born it would be washed and then wrapped in swaddling clothes, generally made from the cast-off clothing of other family members. So tentative was its very existence that no name was given to the child, it being referred to only as 'baby' or 'little one'. Neither the child, nor its mother, would venture out of doors until the end of the first month after the birth, at which time a celebratory feast would be held for family and friends. Red eggs would be, and in Hong Kong still are today, distributed to well-wishers who were then expected to give the child a small gift. These were often presents of jewellery to ward off evil.

At this point, sets of clothing tailored along the same lines as the parents' would be presented by the maternal grandmother to replace the swaddling clothes. These would generally comprise a red centre-opening or side-fastening jacket, a green sleeveless waistcoat and divided trousers, navel cover, and hat (**plate 66**). Underwear for a young child would consist of the navel cover and later, a small triangular embroidered apron called a *dou dou* which fastened with tapes round the neck and waist. Indeed, this apron might be the only form of clothing worn by a child in the hot summer months until it was two or three years old (**plate 67**).

Other gifts were also bestowed on the child. One common tradition during the last century was that of giving the mother small pieces of silk and embroidery for her to sew together to make the child a jacket. This was known as a 'hundred families coat', an old tradition seen on paintings of children of the Song dynasty; all those who contributed joined in wishing the child good fortune and protection from evil (**plate 68**).

The baby would receive his or her first name at this time. It was very common, however, especially with boys, to use an animal's name, or even that of a girl. It was thought that the evil spirits would be fooled into thinking the boy was either an animal or a girl, and, as such, of little value.

The cutting of a child's hair was even governed by superstition, and when the baby was almost a month old a lucky day was chosen for shaving the head. This was said to make the real crop grow thicker, and to prevent it from falling out in later life. At a second shaving some months later, the crown was shaved, but two circular sections of hair, one above each ear or even a whole ring, was left around the bald spot. The purpose of these tufts of hair was said to be to enable the parents to seize them when the child was in danger of being whisked away by bad spirits (**fig. 14.1**).

Fig. 14.1 Children at play showing hairstyles. From a Ming scroll painting by Ch'iu Ying (1494–1552). National Palace Museum.

Young Children's Clothing

A child's first birthday was a time for another great feast. A boy would be dressed in a silk embroidered jacket, either centre-fastening or side-fastening following the style fashionable during the Ming period. This was worn together with embroidered divided trousers comprised of two pieces of cloth attached to a broad waistband, joined from ankle to knee, but leaving the area covering the buttocks free. This style of trousers dates back hundreds of years, and is illustrated in a Ming dynasty children's reader first published in 1436 (**fig. 14.2, plate 69**).

Fig. 14.2 A child on his mother's knee dressed in his finery for his first birthday celebration. Early 20th cent. Valery Garrett.

At the first birthday celebration a son would be expected to indicate his future career (**fig. 14.3**). Chiang Yee remembers that his nephew was set

in the centre of a huge round table, in the midst of an assortment of articles representing the various professions he might enter—inks, brushes, an abacus, a sword, scissors, a very small hammer, an official seal, herbs, and so on. He was encouraged to pick up anything he liked.

Fig. 14.3 The *zhua zhou* ceremony which takes place on the boy's first birthday and supposedly determines his future career. Hubei province, c.1985. China Tourism.

This is called *Cha-chou* [*zhua zhou*], the Grasping Celebration of the first year of age. At first he did not know what was expected of him, and stared round inquiringly at the assembled company. Then, seeming to realize we were all waiting for him to do something, he stretched out both hands . . . and after a while picked up a green herb, which was not actually very near him. Grandmother smilingly announced that he would be a medical man when he grew up.

Fig. 14.4 Young girl with bound feet in oversized *ao*.

Needless to say, Chiang Yee remarked later, when his nephew grew up he never once thought of becoming a doctor.[1]

If little girls took part in the *zhua zhou* ceremony at all, it was to determine their future husband's profession. Indeed, such was the traditional status of women and girls in China, if a man had only girls in his family he was considered to be childless! Young girls wore a scaled-down version of the *ao* worn by their mothers with the *ku*, and their hair was braided into two little pigtails (**fig. 14.4**).

Older Boys' Clothing

Education, literacy, and scholarship were always greatly prized, and from an early age, where possible, sons were groomed to take the civil service examinations. Families employed private tutors, or else the clan would establish a private school or study hall to educate prospective candidates. During nine years of education, a boy was expected to memorize 200 characters a day, totalling about 400,000 by the time he was fifteen.[2] These were culled from essential school texts such as the *Three Character Classic*, the *Analects of Confucius*, and the *Book of Changes*. Reciting from memory to the teacher was known as 'backing the book', and traditionally subjects such as geography, science, and foreign languages were considered irrelevant (**fig. 14.5**).

Fig. 14.5 'Backing the book': students reciting from memory to the teacher. Late 19th cent.

From the age of four or five, boys wore the long gown made of grey or blue silk. Over this would be worn a side-fastening waistcoat, colourfully embroidered and edged with braid (fig. 14.6). Older boys wore a blue sleeveless and side-fastening satin waistcoat, known as a *bei xin*, over their gown at Lunar New Year and on special occasions, but it became increasingly common in wealthier families to wear the *ma gua* with the *chang shan*, or even the *nei tao* and surcoat for formal events (fig. 14.7).

Fig. 14.6 The governor of Shanxi with two of his sons. 1902.

Fig. 14.7 Boy's black satin surcoat with first-rank civil badge and blue *nei tao*. 19th cent. Surcoat 74 cm(L); *nei tao* 80 cm(L); rank badge 16 cm(H) x 17 cm(W). Valery Garrett.

Older Girls' Clothing

It was not customary to give girls any formal education. They were expected to help around the house and with the younger children if the family did not have servants. They were taught to embroider from an early age, both to provide the many articles needed within the household, as well as to contribute to the family income, in some cases. Often, if a family had many girls, a number might

Fig. 14.8 Schoolgirls, wearing the *ao ku,* sewing. Xiamen, c.1900.

be sold into better-off families to work as domestic servants. There was then the possibility that when the girl was of age she might become a wife or concubine to one of the sons in the family.

During the last century girls wore the bulky side-fastening *ao* and trousers cut along the same lines as their mothers', but without the skirt which was the prerogative of married women. By the beginning of the twentieth century, however, amid greater emancipation for women and more outside influences affecting China, many girls were formally educated (**fig. 14.8**). As the century advanced, they began to wear a slimmer version of the *ao* with a plain black skirt. Then, with the development of the female *qi pao* after 1925, young girls began to wear dresses with a shaped waist and fastening down the centre-back (**plate 70**). Older girls wore the *qi pao* like their mothers. Better educational opportunities for girls in the mid-1920s brought the need for a school uniform which reflected the Chinese style of dress. In place of Western-style gym slips, girls wore a plain cotton *qi pao* with wrist-length sleeves and short slits at the side of the hem.[3]

Festive Dress

Today, it is rare to see a child dressed in traditional clothing. A few vestiges remain: an embroidered baby carrier, a silver bell worn round the ankle, a little hat resembling an animal. In the main, most Chinese children wear Western fashions, though in Hong Kong there is more than a little influence from Japan and its passion for Italian and French styling.

Nevertheless, the Hoklo boat people in Guangdong and Fujian provinces, and in Hong Kong, are very superstitious and still preserve their old customs, particularly when related to dress. The women are prolific embroiderers and make many gaily decorated clothes, baby carriers, and hats for their young children to wear throughout the year and especially at festivals. On these occasions, boys and girls up to the age of seven wear black cotton waistcoats trimmed with red, yellow, and blue binding and appliqué. They are worn with shorts by boys, while the girls wear matching skirts. Both wear elaborately decorated crowns and embroidered collars in the festival processions (**plate 71, fig. 14.9**).

Fig. 14.9 Hoklo child's black cotton jacket decorated with blue, yellow, red, and white cotton appliqué around all edges; maroon cotton dungarees trimmed with yellow and green binding. Hong Kong, c.1975. Valery Garrett.

Notes

1   Chiang Yee, *A Chinese Childhood*, London: Methuen & Co., 1940, p. 203.
2   Ichisada Miyazaki, *China's Examination Hell*, New Haven and London: Yale University Press, 1981, p. 16.
3   Even in the early 1990s, several schools in Hong Kong have retained the *qi pao* as their uniform.

15 Children's Accessories

Charms and symbols, historically important to Chinese people of all ages, were considered to be of special benefit to children to protect them from harm, and elaborately decorated accessories, often in the form of fierce animals to scare away evil spirits, were worn by a child with this end in mind. Even so, much of this protective symbolism was reserved for boys.

Hats

Hats were a necessary part of a child's dress, and continue to be so in many parts of China. Several types were worn throughout childhood, the first from the age of one month, when it would be presented to the child, often by the maternal grandmother. Made from a strip of red satin or cotton gathered into a circle at the top with a centre-back seam, it was called a 'rice bowl' style in the south as it resembled an upturned bowl. It was embroidered with designs of flowers, fruit, and Chinese characters wishing the child long life and good fortune.

The second type, also worn in infancy, was similar to the first, but the top of the crown was left open. It sometimes took the form of an animal such as a tiger, dog, or pig, with a face at the front and a padded tail at the back. Another style, worn by Hoklo children in Guangdong province and Hong Kong at the first-month celebration and on other special occasions, comprised a strip of material joined at the back and slightly gathered along the top edge. Above the ears and at the centre-front were pleated fabric rosettes, and braid and beads decorated the edges. The whole effect was very colourful, some hats even having little animals and charms on wire which danced in the breeze.

When the child was about one year old it would wear the 'dog's head' cap to fool bad spirits into thinking it was a dog. This cap was made of black or red cotton, plain or patterned, with a seam running from centre-front to centre-back. A horizontal cut about a third of the way up from the front was folded down to give the impression of dog's ears. The edges were bound with contrasting cotton, and the ears would sometimes have little tufts of fur to further suggest the animal. This was normally a plain style, without much embroidery, although a row of amulets was sometimes placed across the front (**plate 72**).

A hat for winter wear was the 'wind' hat. Shaped like the dog's head hat, or with the crown gathered into a circle, the back extension was there to keep the neck warm in cold weather. This type was often lined and padded, some being embroidered with flowers and birds, while others had a fierce animal face. A long hood was another version of this style.

Another version, made to represent either the lion, tiger, or dog, was worn to emulate the strength and ferocity of the animal. The character for 'king' was placed at the centre-top of the tiger hats as the tiger was considered to be the king of beasts. These were made with an orange satin crown marked with black stripes or 'eyes', and with ears, large protruding eyes, a mouth full of bared teeth, and a padded tail standing up at the back. Lions were usually green with a long silky mane, while dogs were black. Some animal hats had another animal on top of the hat, to give greater protection. An embroidered back flap was often added to cover the back of the neck in cold weather. Some are still worn today in the northern provinces, especially Shaanxi and Shandong.

As the child grew older, hats were worn less to protect against evil, and more to bring success for the future. The scholar hat was given to a boy in the hope that he would do well in the official examinations. Made of black satin, it was embroidered with bats, flowers, and religious symbols. At the back were often two streamers and two pointed 'feathers' like those on the gauze caps worn by scholars and officials during the Ming dynasty (**plate 73**). For everyday wear, boys wore the plain black skullcap. Made from six segments of stiffened black satin fixed to a narrow brim, it was topped with a black or red button, or silk pompom.

Hats worn on festive occasions, and at Lunar New Year, were shaped more like a crown (**fig. 15.1**). Some, called eagle hats, had upturned wings which—as an eagle soars high— would ensure the wearer rose high in office. As this bird also swoops low the hope would be that the wearer would live to become a grandfather. The crown was made of stiffened card covered with fabric and decorated with embroidery, sequins, and chains with streamers hanging down the back. Tassels hung from

Fig. 15.1 Two children wearing crowns, collar, and padlock at the Lunar New Year. Hong Kong, 1909. Public Records Office, Hong Kong.

the sides, with silk puff balls, stuffed toy animals, and birds attached to wire springs to make them dance when the child moved. This style is still worn at festivals and at Lunar New Year by Hoklo children up to the age of six.

A further style had a false fringe and queue made of black twisted silk thread. The crown was made of stiffened cardboard, covered with silk, and often divided into eight sections, each embroidered.

Earmuffs

Padded and lined, and shaped like a heart, earmuffs were slipped over the ears to keep them warm. They were sometimes trimmed with fur at the edges to represent an animal and usually embroidered with bats, a wish for happiness, fish for plenty, or flowers for beauty. Although not confined to any sex or age group, they were generally worn by girls.

Baby Carriers

The carrying of a baby on the mother's back has been the custom in China for centuries, especially in the southern provinces. For any mother who must work in the fields, on the boat, or round the home, it was also a safe and convenient place to keep a child out of mischief. As the family grew, it was then the turn of the older girls to carry their younger siblings in the same manner (**fig. 15.2**).

The traditional baby carrier is made from a decorated square of cloth, with long strips of fabric extending from the corners of the square to form straps. There are four main types. The first, favoured especially by land dwellers in Guangdong province and Hong Kong, has a decorated centre square with straps which

Fig. 15.2 Girl carrying her brother on her back in a baby carrier. Hong Kong, c.1912. Public Records Office, Hong Kong.

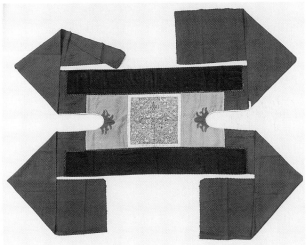

are a continuation of the top and bottom edges. Once the child and carrier are in place on the mother's back, two straps are brought over her shoulders, and two more come under the arms, to tie in a knot in front; the child is carried with the feet encircling the mother's waist. Earlier carriers, dating back to the last century, were much

Fig. 15.3 Baby carrier of black hemp and pink and red coarse cotton, with a pocket at one end of the strap; the centre satin panel is lavishly embroidered with flowers, peacocks, and *shou* characters. Late 19th cent. Valery Garrett

larger, and at the end of one or two straps, the corners would be folded over to the centre to form a pocket in which to carry coins. The carriers were made of cotton or hemp, dyed purple-black or indigo-blue, with centres of embroidered silk, or occasionally wool, or else left plain (**fig. 15.3**). Modern versions of this style are simpler in construction, and usually made of red or patterned cotton with an embroidered centre square. However, those for presentation on a special occasion would be made of red satin or brocade.

The centre designs of these carriers were a selection of good luck symbols: a pair of mandarin ducks symbolizing marital fidelity; pomegranates for abundance in all things, especially sons; lotus flowers which represent purity and fruitfulness; butterflies for conjugal happiness; and the Chinese characters for double happiness, long life, and good fortune. The centres were also made in many other ways: brocade pictures, crochet pictures, white canvas squares with red cross-stitch, and interwoven strips of cotton. On certain carriers, at the centre top of the square was a small folded triangular piece of cloth, five layers thick, but now only one layer. It was considered to be a lucky charm, and originally symbolized the five blessings: wealth, health, happiness, long life, and the right to a natural death.

In other provinces, especially in Guizhou and Yunnan, carriers are made of a large rectangle with a folded flap along the top edge. Floral embroidery or appliqué is arranged in the centre of the square, and/or along the flap. There are long straps along the top part only which cross over the mother's shoulders and chest, then round the child's body at the back; the child is carried with the feet hanging straight down.

Another shape favoured by fishing people has a slightly smaller centre with longer straps fixed diagonally to the four corners of the square, and much reinforcing stitching at these points. The centres on these carriers do not feature embroidery, but are made of many coloured strips and triangles of cotton.

These are appliquéd on to the centre square, and continue up the top straps so that when worn the decoration is visible as far as the knot. This patchwork effect is reminiscent of the 'hundred family coats' of the last century. Special ones still made by the Hoklo boatwomen for festivals and celebrations have bells to frighten away bad spirits, plus tassels, fringing, beading, and appliqué in all the colours of the rainbow.

Head supports were attached to the baby carriers. These were either made of strips of cotton stitched at intervals to form a lattice square, or were a plain piece of cloth attached to the top edge of the carrier to support the baby's head, and to shield it from the sun (plate 74).

The last style is the simplest of all, being a plain, undecorated strip of red cotton or hemp, approximately 3 metres long by 30 centimetres wide. In the past, it was a tradition for the bridegroom to wear a strip of red cloth draped across one shoulder of his long gown and tied on the opposite hip.[1] After the wedding day it was then put aside for later use as a baby carrier: winding the strip of cloth twice round the child, then tying in a knot in front of the wearer. It is seldom seen today, although some fisherwomen use it as an alternative to the more elaborate styles.

Highly decorated baby carrier covers are used to protect the child when the weather is cold, as well as on special occasions. Those made by the Hoklo boat women are embellished with embroidery, appliqué, braid, tassels, and bells like the carriers, and are real works of art which take many months to complete (plate 75). Simpler covers used by other ethnic groups in the past were made of two layers of brightly patterned cotton stitched together so as to be reversible. Red silk ones, padded and embroidered, some with fur lining and hoods, were often given as gifts at Lunar New Year.

Collars

Fig. 15.4 Multisegmented collar embroidered with Peking knot. 19th cent. Valery Garrett.

Collars were worn by very young children. Embroidered examples made of several segments, usually five, were popular, while some were elaborately subdivided into many smaller segments, each decorated with auspicious symbols (fig. 15.4). Five-segment collars, made of plain and printed cottons, are still seen today in Hong Kong.

In the northern provinces, especially Shaanxi, collars shaped like a fierce animal's body, often the tiger or dog, were common. The animal appeared to be coiled round the child's neck to give greater protection. The Hoklo children wore very elaborate collars on special occasions and festivals. The collars were made of a circular piece of cotton with a back opening, and decorated with beads, sequins, braid, coloured cotton appliqué, and beaded tassels hanging all round the edge. These were made by the mother or bought from an embroiderer living locally, and worn by the child up to the age of six or seven.

Footwear

On special occasions very young children would wear satin bootees when carried in their baby carrier. Viewed from the front as mother and child approached, these were most colourful, made of red, orange, or purple satin, often embroidered with designs of the imperial dragon or phoenix, a mythical bird signifying goodness and benevolence and the hope that the wearer would rise high in society. Fish, with the homophonic Chinese sound meaning superfluity and therefore a symbol of abundance in all things, and deer, symbol of advancement and good fortune, were also used. Often padded animals and birds were suspended above the toe on wires and long coloured tassels were hung from the front, together with multicoloured bobbles. Some styles also had a false shoe fixed to the bottom for a slightly older baby.

Like the other accessories, children's footwear was also made in the form of a dog, cat, tiger, or pig to frighten away bad spirits. Large eyes to see evil lurking, large ears to hear it, and whiskers all helped to suggest the creature being represented. Usually made of red cotton or satin, with brightly embroidered uppers and padded cotton soles, some shoes even had bells on the toes to produce an audible warning for the spirits.

When a girl was aged from three to twelve years, she would begin to have her feet bound and to wear the tiny embroidered shoes. A mother who did not impose this barbaric custom on her daughter would render her virtually unmarriageable and a liability to her parents for the rest of her life.

Woven straw shoes were worn in the summer in the southern provinces. Shoes for older boys were made of satin with a thick white sole, similar to those worn by the men, albeit more colourful. The uppers were sometimes embroidered with auspicious flowers and insects, and with a centre seam reinforced with leather extended over the rigid sole to give sufficient spring for walking (**plate 76**).

Jewellery and Charms

Lucky protective charms were an important part of children's dress. Silver, *bai tong*, gilded silver, or brass jewellery was given to the child by family members and friends, usually at the first-month celebration. This is still the custom in many parts of China.

Amulets stamped out of a thin sheet of silver or brass were often stitched across the front of a hat. The most popular were the Eight Immortals worn

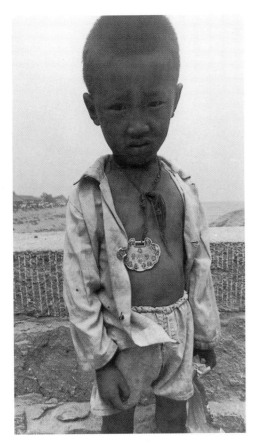

Fig. 15.5 Boy wearing a padlock to 'lock him to earth'. Shangdong, 1980s. China Tourism.

Fig. 15.6 Child's metal neck ring with padlock and peach charms. 19th cent. Valery Garrett.

with the god of longevity, *Shou Xing*, in the centre. These were often shown together because it is said that the group were guests of the Queen at her birthday feast in the Western Heavens. One or more laughing Buddhas were also sometimes placed across the front of the cap as this friendly figure was thought to be able to dismiss misery and unhappiness from the world. Other amulets depicted Chinese characters for good luck and long life, but one which was frequently worn on hats to ensure continued good fortune was the *Ba Gua*, also known as the Eight Trigrams, the basis of an ancient system of divination and philosophy. This mystical symbol showed eight groups of broken and unbroken lines arranged in a circle, sometimes with the *yin yang* symbol of creation in the centre.

Bells to scare off bad spirits were part of the charms given to the baby at the first-month celebration. Two anklets with bells, or a large, single brass bell tied to the ankle with red string, were especially popular for fishing people's children. Bells were also attached to the cap strings at the back of hats.

The god of longevity, depicted either mounted or standing beside a deer or a *qilin*, holding a peach for immortality in one hand and a staff in the other, was also worn as a charm around the child's neck. The *qilin* was often used as an auspicious symbol for children; it is thought to have great wisdom, and represents traditionally a desire for a large family of sons who do well in the civil service examinations.

A very common tradition was the wearing of a silver padlock around the neck inscribed with propitious characters and symbols to 'lock the child to earth'. These are seldom seen nowadays, however the Hoklo children still wear an enamelled *bai tong* padlock in the shape of a butterfly, symbol of happiness and summer. Padlocks were sometimes attached to a chain, or else joined to a metal ring which was large enough to go over

the child's head (**fig. 15.5, 15.6**). This metal ring was also used alone. Meant to be the equivalent of a dog collar, it was again aimed at fooling evil spirits into thinking the child was an animal.

Other charms of silver or carved peach stone kernels were worn in the form of a necklace, and pendants of gold or jade Buddhas are still popular today outside mainland China. Paper charms were also worn, and are still favoured for the children of fishing people. A charm is written on yellow paper then wrapped in red cloth and pinned to the child's clothing, or suspended from a string or metal ring around the neck of a child, who—in summer on the boat—might otherwise be completely naked.

Red thread was also propitious, and said to ensure long life. An old tradition was that after the birth of a baby, neighbours and friends would give pieces of thread which were then combined into a tassel and hung on the baby's clothes. Called the 'hundred families tassel' it signified a wish from many families for good fortune for the child. Another use was the placing of two pins horizontally on the front of the little embroidered cap worn from the age of one month. Round these were wound red and green thread as a wish for long life. Red thread was often tied around the wrists or ankles of the child, and sometimes also fastened to the jade bangle or silver anklet to stop it falling off inadvertently.

Note

1 This red cloth had been a feature of the graduation dress for successful candidates in the imperial civil service examinations.

Part VI
Minority Dress

16 Minority Groups in the North

Although mainland China's population totals more than 1.13 billion, the 55 groups not of the Han race, termed minorities, which total some 91 million people and account for just 8.04 per cent of the whole population, actually inhabit more than half the total land. They are spread in a wide arc, from Heilongjiang and Inner Mongolia in the north-east, to Xinjiang and Tibet in the west, Sichuan and Yunnan in the south-west, through to Hunan and Guangdong in the south-east. Many minority people live in regions, prefectures and counties administered autonomously but supported by the state. In the last decade their population has been increasing proportionately at a faster rate than the Han race, due to the government's policy of not enforcing the one child per family rule in their case. The largest minority groups are discussed in this, and the following chapter.

Exposure to the general uniformity of revolutionary Han Chinese dress inevitably affected the traditional dress of the minority groups, especially during the 1960s and 1970s, and some minorities have been assimilated into Han culture and customs, especially in the cities and their environs. Many similarities with Han traditional symbolism exist anyway, particularly in children's clothing; the genre of fierce animal hats and shoes, and amulets of the Eight Immortals have been common ground. But in recent years the Chinese government has made a concerted effort to encourage and promote minority groups in certain areas, realizing that the traditional customs and dress can be a cultural and tourism asset. Furthermore, dressing up for special occasions such as festivals and weddings retains its importance in the poor, often harsh, living conditions of numerous minority groups.

North-East China

The Manchus

There are 9.82 million Manchus living in Liaoning, Jilin, Heilongjiang, Inner Mongolia, and Hebei provinces, and Beijing. The three north-eastern provinces of Liaoning, Jilin, and Heilongjiang cover the original homeland of the Manchus, who conquered China in the seventeenth century. Shenyang, the provincial capital of Liaoning—formerly known by its Manchu name of Mukden—was the original capital of the Qing rulers, and today more than half the Manchu population lives in Liaoning.

After the fall of the Qing dynasty and the later establishment of the People's Republic, Manchurian customs and language, both written and spoken, were outlawed. Manchus now use the Han Chinese language, and many adopted Han surnames to avoid persecution. However, amid recent encouragement of the minorities, Manchu customs and dress are once more permitted. The elaborate headdress of a wooden frame covered in black silk or velvet and decorated with flowers, the colourful *qi pao,* and the high-soled shoes are worn by girls on special occasions, while the men put on the short jacket and long gown; for everyday wear Han Chinese dress continues to be worn.

The Mongolians

Mongolians total 4.8 million, the majority in Inner Mongolia and the surrounding northern provinces of China, although one group lives as far south as Yunnan. Originally a small group of nomadic tribes, their leader Genghis Khan had unified the different tribes in the northern regions above China by the thirteenth century. Genghis Khan and his followers conquered most of Asia, the whole of China was brought under the control of his grandson Kublai Khan,

Fig. 16.1 Women from the Khalka Mongol group. Early 20th cent.

and the Yuan dynasty was established in 1279. Although overthrown by Zhu Yuanzhang, who became the first emperor of the Ming dynasty in 1368, the threat from the north did not disappear. During the Qing period, the Mongol areas were grouped into leagues and banners, administrative divisions devised to bind the Mongols under Manchu rule.

Those of the clan living north of the Gobi Desert live in a region latterly named Outer Mongolia, once part of the Soviet Union. Inner Mongolia, south of the Gobi Desert, was the first of the national minorities' autonomous regions to be established by the communist government of China. Here, there are vast pasturelands, and animal husbandry, especially stock farming, forms the main base of the economy. The people are nomadic, with excellent equestrian skills. They live in yurts, collapsible round tents made of felt which are quickly assembled and dissembled when the tribe moves on to fresh grassland, and hung with colourful felt rugs for extra warmth inside. The Mongols initially believed in shamanism, but the predominant religion today is a sect of Buddhism known as Lamaism, dating back to contacts with Tibetan Buddhism in the reign of Genghis Khan.

The Khalka Mongols, direct descendants of Genghis Khan, live in both Outer and Inner Mongolia (**fig. 16.1**). In the past, the Khalka Mongol women wore a long gown with horse-hoof cuffs, sashed around the waist if unmarried. Over this a sleeveless long vest with braid or embroidery around the edges was placed, while the headwear was a hat with velvet brim and pointed crown.

Nowadays, the Khalkas wear costume similar to that of the Oirat Mongols (also known as Western Mongols) who are scattered in groups in Qinghai, Ningxia, and Xinjiang provinces. Young women wear brightly coloured gowns, often tied round the middle with a wide yellow sash. Men and older women wear gowns in brown and blue, also with a sash of contrasting colour, and edged at neck, sleeves, and hem with embroidery or narrow piping. Sheepskin coats are worn over the gowns in the winter. Men's hats have a velvet brim with a segmented crown decorated at the centre, while those living in the grasslands wear turbans (**fig. 16.2**). Both men and women wear black leather boots with multicoloured embroidered designs on the uppers.

Fig. 16.2 Young Oirat Mongol man standing outside a yurt and wearing a white robe with green sash and light blue turban.

Fig. 16.3 Buryat Mongol woman with conical hat and fitted dress with deep set-in sleeves. China Tourism.

The Mongols are also skilful silversmiths. Buttons, jewellery, and many silver rings hang at the end of the women's plaits, while some household utensils are even made of silver and copper inlaid with coral, jade, agate, and amber. Very elaborate headdresses are worn by the women, comprising a headband of turquoise or agate placed on top of the head with strings of pearls hanging over the forehead. Longer strings of pearls, turquoise, and coral ornaments hang over each ear.

A third group are the Buryat Mongols, also known as Northern Mongols, who live in the western parts of Shaanxi province and Inner Mongolia. The Buryat Mongols, who emigrated from Siberia at the turn of the century, are still widely spread over Russian territory and Outer Mongolia. The women have a different style of dress from the other Mongolian groups: a fitted top with a skirt gathered at the waist. The sleeves of those worn by married women are gathered at the shoulders and the effect is akin to that of medieval European dress (fig. 16.3). A conical blue woollen hat with earflaps, decorated with embroidery and a tassel on the top, is also worn.

A southern group of Mongols live around the Qilu Lake in Tonghai in Yunnan province. Their ancestors followed Kublai Khan there in the middle of the thirteenth century, later becoming fishermen and woodworkers. These Mongols wear a style quite different from those in the north, due to the different climate and occupations. The women wear cap-sleeved short jackets in a plain colour, usually green or black, meeting edge to edge at the front. Some jackets fasten at the centre-front with many silver coins used as buttons. The jacket with multicoloured stripes around the arms is worn over a white shirt longer than the jacket. Slim-fitting black trousers complete the outfit. The hair is worn braided and wrapped around the head, the ends overlapping at the front and decorated with coloured wool. When working outdoors, a large bamboo hat is worn.

West and North-West China

The Hui

Widely dispersed throughout China are 8.6 million Hui people. About 20 per cent live in the Ningxia Hui Autonomous Region established in 1958, with others in many other provinces, especially Gansu, Henan, Xinjiang, Qinghai, Hebei, Shandong, and Yunnan. They are followers of Islam, and consequently there are mosques in many city centres. Hui people trace their origins to the Arabs and Persians who came as merchants to trade with the cosmopolitan Tang dynasty, but later more Muslims arrived from Central Asia in the early thirteenth century, driven east by Mongol followers of Genghis Khan. Intermarriage with other groups, especially Han Chinese, Mongolians, and Uygurs, means that Hui minority people have long since adopted the Chinese language and Chinese names, although they still maintain their original religious customs.

As Muslims must keep the top of their head covered, traditional dress for Hui men is a white or black knitted, crocheted, or embroidered cotton cap close-fitting to the head (**fig. 16.4**). A front-opening white shirt and black or white trousers are worn beneath a sleeveless front-opening jacket in a dark colour. Older men can wear long overcoats and scarves wrapped round the head over the caps. However, although many Hui men now wear Han Chinese revolutionary-style jackets and trousers with the white cap, beards continue to be cultivated.

Fig. 16.4 Hui men from Ningxia wearing white cotton caps. China Tourism.

Women wear black or white round caps. Over them young women wear green hoods, middle-aged women black ones, and old women wear white hoods which cover the head and shoulders; all are made of silk or cotton gauze, sometimes embroidered. White long-sleeved gowns reaching to the knee are worn with black or blue trousers. Sleeveless jackets or close-fitting vests are worn over the gowns.

The Uygurs

In the inhospitable mountains of the arid north-west of China live the Uygur minority, whose name means 'unity' or 'alliance'. There are about 7.2 million living in the Xinjiang Autonomous Region where the climate is extreme, with temperatures of minus 15°C in winter up to 48°C in summer in the Turpan Basin, and an annual rainfall of as little as 16 millimetres. Although originally nomadic, the Uygurs are now more settled. The climate and soil are especially suited to grapes and melons, and cotton is a major cash crop. Uygur people are also followers of Islam, and in recent years some pilgrims have even visited Mecca.

Traditional clothing for men is a loose tunic of striped cotton reaching to the knee. It is worn over a white shirt with side-fastening collar. The tunic has long, wide sleeves and wraps over to the right, held in place at the waist by a patterned scarf. Black trousers are tucked into knee-high leather boots. Most men grow a moustache.

Women and children wear a wide-sleeved dress with a high yoke, from which a full gathered skirt falls. Traditionally the dress is made of ikat-patterned silk (**plate 77, 78**). The silk warp threads are dyed in a pattern before being attached to the loom, and the weft yarn is completely hidden beneath the warp after weaving. Today, however, the fabric is often cotton merely printed with this pattern. The dress is worn with wide trousers and a black or red vest which fastens at the front. Hair is worn in pigtails; eyebrows and fingernails are painted on special occasions, and some women wear the veil.

Both men and women wear small embroidered hats which are an integral part of their costume. Worn throughout the year, their use is obligatory on certain occasions such as a marriage or festival. The custom is thought to have begun in the Ming dynasty with the influence of Islam from Arabia and Central Asia. Made by the women, these hats are formed by four petal-shaped embroidered pieces sewn together to make a shallow cup. It is then blocked over a wooden mould to set the shape, and edged in black velvet. Sometimes five pieces are used to give a more tailored fit. The decoration is composed of beading, gold and silver filigree work, or embroidery of satin stitch, cross stitch, or a combination of all these. Each section has the same arrangement of motifs, and the design is usually made up of flowers, birds, fruit, and other natural motifs, as well as geometric patterns borrowed from Han Chinese sources.

The Kazaks

Kazaks live in Xinjiang, Qinghai, and Gansu provinces. They are a nomadic people, numbering about 1.11 million, who move around the pasture land as the seasons change, rearing sheep and horses. They live in yurts; three generations will cohabit in the larger ones.

The interior of the Kazak yurt is a maze of colour. All the surfaces of the tent are covered with embroidered panels; chests holding clothing are covered with embroidered cloths, and every possible surface is decorated with embroidery. The women are famous for their embroidery worked in bright colours often on black cloth using a very large frame. A girl is taught to embroider from an early age, and will then begin to amass a collection of items as part of her dowry, as well as to demonstrate her sewing ability to the prospective groom.

Kazak men wear long-sleeved shirts with high embroidered collars. Leather breeches are tucked into boots, and around the waist is a leather belt carrying a flint purse and a dagger. Embroidered sheepskin overcoats are worn in cold weather. Winter hats are made from three pieces of sheepskin or fur covered with silk which hangs over each ear and the back of the neck. At other times a hat made of four segments of fur topped with a tassel is worn.

Women wear dresses with short sleeveless jackets, and cotton padded coats in winter. They also like to wear embroidered leggings to which are attached silver coins and ornaments. On the head is a leather or velvet cap, embroidered at the front and decorated with a bunch of owl feathers (**fig. 16.5**). A large white

shawl, embroidered with red and yellow and reaching down to the ankle, was traditionally worn by most women, but this is now being replaced by a smaller silk scarf. As the Kazaks are Muslim, the married woman will often also cover her head with a scarf.

The Tibetans

Tibetans living in Tibet, Qinghai, Sichuan, Gansu, and Yunnan total 4.59 million. About 2 million ethnic Tibetans live inside the traditional boundaries of Tibet, raising sheep, cattle, goats, and yaks, and growing

Fig. 16.5 Kazak girl wearing a red velvet sequinned cap with a spray of owl feathers. China Tourism.

fruit and grain. In the seventh century, while King Songzan Gambo ruled over Tibet, an envoy was sent to China to pay homage to the Tang emperor. Seven years later, in AD 641, Princess Wen Cheng, the daughter of the Tai Zong Emperor, married the Tibetan king, and thus began Chinese influence in Tibet. The Tibetans' religion is a form of orthodox Buddhism, introduced in the reign of King Gambo, which gradually turned into Lamaism by combining with the native religion, Bon-po.

Tibet was annexed by China during the Yuan dynasty, and then administered by Qing officials; after the founding of the People's Republic it became the Tibetan Administrative Region in 1951. In 1959, following a rebellion, the Dalai Lama, Tibet's spiritual leader, and thousands of his followers fled into exile in India, and Tibet was reformed along communist lines. The Tibet Autonomous Region was officially established in 1965.

There are some differences in dress according to area and, in the past, to social status, but the styles are similar in the main. In the farming areas women wear a patterned blouse with very long sleeves, fastening over to the right. The sleeves are rolled up for working, and worn down for dancing at festivals. Over it a long black sleeveless woollen tunic, side-fastening and tied with a colourful belt, is worn. The herds in the grasslands produce a thick, home-spun wool called *pulo* which is made into clothing, headwear, and boots. There are many different kinds of *pulo*: a popular one with multicoloured horizontal stripes is woven in strips on a very narrow loom, and then made into aprons for married women by sewing three strips together with the stripes intentionally unmatched (**fig. 16.6**).

Fig. 16.6 Tibetan women having a tug-of-war, wearing the sleeveless robe, blouse, and striped apron.

In the pasturelands of the Qinghai-Tibet Plateau, men and women wear the *chuba*, a robe made from sheepskin or woollen cloth, which is long and loose, fastening over to the right with sleeves extending about 30 centimetres longer than the fingertips (**fig. 16.7**). Sometimes, they are edged with a colourful striped border or fur. The robe is worn with a belt from which many items are hung, and is pulled up high to form a loose pouch which is useful for carrying daily necessities, and even a baby. As temperatures fluctuate sharply between day and night, the *chuba* is made loose enough to put on and take off easily, and one or both arms can be slipped out of the sleeves when working. At night the robe becomes a bed cover.

Both men and women wear boots with leather soles and brightly patterned uppers made of *pulo* or leather. Men wear their hair cut short, or in a long queue coiled around the head and over one ear. A felt or fur hat is worn also as protection against the extreme temperatures and strong sunshine. Tibetan women wear their hair long and braided in a variety of different styles according to the region. In Tibet it is braided into two plaits which are then intertwined with two contrasting colours of wool, and coiled around the head. In Qinghai and other areas, the preference is for many braids, traditionally 108, the same as the number of holy sutras. These braids are looped together with silver plaques studded with coral and turquoise.

In the past, Tibetans of different ranks were distinguished by the designs and ornaments on their clothing. These ornaments were made of gold and silver inlaid with coral, turquoise, amber, and other precious stones. In this way a Tibetan would carry his wealth, either in the form of jewellery or accoutrements, on his person at all times. Tibetan women love jewellery, and wear many

Fig. 16.7 Group of Tibetans in Qinghai wearing sheepskin coats. China Tourism.

earrings, necklaces, bracelets, rings, and pendants, all of which have symbolic properties. At festival time the backs of the womens' robes are ornamented with round silver plaques engraved and studded with coral and turquoise (**plate 79**).

17 Minority Groups in the South

South-West China

The Yi

There are about 6.57 million Yi people of whom more than 1 million live in the Liangshan Yi Autonomous Prefecture in Sichuan province, with the remainder in other parts of Sichuan, Yunnan, Guizhou, and Guangxi. The areas are rich in natural resources. Many of the Yi are farmers who tend sheep and goats. There were references to the Yi people in the Han dynasty, and Yi warriors established a slave society during the Tang period, centred in present-day Yunnan, which flourished right up to the 1950s. Under this system, the Yi people (or Lolos as they were known locally) were divided by heredity into four classes. The ruling class, comprising 7 per cent of the total population, was the Nuohuo, or Black Yi, and they owned the three lower ranks: the Quono, or White Yi, comprising about 50 per cent; the Ajia, making up about 33 per cent; and lastly the Xiaxi, accounting for 10 per cent. As intermarriage between the classes was forbidden, a member would remain in one class for life.

Yi costume differs according to area, and there are more than fifteen variations. The styles worn in Sichuan province are most typical, with long pleated skirts with many layers an important feature. Young girls wear a two-tiered red and white skirt which is tightly fitting at the hips, flaring out with pleats at the lower section. Young women have three-tiered skirts fitted to the hips, with the lower tiers of pleats in red, white, blue, yellow, or black (**fig. 17.1**). Older women wear blue or black skirts in three or four sections. The pleated part is made from up to 7 metres of cloth, with the lower section of pleats edged with black and braid. These skirts, which are made of heavy wool, or cotton by those living at lower altitudes, are difficult to wear and usually reserved for special occasions, when several

Fig. 17.1 Group of Yi women wearing full pleated skirts and woollen *charwas*.

layers of skirts may be worn. Those Yi living in the Liangshan Mountains in southern Sichuan mainly use three colours, black, red, and yellow, although plain yellow or white banded with black have become more popular in recent years.

Women living in other parts of Sichuan and western Guizhou wear skirts with a short *shan*, edged with wide bands of contrasting fabric and braid fastening to the right (**plate 80**). The 'false cloud' design, so popular with the Hoklo boat people in southern Guangdong, is used on the upper clothing of festive dress worn at the Torch Festival in Sichuan. A yellow oilskin umbrella is also carried and is an important feature of festival dress. Stiff detachable collars studded with silver ornaments are worn around the neck, and the Yi women are fond of wearing silver bracelets, earrings, and rings. Women from some groups wear a long blue *shan* reaching down to the knee, edged with bright braid and contrasting fabric bands. It is worn over either the pleated skirt or black trousers. Sleeveless, side-fastening jackets are worn over the *shan* and studded with many silver discs, and elaborately embroidered aprons are also worn on some occasions.

A woollen felt cape called a *charwa* hangs straight down from squared-off shoulders, and is an important part of the women's dress in Sichuan province. It is usually made in black edged with narrow coloured piping, or sometimes of patchwork. The shoulders have small round openings or else small sleeves folded back, like a jacket thrown casually over the shoulders. Another type of cape or shawl worn by men, children, and some women is a simple length of woven black or natural wool, gathered at the neck and often with long fringing at the hem. This shawl, sometimes made of sheepskin, is worn to keep out the cold and rain, and also as a covering at night.

Women wear a variety of headgear according to age and district. Young girls wear a folded cotton scarf in either blue, red, and black, or black which is embroidered in bright colours and held in place with a long plait of hair. At a special ceremony which takes place when a girl comes of age, between fifteen and seventeen, she will start to wear two plaits coiled over a black cloth scarf folded and tied at the back of the head. Unmarried women in Yunnan wear a 'cockscomb' hat made of wool, tassels, and embroidery, which symbolizes the rooster and is based on an old folk story. Married Yi women wear a turban, sometimes of black or red wool, while those from the Sani branch in Yunnan wear a striped turban edged with pearls across the front. Some women wear a bamboo conical hat with a red tassel, while those women who have given birth are entitled to wear a most unusual hat. This is like a large dish, narrow at the bottom and wider towards the crown. It is covered with black gauze, and placed on the head over a coloured headscarf.

Men's costume also differs according to the district, and is sometimes indicated by the tightness of the trouser leg which can be flared, medium width, or tight. The upper garment is a tight, side-fastening *shan* in black with neck opening, hem, and cuffs edged with coloured piping and braid.

Fig. 17.2 Yi male with Buddha's lock hairstyle and wearing the woollen cape gathered at the neck. China Tourism.

The Buddha's lock is a famous hairstyle still worn by Yi men of all four classes, although it was originally said to have been imposed on their captives by the Black Yi. The head is shaven, except for a long lock knotted in a horn pointing towards the front over the forehead (**fig. 17.2**). In the left pierced ear, an earring made of three beads will be worn— one large yellow, with a smaller red one above and below. Some also wear a black turban with a horn-like twist on the right to symbolize heroism.

The Bai

There are 1.59 million Bai people, with approximately 80 per cent living in the Dali Bai Autonomous district in Yunnan province, and the remainder in

Plate 77   A Uygur family wearing embroidered caps, the woman in an ikat woven dress.

Plate 78 An ikat woven gown of silk, with set-in sleeves, a centre-front opening edged with cotton and stitched detailing, welt pockets, yoke, and gored skirt. 98 cm(L), 1930s. Eric Boudot.

Plate 79 Tibetan women from Qinghai province with many hair plaits decorated with silver plaques studded with coral. China Tourism.

Plate 80   Yi women wearing the short *shan* and turban headdress.

Plate 81   Bai women in Yunnan province.

Plate 82   Dai woman from the Dehong area in western Yunnan wearing the tight-fitting sarong and silver studded *dou dou*.

Plate 83   Hani woman from the Aini subgroup wearing silver ornaments and headdress.

Plate 84   A group of Dong women wearing elaborate silver headdresses and embroidered aprons. China Tourism.

Plate 85   Miao women of the Xiangxi subgroup with their large turbans and embroidered aprons. Western Hunan province.

Plate 86 White-trousered Yao men and women threshing rice. China Tourism.

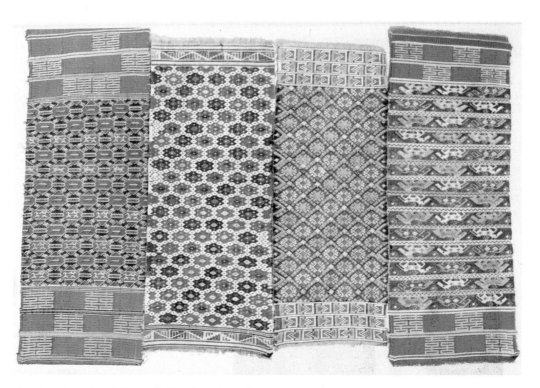

Plate 87 Examples of Tujia *xilankapu* brocade. Hubei province.

neighbouring Sichuan and Guizhou. The ancient city of Dali was the capital of the Bai kingdom for three hundred years until 1253 when Kublai Khan moved the regional capital of Yunnan from Dali to Kunming. Bai architectural, musical, and literary skills date back to the Tang dynasty.

The word Bai means white, and the women wear a white *shan*, edged with contrasting bands of colour at the sleeve cuffs, with a sleeveless red or black *shan* over it (**plate 81**). This is worn with an apron with embroidered edges, and a wide waistband with embroidered ties which wraps around the waist, fastening in front. Dark coloured trousers and embroidered shoes complete the outfit. Unmarried women wear long plaits bound with red wool which they wind around the head and over an embroidered headcloth with white tassels falling over the left ear. Married women wear their hair in a bun with a headscarf over it. A 'cockscomb' hat of stiff black cloth decorated with silver ornaments and red silk pompoms is also worn in some areas.

Men wear a white or blue turban. A front-opening jacket in white is worn under a sleeveless soft leather or embroidered waistcoat. Black or blue trousers, with white cotton leg wrappings and a short black vest, complete the outfit.

The Dai

About 1.02 million Dai people live in Yunnan province, with the majority in a reserved area in the south known as Xishuangbanna, meaning twelve districts. The area is subtropical, much of it taken over by jungle where monkeys, tigers, and elephants roam. Peacocks are also common and are celebrated in the Dai's Dance of the Peacocks. Those living in this area are known as the Water Dai, while others in the district of Dehong in western Yunnan close to Burma are known as Land Dai. Their main occupation is farming the very fertile land, and the famous *Pu'er* tea is grown there. The name Dai in their dialect means 'freedom' and they are strict followers of Hinayana Buddhism. Their history can be traced back to the Han dynasty when the Dai sent tribute to the court at the capital, Luoyang. In later years, the land was divided between hereditary headmen who ruled according to feudal systems. In some areas social status from the past is still indictated by the richness of the dress.

Men wear a short front-buttoning jacket with narrow sleeves and loose trousers with a blue sash around the waist. Round the head is wrapped a long piece of blue or white cloth to form a turban. Tattooing the body is still common.

The Dai women from Xishuangbanna wear a patterned sarong which wraps closely around the hips. These are often made from brocade which the Dai have made for over 1,000 years (**plate 82**). A short, collarless, close-fitting jacket, front or side-fastening with slim sleeves, is made from sheer fabric and worn over an embroidered bodice which is worn next to the skin. Young women wear their hair in a bun at the top or side of the head, sometimes dressed with flowers and combs.

Married women from the Dehong area in western Yunnan wear black skirts which have a wide embroidered waistband and rows of coloured woven pattern round the hem. Unmarried women wear black trousers. A short front-fastening jacket with narrow sleeves is worn by both, with or without a *dou dou* heavily studded with silver discs. Women wear a black scarf tied like a turban. Silver neckrings, earrings, and bracelets inlaid with semi-precious stones or glass are favoured by all Dai women.

The Hani

The 1.25 million Hani people live and farm in the fertile, subtropical regions of southern Yunnan. Most live in the Mojiang and Honghe counties in the Ailao mountains, with the rest in the Wuliang mountains and Xishuangbanna prefecture. They have a long history, and are noted in Tang dynasty records as having paid tribute to the Tang court. Hani people are subdivided into more than twenty groups and subgroups, each having different names according to the region they are from, and each with its own style of dress and customs. Unusual forms of dress are worn to indicate marriageability, and a woman will change her hairstyle and headdress many times before and after marriage.

The common outfit for women is a black or indigo jacket edged with colourful braid and silver ornaments (**plate 83**). Some groups wear short pleated skirts with embroidered leg wrappings. Those women in the branch of the Hani called the Yeche wear tight shorts shaped like a close-fitting loin cloth. Their top, which has narrow elbow-length sleeves, wraps over and is held in place round the waist with a woven fringed belt. These women sometimes wear as many as ten layers of this bodice at once as a sign of beauty and wealth. The top and shorts are made of homespun cotton, dyed black and decorated with many silver ornaments. They also wear white peaked hoods.

The Aini subgroup living in Xishuangbanna are especially known for their elaborate silver headdresses, and depending on the style are known as 'flat head' or 'round head' Aini. Hani women of all groups enjoy wearing a large variety of silver necklaces, earrings, and headdresses.

Men wear indigo-dyed cotton jackets opening at the front or to the side. Those living in Xishuangbanna decorate their jackets with silver coins and ornaments. They are worn with loose trousers and a black or white cloth turban.

The Bouyei

Bouyei people living in communities with the Miao and Dong minorities in remote regions in south and west Guizhou, especially on the Yunnan-Guizhou

Plateau, total 2.54 million. The Bouyei, who can trace their history back to before the second century BC, were recognized as a separate minority group at the end of the Tang dynasty.

Although skilled in many arts and crafts, the Bouyei have been famous for centuries for the art of batik dyeing. Girls are taught from a young age to use a copper tool, piece of bamboo, or even a blade of grass to apply the melted wax to the parts of the design to be left white. After the wax hardens the cloth is immersed in indigo dye. Often designs are embroidered on top of the batik. What began as a cottage industry is now produced in factories both for export as well as home consumption.

Batik-printed material is used both for household items as well as women's dress. Women wear a side-fastening, collarless *shan* edged with batik and embroidered bands. This is worn either with trousers or with a long finely pleated skirt also made of batik. The garments, made of cotton, are dyed in varying shades from a very dark blue-black to a light turquoise. Outer garments are often worn over a white shirt with longer, narrower sleeves. A long apron, edged with braid and contrasting-coloured fabric, completes the outfit (**fig. 17.3**).

Fig. 17.3 Bouyei women dyeing cloth as part of the batik designing process. China Tourism.

Unmarried girls plait their hair which is then wound into coils under a scarf. After several years of marriage a headdress is worn made from a dark cloth placed over a bamboo frame about 30 centimetres long which raises the scarf to symbolize status.

Men wear a front-opening jacket with narrow band collar and loose trousers, following the style of the Han Chinese. The jacket is often sashed around the waist. Blue or blue and white checked cotton turbans complete the outfit.

The Dong

A total of 2.51 million Dong people live primarily in Guizhou province, with the remainder in Hunan and Guangxi. They are descendants of a tribe with origins in slave societies of the Qin and Han dynasties. Main occupations today are farming and the cultivation of fir trees for market. Their architecture is spectacular, with two- and three-storey houses built of fir wood being a feature, as are the roofed, highly decorated bridges called 'wind and rain' bridges.

Dong women are famous for their brocade designs. Girls learn to weave and embroider from childhood to master designs of flowers, birds, and many geometric patterns. Homespun cotton and hemp, indigo-dyed to shades of light through to dark blue, some soaked in ox or pig blood to give a purple sheen, are used for clothing. Women wear the side-fastening *shan*, edged in contrasting shades of blue and braid. It reaches to the thigh and is worn with trousers similarly decorated. Alternatively, especially in warmer weather, they will wear a front-opening jacket with bands of brocade edging front, cuffs, and trouser hems. Around the neck a long apron or *dou dou* with embroidery across the top is worn (plate 84). This is complemented by a short pleated skirt trimmed with braid, and blue puttees.

Hairstyles differ according to district, and hair is either worn in a knot at the front, back, or sides, or in plaits wrapped around the head. Scarves and turbans are also worn. Dong women are fond of wearing silver ornaments in their hair, necklaces, earrings, and apron chains; correspondingly, their children wear many amulets in their hats.

Men wear Han-style jackets fastening with buttons at the front, but a collarless *shan* fastening over to the right with a sash round the waist is worn with large turbans in mountainous areas.

The Miao

Miao people, with a population of 7.39 million, comprise one of the largest and best-documented minority groups. Among the oldest ethnic groups, dating back over 4,000 years, they principally live in Guizhou, with others in Yunnan, Hunan, Sichuan, Guangdong, Hubei, and Guangxi in the high mountainous areas, speaking a large variety of dialects according to tribe and region. The Miao supported the Taiping rebels in the mid-nineteenth century, and sustained the Communists during the Long March of the mid-1930s.

Traditionally, the Miao people have been grouped according to the dominant colour of their clothing: Red Miao from north-east Guizhou and north-east Hunan; Green Miao in central and western Guizhou; Black Miao in central, eastern, and south-eastern Guizhou, and White Miao and Flowery Miao in central, western, and north-western Guizhou. Clothing styles still vary considerably from village to village and are said to number over a hundred varieties, but in recent years the Miao have been classified into five main groups according to geographical area and renamed Xiangxi, Qiandong, Qianzhongnan, Chuanqiandian, and Hainan.[1]

Clothing is made from cotton, indigo-dyed in shades from almost black to paler blue, and calendered to produce a smooth, shiny appearance. Material is very often then dipped in pig blood to give it a purplish sheen, or else soaked in egg whites to add lustre. Some groups of Miao also use batik cloth.

Xiangxi, or western Hunan group, is the name given to those whose dialect belongs to western Hunan, though this style of dress is also found in parts of Hunan, Guizhou, Sichuan, and Hubei provinces. The dress for women is the *shan* edged with contrasting fabric and braid at neck-opening and sleeve cuffs. It is worn with trousers decorated to match, and an embroidered apron. Sleeveless jackets and turbans are worn in the cooler weather. The turbans worn by women in Shanjiang, in Fenghuang county in western Hunan, are often more than 10 metres in length and wound round the head to create a cylindrical coil—the bigger and taller the better (plate 85). Men wear jackets buttoned in front, with long trousers, turbans, and puttees.

The Qiandong, or eastern Guizhou group, is distributed mainly in parts of Guizhou as well as Guangxi where the largest concentration of Miao people are found. Men's dress comprises a short jacket open down the front, or a long gown fastening to the right. These are worn with long trousers and a belt, with many layers of cloth utilized for a turban. Women's styles are more diverse according to the region, and can be a short jacket with a large collar buttoning on the right, or centre-opening jacket with no buttons and a large collar. Pleated skirts are worn whose lengths vary according to area. The ankle-length skirt takes 12 metres of cloth which is starched in rice water, then dried, folded, and rolled tightly inside a bamboo tube. The hem of the skirt is decorated with bands of cross-stitch embroidery. Embroidered aprons are worn, as well as puttees, but trousers are only worn in certain areas.

A great variety of silver ornaments are worn on festive occasions, in particular towering horn-shaped headdresses, earrings, combs, and necklaces. A complete set can weigh as much as 5 kilograms. Silver is a symbol of wealth, and the ornaments, which have motifs based on dragon and phoenix, animal and plant forms, show superb workmanship (fig. 17.4).

The Chuanqiandian group is found mainly in Sichuan, Guizhou, and Yunnan. Women's dress is made of hemp, usually in lighter colours. They wear a jacket buttoning to the right or down the front, with a pleated batik skirt richly decorated with geometric patterns. Puttees are worn to protect the legs from rough grass (fig. 17.5). Festive clothing and silver ornaments are not popular, and wooden combs and turbans are more common.

The Qianzhongnan group is found mainly in the dialect region of the Chuanqiandian in central and southern Guizhou. Due to their geographic location,

Fig. 17.4 Miao women from the Qiandong subgroup wearing spectacular silver headdresses and ornaments. China Tourism.

the clothing tends to be a combination of both Qiandong and Chuanqiandian styles. In general, women wear jackets fastening at centre-front with pleated skirts of medium length. Embroidered or woven back panels with fancy shoulder ribbons are worn over the jacket, but fewer silver accessories are worn.

The fifth group, the Hainan, is found on subtropical Hainan Island close to southern Guangdong. Men wear a short light-blue jacket with a stand-up collar, a turban in the same colour, and long trousers. Women wear knee-length collarless jackets fastening· over to the right, and short batik skirts with little decoration. Woven sashes are worn, and puttees in cooler weather.

The Yao

Around 2.13 million Yao people, the majority living in the mountainous regions of Guangxi in the Guangxi Zhuang Autonomous Region, are also spread out into Hunan, Yunnan, Guangdong, and Guizhou provinces. With a recorded history dating back to the Han dynasty, many live in rural stockaded villages, and continue beliefs rooted in animism. There are many different tribes, each one characterized by its own distinctive type of dress. Colour is common to all, as are well-developed skills in embroidery, weaving, beadwork, and silverwork.

Fig. 17.5 Miao women from the Chuanqiandian subgroup. Guizhou province, c.1920.

The men of the White-Trousered Yao (Baiku Yao) in Nandan in Guangxi, one of the better-known groups, wear knee-length white trousers with five red stripes sewn just above the knee representing a bloody handprint which celebrates the bravery of a legendary Yao king. These are worn with black wrap-over jackets edged with blue, leg wrappings, and turbans. Yao women of this tribe wear stiffly pleated skirts of batik in blue and white horizontal stripes, with a patterned patchwork tabard joined at the shoulders which, in summer, is worn next to the skin (plate 86). Puttees and turbans complete the outfit.

Fig. 17.6 Hualan Yao girls sewing. Jinxiu Yao Autonomous County.

In another group in the Jinxiu Yao Autonomous County in eastern Guangxi, the Hualan Yao women wear black jackets edged with embroidered bands, worn with blue or green trousers. Turbans are also worn, made from bands of embroidered and beaded white cloth finished with red tassels (fig. 17.6).

The Yao people from Liannan in northern Guangdong are called Ba Pai Yao meaning the eight largest, leading tribes. Red and black are the common colours, although the dress of each tribe differs. Men wear their hair long, coiled into a bun, covered with red cloth, and decorated with pheasant feathers. Women wear black wrap-over jackets edged with blue bands, black skirts, and red puttees, while unmarried women wear white feathers on their heads. Older married women wear a very tall hat made of a bamboo frame covered with black and white cloth. Women from another tribe wear broad red yokes and deep hem bands on their black jackets, and a red folded head scarf with many silver ornaments.

The Zhuang

The Zhuang are the largest of the minority groups in China. The majority of the 15.48 million population live in the Guangxi Zhuang Autonomous Region, but others have settled in Guangdong, Guizhou, Yunnan, and Hunan provinces. The Zhuang people are polytheists, worshipping rocks, trees, high mountains, and birds, as well as Daoists who worship their ancestors. Their recorded history spans some 2,000 years, and early frescoes found in south-west Guangxi depict the daily life of the Zhuang people. By the Tang dynasty they were already famous for their detailed and beautiful brocade used for many household articles as well as clothing. In common with the Han Chinese, the Zhuang prefer decorative designs which symbolize good fortune: the dragon, phoenix, and auspicious animals and flowers.

Contemporary Zhuang men tend to dress in black trousers and centre-fastening jackets with a sash round the waist. Women wear black trousers with bands of embroidery above the hem. A collarless jacket opens down the front, and is decorated with bands of brocade or embroidery at the neck and the arms. Alternatively, a side-fastening *shan* is worn with an embroidered apron, sometimes with a black pleated skirt. A black cloth turban and embroidered shoes complete the outfit (**fig. 17.7**).

Fig. 17.7 Zhuang women washing in a stream.

Central and South-East China

The Tujia

Tujia people, living in western parts of Hunan and Hubei in the Tujia-Miao Autonomous Prefectures, total 5.7 million. Said to be descendants of an ancient tribe called Ba dating back some three thousand years, they were known traditionally as the Tumin people, and it was only in 1949 that they received the name Tujia. With a long period of assimilation into Han culture, however, Tujia clothing—particularly for women—is very similar to that worn by Han Chinese women in the Qing dynasty.

Tujia women wear the side-fastening *shan* with wide bands of contrasting fabric or braid around the neck, side, hem, and sleeves (**fig. 17.8**). It used to be worn with a pleated or gored skirt with decorated panels at back or front, but today trousers are more common. Young girls wear their hair in a long plait, but after marriage it is wound up into a bun and covered with a turban. Many silver earrings, pendants, bracelets, and other ornaments are worn.

Traditional dress for men is a blue or black jacket made of cotton or hemp buttoning down the front. The edges are decorated in similar fashion to those worn by women, with contrast-fabric appliquéd designs, especially the *ruyi* design, around the neck and front opening. Matching trousers have a similar design at the hem. A black or white cotton scarf is worn as a turban.

Xilankapu brocade is a speciality of the Tujia people, and has a long history dating back to the Qin and Han dynasties when it was produced as tribute cloth; it continued to be an important part of trade even in

Fig. 17.8 Two women of the Tujia minority. Hubei province.

Qing times. In the Tujia language *xilan* means 'bed cover', and *kapu* means 'flower' or 'pattern'. Most families have a back-strap loom on which to weave the brocade, made of cotton 50 centimetres wide and about 1 metre long. Designs of animals, plants, Chinese characters, and a variety of scenes from daily life are used for clothing, including wedding dresses. Like the Han Chinese, the Tujia people like designs which symbolize good fortune: dragon, phoenix, and the Buddhist *wan* symbol. The colours of the brocade are bright, contrasting against a dark background. At the beginning and end of the piece, three rows are woven in a quieter pattern. The material is also used for shoulder bags, and around the house for door curtains, wall hangings, quilt covers, and pillowcases (**plate 87**).

The Li

Li people live on Hainan Island, now a separate province, off the coast of Guangdong; with a population of 1.11 million they account for about 15 per cent of Hainan's population. Historical records date back to the Tang dynasty, but archaeological finds on Hainan show evidence of Li settlers as far back as the late Shang or early Zhou period.

The women are skilled weavers, and their traditional dress is a front-opening jacket with geometric patterned bands on the sleeves. Worn with a short tight tubular skirt woven with bright geometric designs, especially in red, the length of the skirt differs from place to place, some reaching down to the ankle. The hair is worn in a bun, and dressed with bone ornaments. Additionally, a richly woven turban is often worn. In the past, tattooing was a common part of the initiation ceremony for a girl reaching puberty. Large silver neckrings continue to be popular, as are bracelets and earrings (**fig. 17.9**).

Men wear a collarless undyed hemp top with long sleeves which wraps over to the side. Two pieces of cloth resemble an apron and cover the lower body, one at the back and one at the front. The hair is wrapped up in a headcloth like a turban, and men from some tribes wear earrings.

Note

1   See *Ethnic Costumes of the Miao People in China*, Hong Kong: Urban Council, 1985. Another branch of the Miao is the Gejia people, said by some to be a separate group although they are not classified separately by the Chinese authorities. There are large communities of Gejia living alongside the Miao in the Huang Ping area of north-east Guizhou.

Fig. 17.9 Woman from the Li minority group on Hainan Island.

Part VII
Materials

18 Fibres and Fabrics

Three main fibres were utilized in the construction of traditional Chinese dress, with hemp and cotton generally worn by working people, while silk was favoured by the more wealthy. Wool was seldom used until the twentieth century, except by some minority groups in the north-west who raised sheep.

Hemp

Hemp had been grown in China since the Zhou dynasty and was mentioned in several literary sources of the time.[1] The planting of hemp to clothe the peasant population was a major farming occupation in the Han dynasty, and it continued to be an important fibre until the middle of the thirteenth century, when cotton began gradually to become the main fabric for the common people. During neolithic times hemp was grown principally in the northern part of China, while ramie, sometimes known as nettle cloth, was grown in the south, but by the Song period both fibres were grown throughout the land.

Hemp continued to be cultivated domestically up to the early part of the twentieth century. The plant

Fig. 18.1 Stripping the bark from the hemp plants. The strips are then hung to dry.

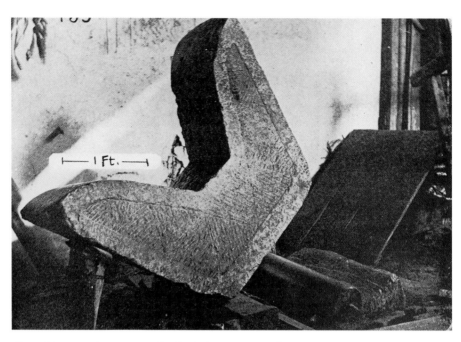

Fig. 18.2 Rocking-stone and roller for calendering fabrics.

Cannabis sativa is an annual which has a stem of 2 centimetres in diameter, and grows to a height of between 1.5 and 3 metres. Guangdong province was a well-known producer of hemp, with many bolts of cloth sent as tribute to the Qing court. Three crops a year were harvested: the first in June, the second about six weeks later, and the final one in October which was expected to produce the finest cloth (**fig. 18.1, 18.2**).

> On being cut the leaves are soaked in water for an hour, and the fibre stripped by breaking in the middle; whilst the operator, generally a woman or a child, separates the filaments skilfully from one end to the other with the finger-nails. The next process is scraping the hemp with a knife by drawing the strips over the blade from within outwards, taking off all the mucilaginous parts; then it is rolled up into bundles, exposed for a day in the sun, then assorted and the whitest selected for fine cloth. A partial bleaching is effected on the fibres before they undergo further division, sometimes by boiling, and at others by pounding on a plank with a mallet. When the cloth is finished it undergoes a process of glazing, which is done by a rude machine most effectively. A sort of bed or tray is laid down firmly in the ground, the inside curved or scalloped, and made very smooth. Upon this the cloth is carefully spread; a small cylinder is laid above, and upon that a stone with a smooth face, having the ends turned upwards. A man mounts this stone, and places one foot at each end, giving it a see-saw motion working the cylinder backwards and forewards with great power, and imparting a fine glaze to the cloth, equal to hot-pressing in European factories.[2]

It was usual for the women of a village to spin the fibres and prepare the yarn for weaving. However, the task of actually turning the yarn into cloth fell to groups of itinerant weavers, generally Hakka people, who travelled from village to village during the autumn following the hemp harvest. They would stay in an empty house in the village, and weave the cloth on simple looms, using tools they brought with them.[3] Afterwards, the cloth would be dyed and made into clothing or mosquito netting. Hemp cloth felt stiff when first worn, but it softened with age and was popular because it felt cool in summer. Coarse undyed hemp is still used for funeral clothing today.

Ramie, *Boehmeria nivea, Gaudich*, was also an important textile plant, a perennial capable of producing a higher yield than hemp over a longer period of time. It had great tensile strength, and could produce coarse to very fine yarn which took dye well to give a lustre equal almost to that of silk. It was produced by hand in a similar way to hemp, and the finer fibres of the third crop of the year were used to make summer robes for the more wealthy.

Silk

There is a long tradition of sericulture in China with remnants of silk being found together with bronzes dating back to the Shang dynasty. In Chinese legend the discovery of silk fibre has been attributed to Lei Zu, wife of Huangdi, the Yellow Emperor, who saw caterpillars in the garden eating mulberry leaves; some days later she discovered the caterpillars had spun cocoons made up of a web of gossamer-like fibres. Experimenting, she found that by boiling the cocoons in water the threads unravelled easily; from this the first silk fabrics were produced. However, recent archaeological evidence indicates that silk was first produced in China in neolithic times.

By the Zhou dynasty there were imperial workshops producing silk fabrics supervised by court officials. As the wearing of silk spread outside the court circle it began to be traded, and by the second century BC a route was opened from Chang'an (present-day Xi'an) in Shaanxi province, through Xinjiang in northwest China, to Syria 11,000 kilometres away. This became known as the Silk Road, and it was by this means that China exported silk to the West. The secret of silk production stayed with the Chinese until around the middle of the fifth century AD when, again according to legend, a Chinese princess carried silkworm eggs hidden inside her headdress when she went to marry the king of Khotan.

Silk was an important cottage industry by the Han dynasty. The 1972 discovery at Mawangdui, near Changsha in Hunan province, of the tombs of the Marquis of Dai and his family proved conclusively that the silk industry in China had reached a high level of sophistication by the Han period. About fifty pieces of clothing were found in the tomb, including shoes, stockings, and gloves, as well as a similar number of silk fabrics. There were plain silks, gauzes, and brocades, dyed, embroidered, woven, or painted with animal, cloud, flower, and geometric designs. The silk gauzes were as light as a feather: a piece of silk 49 centimetres wide and 45 centimetres long weighed just 2.8 grams.[4]

Many different types of silk fabric were produced. Satin, first developed during the Han dynasty, became very popular during the Ming and Qing dynasties. Suzhou, Hangzhou, and Nanjing were the centres of production, with the latter being the originator of tribute satin. This was made especially for formal robes for the imperial household, was plain black in colour, and was always the first and finest bolt of the season.

Another new weaving technique introduced by the Uygurs during the Tang dynasty was called *ge* silk weaving, or more commonly *kesi*, literally 'cut silk'. Each colour doubled back on itself, without any floating threads behind, giving small gaps between each colour and making it quite fragile for frequent use. It was later further refined by Suzhou weavers and given as tribute to the imperial household. This tapestry weave was highly prized, reaching its peak in the Qianlong emperor's reign, after which it declined, re-emerging once more towards the end of the nineteenth century (**plates 88, 89**).

By the Ming dynasty, silk-weaving centres established during earlier reigns were thriving at Suzhou, Hangzhou, Nanjing, and Chengdu. Imperial silkworks were established in the first three cities at this time, and supervised by the Office of the Imperial Household until they went out of service in 1894. Their function was to produce silk fabrics for use by the imperial family and court officials, as well as tribute silks and bolts of silk for barter in border trade. Once the silkworks had fulfilled their annual quota they were then free to take other orders from wealthy families.

Silkworm eggs and larvae were selected with great care, and the rooms reserved for breeding were kept at a constant temperature. The larvae were weighed and distributed evenly on trays, then mulberry leaves were washed and shredded and spread over the worms. It took a few days for the worm to spin its cocoon; the cocoons were then sorted, and those selected for future breeding purposes were removed. Cocoons which were to be spun were put into boiling water which softened the gluey protein holding the fibres together, after which they were removed, the ends snipped off and the silk 'pulled' (**fig. 18.3**). Strands from several cocoons were

Fig. 18.3 Boiling the silk cocoons to unravel the thread. FormAsia.

Plate 88   Ming *kesi* wall-hanging depicting a gathering of Immortals in the Kunlun Mountains.
219 cm(L) x 173 cm(W), c.1600. Plum Blossoms (Int'l) Ltd.

Plate 89   The reverse side of an uncut *kesi* neckband depicting butterflies and lotus flowers. 19th cent. Valery Garrett.

Plate 90   Selection of Manchester cotton prints used as lining or waistbands for children's clothing. Late 19th cent. Valery Garrett.

Plate 91 *Bao fu* or parcel carrier of cotton with stencil print of four colours plus black outline. Jiangsu province, early 20th cent. Valery Garrett.

Plate 92 Multicoloured stencils applied to white cotton cloth to be made into household furnishings and *bao fu*. Shandong province. China Tourism.

Plate 93 Batik patterns produced by the Bouyei in western Guizhou. China Tourism.

Plate 94   Peony, from the famous embroidery school of Gu Han Ximeng. Ming dynasty. Liaoning Museum.

Plate 95   Patchwork design of coins to be used for centre and straps of a baby carrier. Made by Tanka fishing women in Hong Kong, 1990. Valery Garrett.

Plate 96   Appliqué banner with the 'false cloud' design to be hung over the doorway to bring good fortune for the coming year. Made by Hoklo fishing women, Guangdong, 1980s. Valery Garrett.

Plate 97   Miao satin stitch embroidery, the top row depicting two fish changing into dragons on either side of fruit with a human face; the centre, vertical stripes showing birds, butterflies, and fish; the bottom row, two oxen being transformed into dragons on each side of the mother butterfly with a human face. Franck Vassal.

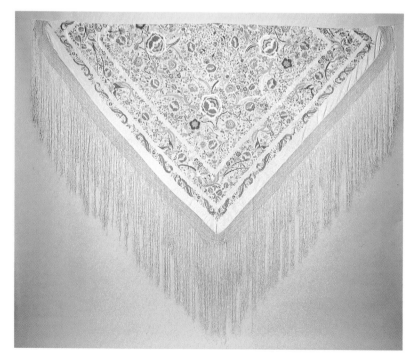

Plate 98   Silk embroidered 'Canton' shawl. c.1900. Teresa Coleman Fine Arts.

Plate 99   Needleloop embroidered rank badge depicting two cranes. 38 cm square, c.1400. Plum Blossoms (Int'l) Ltd.

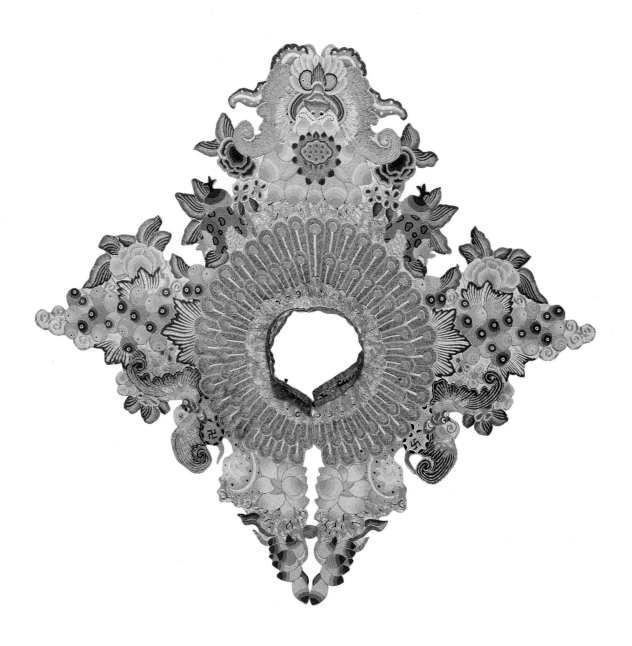

Plate 100 Woman's two-tiered wedding collar embroidered in Peking knot in a design of peacock feathers, bats (a homonym of *fu*, 'happiness'), and pomegranates (which, having many seeds, denote a wish for many sons). c.1850. Teresa Coleman Fine Arts.

Fig. 18.4 Reeling silk thread. c.1870.

unwound together to make a single stronger thread. The skeins were then dyed, reeled, and woven into cloth (**fig. 18.4, 18.5**).

By the end of the nineteenth century, silk had overtaken tea as the leading export commodity. The great silk-producing regions were Zhejiang province, where Hangzhou and Huzhou were the main centres, and Jiangsu province, with Suzhou and Wuxi as important producers. In Huzhou alone in 1879, 4,000 looms produced nearly two million kilos of silk.[5] Huge quantities of silk were exported, but even larger quantities were needed for the home market and many different varieties were woven: crêpe, brocade, raw silk, satin, damask, velvet, pongee, and gauze.

Fig. 18.5 Woman weaving. Shanghai, 1870s.

Another type of silk popular in southern Guangdong was black gummed silk, *hei jiao chou*, also called gambiered silk from the plant of that name. The production of this cloth goes back several centuries when it was said 'the common people wear pongee and senshaw (*sien-sha*) which they frequently dye in gambier to a dust or black colour'.[6] The silk has a small geometric weave of varying designs and a distinctive black shiny surface with a matt brown underside. It is still made in the district of Shunde in Guangdong province and has water-resistant properties which make it especially popular with boat people as it does not cling to the body when wet. It also became very fashionable during the 1920s and 1930s when it was worn by all levels of society in many parts of China and Hong Kong.

Cotton

The cotton plant is not indigenous to China, having been introduced into the country from Burma and Turkestan during the Song dynasty. There are references to cotton robes existing in China before that time, but it seems likely that the cotton was brought into the country as tribute cloth. Cotton was first grown in the northern provinces in the eleventh century, but later spread south proving adaptable to different climates. There was initial opposition from silk and hemp producers, and not until the Yuan dynasty was cotton fully accepted. It eventually replaced hemp as the main fabric worn by the poorer classes.

By the mid-nineteenth century the demand for raw cotton was great, and it was grown on a large scale throughout the country, especially in the Yangzi and Yellow River deltas.

> The seeds are planted [in April], after sprouting . . . the shoots, which while growing, are carefully tended, thinned, hoed, and weeded until the flowers begin to appear about August. As the pods begin to ripen and burst, the cultivator collects them before they fall, to clean the cotton of seed and husks . . . The seeds are separated by a wheel turning two rollers, and the cotton sold by each farmer to merchants in the towns. Some he keeps for weaving at home; spinning-wheels and looms being common articles of furniture in the houses of the peasantry. Cotton is cultivated in every province, and most of it used where it grows.[7]

Women and children were employed throughout the largely cottage industry, picking, ginning (separating the cotton from the seeds), scutching (separating the fibres), spinning, cording, winding, and starching (**fig. 18.6**). The men of the family planted, and then helped with the weaving which went on around the clock. The looms were between 30 and 40 centimetres wide and a 20-metre length would be woven. Men were also usually responsible for the tiring operation of carding which was done by means of a large bow more than a metre in length held by, or fastened to the body of, the worker who vibrated the

Fig. 18.6 Cotton spinning and ginning. 1880s.

string amidst the cotton, thus producing a very light floss (**fig. 18.7**). This was then spun or used for wadding in winter garments. This method of cotton-bowing is still used in China today to make cotton quilts for bedding.

By the end of the nineteenth century, cotton had become so well accepted that it was estimated that 90 per cent of the peasant population of China wore cotton clothing. A well-known type of native-grown cotton was nankeen, so named because it was grown around the city of Nanjing. It was a plain, natural-coloured twill cloth used for making pockets, stockings, and items of clothing which needed a hard-wearing cloth. Initially, it had a peculiar yellow tint which faded with time. As insufficient cotton was grown to supply local demand, it was also imported from India, America, and

Fig. 18.7 A woman posing for the camera and holding a cotton bow. 1930s.

England. Manchester cotton prints, so-called because they were printed in that Lancashire city on cotton grown in India, were also sent to China in great quantities in the mid- to late-nineteenth century, and many were used as lining material or waistbands for children's clothing (plate 90).

From a cottage industry, the production of cotton had developed into a large commercial enterprise by the 1920s with more than seventy mills in China, six of the main ones being in Shanghai, the centre of the cotton-growing district of the Yangzi River basin. In the early twentieth century cotton clothing continued to be a material of importance for the peasantry, and a more general use was encouraged by the Communists as a practical and hard-wearing fabric. Today it is widely supplemented with synthetic fibres.

Notes

1   Dieter Kuhn, 'Bast Fibres as Raw Material for the Production of Textile Fibres', *Science and Civilization in China*, vol. 5, part IX, *Textile Technology*, Cambridge: Cambridge University Press, 1988, p. 15.

2   Samuel Mossman, *China, A Brief Account of the Country, its Inhabitants and their Institutions*, London: SPCK, c.1867. This process is known as calendering.

3   J. W. Hayes, 'Itinerant Hakka Weavers', *Journal of the Hong Kong Branch of the Royal Asiatic Society*, 8 (1968): 162–5.

4   *New Archaeological Finds in China*, Beijing: Foreign Languages Press, 1973, p. 48.

5   J. Dyer Ball, *Things Chinese*, 5th edn., Shanghai: Kelly and Walsh, reprint, Hong Kong: Oxford University Press, 1982, p. 577.

6   S. Wells Williams, *The Middle Kingdom*, New York: C. Scribner's Sons, 1895, vol. 1, p. 35.

7   Ball, *Things Chinese*, p. 161–2.

19 Dyes

There is little written information concerning Chinese methods of dyeing. There were no formal recipes, and details such as the proportion of the ingredients, the length of time it took to dye cloth, and the number of times the fabric was immersed to achieve the desired colour were all secrets known to individual dyers and often jealously guarded.

As far back as the Warring States period there was evidence that the Chinese were using mineral and vegetable dyes. In the Han dynasty there were more than twenty hues in existence, and by the Qing this had grown to several hundred. Until the late nineteenth century, most were vegetable dyes made from plants. Some plants gave a fast dye, that is, the colour would not wash out, but many were not fast and required a mordant, a substance used to fix the colour into the fabric.[1] It also enabled the fabric to take the colour successfully, thus enhancing it. Mordanting is done before dyeing, the wet yarn or fabric being immersed in the solution for the required length of time. Different mordants could produce different shades from the same plant dyes.

The main mordants used in China were alum or potash, obtained by boiling hemp or rice straw; iron, obtained by boiling iron shavings, nails, etc; and slaked lime, obtained from sea shells. Chrome and tin were also used as mordants, as was the tannic acid present in some dye plants such as sumac and gall nuts.

Dye Sources

Blue, the most common colour worn by peasants, was obtained from the indigo plant *Indigofera tinctoria*, known as *lan cao*, meaning 'blue grass'. The plant has been used for centuries in China: fragments of cloth discovered in the Mawangdui tomb of the Western Han period were found to have been dyed with indigo. Planted in the first lunar month, harvested in the seventh at the flowering stage, it was thrown into large tanks filled with water. Lime was added and the plants left to soak for some days, during which time they were stirred to release the dyeing matter. When ready, the pigment sank as a precipitate. This residue, initially a greenish-yellow, was removed and churned up to expose it to air, and through oxidization it changed to deep blue.

The cloth to be dyed was thoroughly soaked in water to remove the size. It was then washed, and 'placed in the vats containing the dye and well immersed in the dye solution, being stirred occasionally. Sometimes the cloth [was] given only one dip, which last[ed] for about 15 minutes or more, after which it [was] at once exposed to the air for a few minutes in order to oxidise the colour. As a rule, however, it [was] immersed several times' to increase the density of the colour, 'the cloth being exposed to the air after each immersion. (The solution left after the cloth [had] been removed [was] kept and used again for the next batch of cloth to be dyed, more indigo being added as required.)' The cloth was washed, 'and afterwards sized if required, the size being usually tinted with methyl violet (a coal tar dye), which imparts a copper lustre to the cloth.'

'The cloth [was] dried in the open air by being suspended from a bamboo framework at a height of from 30 to 60 feet. When almost dry, it [was] usually spread on the grass and exposed to the sun for several hours, which completes the oxidation of the colour and probably increases the fastness of the dye.'

'After having, in some cases, been calendered with a heavy stone roller, or otherwise finished, the cloth [was] folded and then packed for the market'.[2]

Another much-used colour was red produced from the mineral cinnabar, or the safflower plant, *Carthamus tinctorus*. The flowers of this plant were gathered and washed in running water until the resulting yellow juice disappeared. They were then dried, and pressed into small cakes to be used for dyeing with a mordant of potash which would produce a fast red dye. Sappan wood, *Caesalpina sappan*, or betel nut, were also used.

Black could be achieved from sulphite of iron, or from gall nuts which were the woody swellings caused by attacks of gall flies on certain trees, mostly oak. For centuries, both were important agents for mordanting and dyeing. Primarily, they produced brown and grey, and to achieve black the cloth had to be dyed blue first. Acorns from the chestnut oak, *Quercus serrata*, also made a good black when mordanted with iron. Another method was to heat ivory shavings in a closed container: this produced ivory black. Animal bones were sometimes used, but the black was not as deep and velvety.

Green came from the scholar tree, *Sophorica japonica*. The flowers were used with alum to produce yellow, then dyed with indigo to give green. The yellow was fugitive in many cases, so that after a number of years the appearance of the cloth was more blue than green. A sap-green colour could be obtained from the leaves or bark of *Rhamnus tinctorus*, which was boiled to give the dye. It was expensive to produce, and not used often, mostly 'to colour shark skin for covering spectacle-cases and the like'.[3] Yellow could be produced from safflowers and *Sophorica japonica*. It could also be achieved from the powdered roots of the turmeric plant, *Curcuma longa,* with a mordant of potash.

Brown was made from the bark of the wax myrtle tree with a mordant of ferrous sulphate. It could also be produced from the false gambier plant *shu liang* to give a dark brown dye used for cotton, hemp, and silk. The dye plant was commonly grown in the southern provinces, especially in Shunde in Guangdong. To produce the dye, the fruit, which resembles the potato, was cut in half, mashed, and mixed with water. The orange-brown mixture was strained, the fabric then dipped in the dye and left to dry in the sun. It was also used to produce black gummed silk. The silk was dyed and dried many times, after which the fabric was plastered with mud from a nearby river said by the residents of Shunde to have special properties not found elsewhere. Left to dry in the sun, the silk was washed to reveal the familiar black glaze. The juice of unripe persimmons was then applied as varnish to the outside of the cloth to make it waterproof.

Purple could be made from blending red with blue, for example, indigo mixed with sappan wood. Gromwell, *Lithospermum crythrorhizon*, roots gave a violet shade, and when mixed with sappan wood produced a wine red colour. The gromwell shade should not be confused with the later very virulent purple produced from aniline dyes known as Perkins violet. These chemical dyes were developed in England in 1856 and reached China in the 1870s. This signalled the demise of plant dyes, and the rise in popularity of synthetic aniline dyes which could be obtained relatively easily and inexpensively.

Dye-resist Prints

Although China is famous for its wonderfully detailed embroidery on clothing worn by the more well-to-do, and especially on children's dress, far less attention has been paid to the resist-dyed prints which were used by many poorer families in place of embroidery. Resist dyeing occurs where the design is applied to the fabric, usually cotton, by a water-repellent substance. After dyeing, normally with indigo—although other colours were used, particularly in earlier times—this substance was removed with the result that the design showed up as undyed white cloth.

There were several ways of achieving this effect. The first method required the use of a stencil through which a dye-resist paste was applied. A very old method, it is well illustrated by a piece of wool with a white flower pattern stencilled on it. Found in 1959 in Xinjiang province, it dates back to the Northern and Southern dynasties of the fifth century AD.

> After a design has been decided upon, it is sketched onto and then cut out
> of a thick paper stencil. If the design is to appear clearly on both sides of
> the material, two identical stencils must be cut and the fabric subsequently
> squeezed between them. This is the proper pre-Song method known as

jiaran. In the nineteenth and twentieth centuries, in rural areas, one side was usually sufficient. A thin net may be placed between the stencil and the fabric to help the pastes adhere to the material. Oil has also been applied to the stencil so that it can be used several times before deteriorating from the moisture of the paste. After laying the stencil on the fabric, the artisan spreads a mixture of bean paste and lime through the perforations. If the design has been created from a number of stencils, or if one small stencil has been used over and over again, the paste is applied piece by piece. After the whole design has dried completely, the fabric can be slipped into the indigo dye bath.[4]

Care had to be taken at every stage not to break the crust of lime. After dipping, the cloth was laid on the ground to dry in the sun. The white paste was then scraped off with a knife, and the fabric calendered if required.

Another method of resist dyeing was by means of wooden boards which had the pattern incised on them. Two identical boards were clipped firmly together with the fabric to be printed placed in between. The boards and fabric were dipped in the dye which ran into the channels and dyed the cloth, except for those parts which it could not penetrate. Dye-resist prints were popular particularly in Zhejiang and Jiangsu provinces, where they were made into household items such as door curtains, bed covers and hangings, *bao fu*, a square cloth used for wrapping and carrying items slung over the shoulder, as well as children's dress, especially for young girls (**fig. 19.1, plates 91, 92**). There has been a recent revival in Nantong in Jiangsu province, which has long been a centre for this type of dyeing, but the blue and white patterns are quite repetitive. However, in Shandong province the multicoloured designs on cotton now made by girls for their *bao fu*, used to wrap their dowry items, are more individual.

Fig. 19.1 Aprons for young children made of resist dye on cotton with the design of a padlock to 'lock' the wearer to earth. c.1940.

To gain a finer, more detailed effect, where a stencil would have to be cut so much that it would fall apart, the batik method was used. Here, melted beeswax or pine resin was applied to the fabric according to the design. The fabric was dipped into a cold dye, and when the dye was fixed it was put into boiling water to remove the wax, thus leaving a white design, a much slower method as every detail had to be applied by hand. A piece of cloth dating back to the Eastern Han period, with a pattern thought to have been applied by the batik method, was found in Xinjiang province in 1959.[5] Batik printing was not much used by the Han Chinese after the Song dynasty, but several minority groups such as the Miao and Bouyei still employ the technique (**plate 93**).

A further method of dye-resist patterning was produced by tie-dyeing—not a difficult process, but a tedious and time-consuming one. The design was first drawn on white cotton cloth, then fine string would be tied in knots around the drawn design. After the fabric was dyed the knots were removed, and a dotted flower-like pattern would appear where the dye was unable to penetrate. Designs on cloth produced by tie-dyeing can be dated back to the Northern and Southern dynasties, and were popular during the Tang dynasty, when many colours were used. However, dye-resist patterns formed by stencils or tie-dyeing were suppressed during the Song dynasty because only the imperial army was allowed to wear them during the reign of the Zhen Zong Emperor (r.998–1023). These techniques disappeared for a while in consequence, and tie-dyeing never regained its popularity for the Han Chinese, although some minority groups in remote areas, such as the Bai in Yunnan, inherited and preserved the practice (**fig. 19.2**).

Fig. 19.2 Tie-dyeing done by Bai girls in Dali, Yunnan province. China Tourism.

Notes

1   This term comes from the Latin *mordere*, meaning 'to bite'.
2   E. Watson, *The Principal Articles of Chinese Commerce*, Shanghai: Inspectorate-General of Customs, 1930, p. 196.
3   Watson, *The Principal Articles of Chinese Commerce*, p. 185.
4   Nancy Zeng Berliner, *Chinese Folk Art*, Boston: Little, Brown and Co., 1986, p. 187.
5   Berliner, *Chinese Folk Art*, p. 183.

20　Embroidery

Symbolism has always been an important part of Chinese life, and embroidered symbols on clothing were a way of indicating a person's rank, as well as putting him in good favour with supernatural powers. Embroidery was also used for ornamenting all kinds of furnishings and accessories used in the home.

There is evidence of embroidery dating back to the Shang dynasty from traces found on a bronze urn at Anyang in 1929,[1] and an example of chain-stitch found in a Western Zhou tomb in Shaanxi province dating from around the sixth century BC.[2] Embroidery flourished due to court patronage during the Han dynasty, and the discovery at Mawangdui in Changsha in 1972 of the Han-period tombs of the Marquis of Dai and his family brought to light many examples of sophisticated and well-executed pieces of embroidery. The craft continued to be refined over the centuries, becoming more diverse in subject-matter and stitches, and by the Song dynasty wall hangings of landscapes or calligraphy embroidered in satin-stitch had reached a high level of skill.

Unfortunately, fabric and embroidery do not survive the ravages of time intact, and little from earlier times is extant today, although a number of examples of embroidery from the Ming dynasty have come to light in recent years via Tibet where they were taken during the sixteenth and seventeenth centuries. Many of the pieces were used as *sutra* covers, banners, and hangings in temples and monasteries, and have been preserved in a state close to the original due to favourable climatic conditions. Other highly prized examples come from the famous Gu school of embroidery, which took its name from the wife, Han Ximeng, and family of Gu Shouqian, and was established in the reign of the Jiajing Emperor in Luxiangyuan near Shanghai (plate 94). Rich colours, fine detail, and a greater use of light and shade are distinctive of this period, and a variety of materials were used with the silks, including baby's hair, cock feathers, gold thread, and precious stones.

In the Qing dynasty, the designs and application of embroidery reached a peak during the relatively stable and peaceful reigns of the Kangxi, Yongzheng, and Qianlong emperors, especially under Qianlong who did much to foster the arts. Embroidery became an industry in itself, with men, women, and children engaged in its manufacture. Almost every garment worn by middle- and upper-class Manchu and Chinese would be embellished with embroidery, as well as all the necessary soft furnishings for their homes, such as bed hangings, door curtains, table covers, bed covers, and pillow-ends. Although a lady in a well-to-do household would learn to embroider as an accomplishment and would be required to prove her skills to her prospective husband and mother-in-law, such households would also employ an embroiderer to produce the many articles required. The task was given to the wives and daughters of tradesmen and artisans whose embroidery could contribute to the family income.

From the middle of the nineteenth century, the quality of embroidery began to decline, in common with other arts, due to the tumultuous social changes taking place in the country. By the twentieth century, embroidered articles had been eclipsed by the invention of new fabrics and improved printing methods. Apart from embroidered wedding garments and evening wear, the craft was largely restricted to children's clothing. During the Cultural Revolution many embroidered works of art were destroyed as a result of Red Guard activities. Some people took the precaution of sewing valuable or sentimental pieces into their clothing in an attempt to avoid detection, and it is remarkable that so much did survive.[3] Today, minority groups still embroider their clothing and household articles, and other smaller ethnic groups among the Han Chinese, particularly boat people, continue to decorate their homes with embroidered textiles with auspicious emblems (**plates 95, 96, 97**).

Embroidery Centres

By the Ming dynasty, centres for embroidery had been established at Suzhou in Jiangsu, Chengdu in Sichuan, and Guangzhou in Guangdong province. The first of these, Suzhou, had been established in the third-century AD period of the Three Kingdoms when, it is reported, the state of Wu, whose capital was Suzhou, needed a military map when fighting the Wei and Shu. The wife of the emperor decided to embroider the map, thinking that paint would not be durable enough. The result was a masterpiece of detail and delicacy, and she became known as the 'supreme mistress of the needle'. Very delicate shading which gives a three-dimensional effect is typical of traditional Suzhou embroidery. It is also famous for its double-sided work where the picture is identical on both sides of the silk gauze. To achieve this effect, and to ensure that no thread ends were visible, the embroidery frame would be set between two people and the needle pushed through the silk alternately. The first recorded example of this skill is an embroidered *sutra* wrapping dating from the eleventh century, which was excavated in Zhejiang province. As recently as the early 1980s, experts in Suzhou, and then Hunan, acquired the skills to create embroidery with different pictures and colours on either side using two needles with different coloured threads.

Embroidery in Sichuan developed during the Three Kingdoms period, and was a specialized discipline by the reign of the Daoguang Emperor (r.1821–50). In Chengdu, at that time, there were about ninety workshops, as well as many individual embroiderers, making everything from official robes and wedding garments to household furnishings and scrolls.

Guangzhou was famous for its gold and silver couching, especially on opera costumes, though much of the embroidery produced there in the late nineteenth century was considered by some to be garish compared with that of the other centres. Gold-shadowing embroidery was a feature of this region, as well as further north around Shanghai, where the stitches were embroidered over an area already covered with gold foil to give a sparkling effect. Embroidered silk Canton shawls were also very popular, so-called because they were produced in and around Canton (Guangzhou), the only city in China open to foreigners before the opening of the Treaty Ports in the mid-nineteenth century. They were frequently purchased as gifts by traders who had to leave their families behind in neighbouring Macau or in their home countries. Shawls were fashionable during Victorian times, and those from Canton were highly prized (**plate 98**).

Specialist embroidery skills could be found in numerous centres, but a fourth important centre was founded in Hunan during the Qing dynasty, although Hunan embroidery can now be dated back more than two thousand years following the discovery of the Mawangdui tombs at Changsha. Hunan embroidery was noted for its strong colours, a wide range of over seventy different styles of stitching, and hundreds of colour shades and tones. The silk was split into more than twenty strands, and the colour gradations of the embroidery gave a very painterly look.

Embroidery Methods

Silk of every weight from gauze to satin was usually the base cloth for embroidery. Cotton was used by the poorer people, usually as a base for appliqué work. Men worked standing at an embroidery frame made of bamboo suspended from the wall with the material to be worked on stretched tightly across. Because bound feet made lengthy standing difficult, women worked sitting down with the frame supported by their legs, while children sat at a high table frame (**fig. 20.1**).

Fig. 20.1 Young girl working at an embroidery frame. Suzhou, early 20th cent.

Very short fine needles were used. About 3 centimetres long, they were made of ivory or bone at first, then of copper, bronze, or steel. Embroidery silks were purchased from itinerant pedlars who walked the streets announcing their wares by twirling a rattle. They carried small drawers of every shade of floss and twisted silk imaginable, as well as silver and gold thread. Metal threads were said to have a special coating which prevented them from tarnishing in the heat and humidity, and this secret was long sought after outside China. Even so, the following description of making gold and silver thread in Guangzhou makes no mention of the special coating:

> Several long, and narrow sheets of paper having been coated with a mixture of earth (well pounded) and glue are, in the next instance, covered either with gold, or silver leaf. In order that a bright glossy appearance may be imparted to these sheets of paper, which, with gold, or silver leaf have been covered, men rub them, heavily, from one end to the other, with pieces of crystal, which, for this purpose, are, to the ends of the bamboo rods, attached. This polishing process having been accomplished, the gilded, or silvered sheets of paper are, now, cut, by means of large knives, into very thin strips, which strips, are, then, by a twirling process, carefully entwined round ordinary threads of silk.[4]

Birds and flowers, landscape and genre scenes, figures from history and folklore, and, above all, objects and characters with auspicious connotations, formed the repertoire of embroidery motifs. Books of woodcuts, in which the approved styles of embroidery and the arrangement of colours and patterns were set out, were being printed in the Song dynasty and continued to be a popular source of reference. Rice-paper cuts, made to be pasted on to the paper windows found in Chinese homes, were also used as a base for design. Stencils of the most popular designs and symbols were made, and most large embroidery studios had a selection of cardboard templates which were used to give uniformity in design, to assist in the placing of the design, and to save time. All the popular symbols such as the *shou* character, bat, cloud filler, and common Buddhist and Daoist emblems, were made in this form.

To embroider small items such as shoes, a loom with pieces of silk of the required size were stretched across it. The outline of the upper was spread flat, and paper cuts of various designs were moved around until a pleasing arrangement was reached. The paper cuts were then tacked down, and the designs embroidered over until the paper was completely covered and sewn into the fabric. Gold paper cuts were also used, especially on children's hats, the edge being left visible around the design as definition. Alternatively, the edge of the paper design was sewn round as an outline and the paper then ripped out. Another method entailed the use of a white powder made of ground oyster shells which was dusted through a stencil, leaving a powdery outline. More powder was mixed with water and a fine line painted over the outline to render it more permanent; the design was then embroidered.

When embroidering a large garment such as an important robe, the main design would be drawn on to heavy rice paper, with one half drawn in black ink and the colours filled in as appropriate, and the other left as drawn areas. With a less-important robe, the outline would be drawn but the colours just noted on the appropriate areas and not coloured in. The designs were placed on the fabric which was then stretched over a rectangular frame. Roller frames were not used for large important pieces of embroidery as the rolled areas could be flattened and spoilt.

Embroidery Stitches

Although the number of stitches was not large, each stitch often had many variations, as well as different names. On each embroidered item, however, the stitches were usually limited to a few; the most common ones are noted below:

Buttonhole stitch was used to cover cut edges, particularly on cotton appliquéd work.

Chain stitch was well-known by the Han dynasty: thirty-nine of the forty pieces of embroidered garments, banners, and accessories found in the Mawangdui tomb had evidence of this stitch, and it continued to be the predominant stitch up to the Song dynasty. Also called the *suo*, or lock stitch, it is used to give a more textured effect on curving lines.

Couching was a way to anchor gold and silver threads or thin strips of material or paper which could not be sewn on directly, as they might break or split the silk cloth. The threads or strips were laid in rows on the surface of the cloth, and a toning silk thread was employed to anchor them in position. Towards the end of the nineteenth century, red and green silk were used for couching as these colours were thought to enhance the colours of the metal.

Counted stitch was also called tent stitch, petit point, or half-cross stitch. It was a short, straight, slanted stitch, usually on an open-weave cloth like canvas or gauze, and was good for covering large areas of background.

Fig. 20.2 Woman embroidering a child's *dou dou* with cross stitch. Beijing, c.1930s. Hedda Morrison.

Cross stitch was used mainly in parts of Sichuan, Shaanxi, Guizhou and Hebei provinces by Han Chinese and the minority groups living there (fig. 20.2, 20.3). It is also found on the centre squares of baby carriers, using red thread on white canvas, in Hong Kong and Guangdong.

Florentine stitch was usually worked with silk thread on canvas ground. Vertical, parallel, straight stitches rise or descend according to the pattern being followed, and each line is often worked in a shade or colour different from the one before.

Fig. 20.3 Child's blue cotton *dou dou* with cross stitch embroidery depicting a padlock and figures. Miao. East Guizhou, c.1950s. Valery Garrett.

Needlelooping, a very rare technique first developed during the Song, had become an important stitch by the Yuan period, but was seldom seen after the early Ming. A layer of plain woven silk and a sheet of gold on paper of the same size formed the base on which the needlelooping was done. This resembled lace knitting or crocheting, and allowed the gold on the paper between to shine through (plate 99).

Pekinese stitch, seen extensively during the Han dynasty, was used to give a neat textured effect. It was also called couched twist, and was formed when a back stitch was interlaced with a looped second thread. Another name was *wan* or roll stitch.

Satin stitch dates back to the Shang dynasty, and examples were found in the Mawangdui tomb of the Han period. It became an important part of an embroiderer's repertoire in the Qing dynasty. The stitches must be very flat and even to give the characteristic satin-smooth appearance. Voiding, leaving a hair's breadth of fabric between adjacent areas of satin stitch, was very popular to give definition to the design.

Another variation was *brick stitch*, a flat satin stitch used in a staggered sequence giving an interesting textured effect when used for filling large areas. *Long and short stitch* was a further type made by sewing the first row of stitches alternately long and short; thereafter all the rows have stitches the same length. It was used to give gradations of colour and shade.

Seed stitch, also called Peking knot, is similar to French knot. It is known as *da zi* in Chinese, meaning 'making seeds', due to the smallness and evenness of the stitch. Although no evidence of a ban has been found, it was also called 'forbidden stitch' by some Westerners because it was thought to have been out-lawed as it was said to ruin the eyesight of the embroiderers. The stitch was used to give a soft texture, to fill in small areas, or to define details. The stitches had to be absolutely even, next to each other, and the rows completely straight (plate 100).

Stem stitch was used to outline a design, and for fine detailing.

Notes

1   V. Sylwan, *Silk from Yin Dynasty*, Stockholm: The Museum of Far Eastern Antiquities (Bulletin No. 9), 1937, pp. 119–126.
2   Li Yezhen, et al. 'An Important Discovery Concerning the Silk Weaving and Embroidery of the Western Zhou', *Cultural Relics*, 4 (1976).
3   Wang Yarong, *Chinese Folk Embroidery*, London: Thames and Hudson, 1987, p. 158.
4   J. H. Gray, *Walks in the City of Canton*, Hong Kong: de Souza, 1875, p. 290.

Afterword

Few countries in the world have had such a rigid dress code as that which was imposed in China for several thousand years. Dating and identification of ownership, therefore, ought to be relatively easy, but for all the regulations issued by successive governments, it seems a fair amount of individual interpretation was permitted. This was due, in part, to the cost of the sumptuous robes to be worn, to the natural desire to outdo one's neighbour, and to the size of the country itself, where deviations in areas far from the capital could go unchecked.

Unlike other art works such as porcelain or paintings, costume and textiles have many possibilities for adaption to other uses or styles. Over the years subsequent owners added their own modifications to earlier pieces. This was particularly the case with early Ming textiles which were taken as gifts into Tibet and there used as banners, or with dragon robes, recut in the Tibetan style. In the early years of this century, after many robes were brought out of China following the fall of the Qing dynasty, they became sought after as fancy dress for soirées in the West. This, compounded by the amount of leeway applied in the making of the garment by the imperial workshops, the embroidery studios, or within the family, make it difficult to match robes to original owners or to date the garment with any high degree of accuracy.

Today, now that Western-style dress has replaced traditional dress for the majority of Han Chinese, the only examples regularly seen are those in minority groups. Here, there is a feeling of colour and vigour in the styles, and because minority areas are generally less accessible, traditional methods of manufacture still apply in many cases. Even so, modern materials and dyes are gradually changing the look of the dress, to its detriment.

Relatively little regard has been paid to the importance of textiles in the past. Museums around the world tend to have few robes and related dress on display even though, in some cases, the storerooms behind may be bursting with undisclosed treasures. But in recent years, a growing interest and awareness has developed among collectors of textiles and costume. In this manner, if in no other way, will the traditions and splendour of Chinese dress be kept alive into the twenty-first century.

Glossary

ao   upper garment worn by urban Han Chinese women in the Qing dynasty and early years of the Republic.

ao gun   upper garment and skirt worn by married urban Han Chinese women in the early years of the Republic.

ao ku   upper garment and trousers worn by Han Chinese women in the Qing dynasty and early years of the Republic.

Ba Gua   Eight Trigrams, an ancient system of divination.

Ba Qi   Eight Banners, the Manchu Army.

bai   side extensions on the lower skirt of a Ming robe to add bulk.

bai shou yi   'one hundred longevity character garment', a type of burial dress.

bai tong   'white copper', an alloy which resembled silver.

bai tou dao lao   'white head, old age', a fanciful way of referring to the white waistband, as well as a wish for long life and a blessing in a Chinese marriage.

bai ze   a mythical animal with two horns, a scaly body and a dragon-like head depicted on rank badges worn by some Ming noblemen.

bao fu   a square cloth used for wrapping and carrying items.

bao tou   'head wrap', a headcloth worn by Hakka (Kejia) women.

bei xin   sleeveless waistcoat worn by boys over their *chang shan*.

bei yun   'back cloud', the counterweight back extension on the court necklace.

bei zi   a narrow-sleeved or sleeveless dress which opened down the front and was worn by men and women during the Ming dynasty.

bi xi   a narrow apron, part of formal attire worn during the Ming dynasty.

chang shan   'long gown' fastening over to the right.

chang fu   'ordinary dress', everyday wear for nobility and officials in the Qing dynasty.

chao dai   'court belt', a girdle with belt plaques from which items were hung; worn as part of Qing court dress.

chao fu   'court dress', the most formal attire of the Qing dynasty.

chao gua   'court vest', a sleeveless garment worn by women.

chao guan   'court hat' worn as part of court dress.

chao pao   'court robe', a side-fastening, full-length robe worn as part of court attire.

chao zhu   'court necklace' based on the Buddhist rosary.

charwa   a woollen felt cape with squared-off shoulders worn by Yi women.

chi   a unit of measure, one *chi* equalled one Chinese foot or about 35 centimetres.

chuba   loose robe with narrow sleeves worn by Tibetans.

Da jiao   a Daoist ceremony held in some rural communities every ten years to pacify the dragon.

da lian   a purse with two flaps worn over a belt.

Da ming hui dian   Ming dynastic statutes governing dress and other matters.

da zi   'Making seeds', Peking knot embroidery stitch.

dai kou   'pockets openings' or 'pocket mouths', the pockets of a man's jacket, especially the inside ones, a punning reference to the number of mouths to feed.

dai xiao   the custom practised of wearing a white, blue or green wool flower in the hair by a woman in mourning for a husband or parent, a grandparent or a great-grandparent, respectively, and of a pink wool flower to denote the end of mourning. Also refers to the black ribbon fastened to the upper garment by a man in mourning.

diao wei   sable tail worn by Manchu soldiers in active service.

dou dou   small triangular apron worn as underwear.

dou niu   'dipper ox', a type of three-clawed dragon with down-curving horns.

duan zhao   'ceremonial overcoat', a surcoat made of fur.

fei yu   'flying fish', a kind of winged dragon-fish.

feng huang   phoenix, a mythical bird said to be king of birds.

fo tou   name given to the four large beads on the court

necklace, representing the four seasons.

fu   one of the Twelve Symbols, representing the two forces of Good and Evil.

fu   a bat, a homonym for happiness and good fortune.

fu, lu, shou   three mythological figures denoting, respectively, good fortune, an abundance of good things, and long life.

fu tou   a type of hat with two stiff wings projecting apart at the sides, worn by officials in the Ming dynasty.

guan   scholar official, a mandarin.

gun   woman's skirt.

gun fu   'royal robes', the term give to the imperial surcoat.

gun mian   ceremonial attire worn for sacrificial rites during the Ming dynasty.

hei jiao chou   black gummed silk.

hong gua   red jacket and skirt worn by a bride.

hua dai   patterned, woven band used by Cantonese and Hakka women.

hua yu   peacock feather plume, a decoration awarded by the emperor for special services.

Huangchao liqi tushi   'Illustrated Precendents for the Ritual Paraphernalia of the Imperial Court', an illustrated catalogue of court dress and regalia commissioned by the Qianlong Emperor.

huang en qin zi   literally 'conferred by imperial grace', the four characters on an insignia square awarded to elderly men who had tried and failed to pass the civil service examinations.

huang ma qua   yellow riding jacket, an award for bravery.

hui shi   the civil service examination held in the metropolis.

ji fu   'festive dress', semi-formal style of Qing court dress.

ji guan   'festive hat' worn as part of the semi-formal court dress.

jian sheng   a title purchased as a short cut to military office.

jiao dai   rigid hooped belt decorated with ornamental plaques, worn by Han Chinese women.

jiaran   a type of dye-resist stencil printing dating back to pre-Song times.

jin huang   'golden yellow', an orange colour, in fact, worn by the emperor's sons in the Qing dynasty.

jin shi   'finished scholar', a graduate of the metropolitan examinations.

ju ren   'promoted man', a graduate of the provincial civil service examination.

kai mian   literally 'to open the face', to remove hairs from over the forehead with two red threads.

kang   a brick or earth platform in northern Chinese homes which is heated with a fire underneath, to serve as seating or as a bed.

kao liang   millet, the stalks of which were used to make straw raincoats.

kesi   'cut silk', a method of weaving silk tapestry.

kou niu   literally 'to do up a button', the phrase is a homonym of *kou liu* meaning 'to detain against one's will'.

ku   loose-fitting trousers.

ku li   literally 'bitter strength', the transliteration for coolie.

lan cao   'blue grass', the indigo plant producing a blue dye.

lan yu   blue feather plume, crow feather and horse-hair plume worn by imperial guards and awarded to officials below the sixth rank on merit.

li shi   money given in a red envelope for a special occasion, usually at Lunar New Year; also known as *laisee* in Cantonese.

li shui   'standing water', the diagonal stripes at the bottom of a dragon robe or rank badge.

liang mao   'cool hat', circular straw hat with black cloth fringe worn by Hakka (Kejia) women.

ling tou   small plain stiffened collar worn with the surcoat or jacket.

ling yue   a gold or gilt torque collar worn by Qing noblewomen with court dress.

long   five-clawed dragon.

long gua   'dragon coat', a front-opening surcoat decorated with dragon medallions and worn by Qing noblewomen.

long pao   'dragon robe', side-fastening robe with five-clawed dragons for official semi-formal wear.

lu   'deer', a homonym for an official's salary; good fortune.

lu gun   'green skirt' worn at marriage by Han Chinese women in Qing dynasty.

Lu Ying   Chinese Green Standard Army.

luan   a lesser type of phoenix.

ma gua   'riding dress', a short front-opening jacket.

ma xue   'horse boots', knee-high black satin boots with stiff white soles.

mang   four-clawed dragon.

mang ao   'dragon jacket', side-fastening jacket decorated with dragons and worn by wives of Han Chinese officials.

mang chu   'dragon skirt', pleated skirt decorated with dragons and worn by wives of Han Chinese officials.

mang pao   'dragon robe' depicting four-clawed dragons.

Ming Shi   the official history of the Ming dynasty.

nei tao 'inner tunic', side-fastening long gown with horse-hoof cuffs worn by men as part of official informal dress.

pao full-length robe.

pau hua a type of wood which, after steeping in water, makes a hair gel.

pi bian a leather hat worn by the emperor and high officials in the Ming dynasty.

pi ling flaring collar worn with the court robe.

pu kui leaves from this tree (*Livistonia chinensis*) were used to make palm-leaf fans.

pu fu 'garment with a patch', centre-opening surcoat with insignia badges on chest and back.

pulo a Tibetan word for a type of woven woollen cloth.

pu zi 'garment patch', the insignia badge worn on the surcoat.

qi 'banner', a colloquial term for Manchu, a banner being one of the divisions of the Manchu army.

qi pao 'banner gown', close-fitting woman's dress with high neck and slit skirt; the term indicates the Manchu origin of this garment. Also known as *cheung sam* in Cantonese.

qilin a mythical beast having the head of a dragon with two horns, a scaly body and a bushy tail; symbol of a first-rank military mandarin.

ren small square flap on the man's court robe.

ru yi sceptre, one of the Eight Precious Things.

san lan 'three blues', three shades of blue used together on embroidery.

shan upper garment fastening over to the right.

shan ku side-fastening upper garment and trousers.

shang seven-panelled skirt worn by Ming emperors for ceremonial attire.

shen yi wide-sleeved burial clothes styled after the under-robes worn in the Ming.

sheng yuan government student.

shui tian yi 'paddy field dress', name given to patchwork style of ladies dress worn in the Ming dynasty.

shou 'longevity', a wish for long life.

Shou Xing God of Longevity.

shou yi 'long-life dress' worn for sixtieth birthday celebrations and, after, for burial.

shu liang false gambier, a dye plant.

shuang xi 'double happiness', a character used especially at weddings.

suo lock or chain embroidery stitch.

suo yi straw raincoat.

Taiping Tian Guo Heavenly Kingdom of Great Peace.

ti du commander-in-chief in the Green Standard Army.

tian ze Manchu women's headdress made of wire or rattan, lattice-shaped like an inverted basket.

tou jin curved neck opening fastening to the right.

Tung Men Hui Revolutionary Alliance Party founded by Dr Sun Yatsen to overthrow the Manchu government.

wai tao 'outer tunic', surcoat without rank badges.

wan 'ten thousand', a Buddhist emblem like a reverse swastika, a wish to live to a great age.

wan pekinese or roll embroidery stitch.

wu bian 'tailless', lacking the queue.

wu fu five grades of mourning clothing.

wu ju ren military graduate of the provincial level examinations.

wu sheng yuan military government student.

xia pei stole worn by wives of nobility and officials in the Ming and Qing dynasties.

xiang se 'incense colour', a greenish yellow colour worn by daughters of the emperor and imperial consorts.

xiang shi 'deserving promotion', the second degree for the civil service examinations taken in the provincial capitals.

xie literally 'shoes', also a homonym for 'together', a punning reference for a couple to live together for a long time.

xie zhai a mythical beast said to be able to tell right from wrong, with a horn to gore the wrongdoer; the insignia of the censors.

xilankapu 'quilt cover, flower pattern', brocade weaving which is a speciality of the Tujia people.

xiu cai 'budding talent', the name applied to those who passed the first degree of the civil service examinations.

yamen a walled establishment containing a mandarin's home and offices.

yin, yang negative and positive cosmological symbols; *yin* also represents earth and the female, while *yang* represents heaven and the male.

ying long a five-clawed dragon with huge bat-like wings depicted in the Ming dynasty.

yue bai 'moon white', the colour of a dragon robe worn for a ceremony at the Altar of the Moon during the Autumn Equinox.

yun jian 'cloud collar', a four-pointed collar covering shoulders, chest, and back and worn by Han Chinese women as official dress. Also describes the placement of dragons on men's official robes.

yung 'braves', volunteers in the Green Standard Army.

zai shui ceremonial kerchief worn by women as part of Qing court dress.

zhi ri sheng gao 'point at the sun and rise high', a rebus which refers to the sun disk on the badge of rank and a mandarin's hope for advancement.

zhua zhou the 'grasping' ceremony held when a child is one year old to determine his future occupation.

Select Bibliography

Ball, J. Dyer, *Things Chinese*, fifth edition, Shanghai: Kelly and Walsh, 1925; reprint, Hong Kong: Oxford University Press, 1982.

Berliner, Nancy Zeng, *Chinese Folk Art*, Boston: Little, Brown and Company, 1986.

Burkhardt, V. R., *Chinese Creeds and Customs*, Vols. 1-3, Hong Kong: South China Morning Post, 1955–9.

Cammann, Schuyler, *China's Dragon Robes*, New York: Ronald Press, 1952.

———, 'The Development of the Mandarin Square', *Harvard Journal of Asiatic Studies*, 8 (1944–5): 71–130.

———, 'Ming Festival Symbols', *Archives of the Chinese Art Society of America*, 2 (1953): 68–9.

Chiang Yee, *A Chinese Childhood*, London: Methuen and Co., 1940.

Dickinson, Gary and Wrigglesworth, Linda, *Imperial Wardrobe*, Hong Kong: Oxford University Press, 1990.

Doolittle, Rev. Justus, *Social Life of the Chinese*, Vols. I and II, New York: Harper & Bros, 1895.

Editorial Committee of Shanghai Theatrical College, *Ethnic Costumes and Clothing Decorations from China*, Hong Kong: Hai Feng Publishing Co. Ltd, 1986.

Hucker, Charles O., *The Traditional Chinese State in Ming Times (1368–1644)*, Tucson: The University of Arizona Press, 1972.

Johnstone, Reginald F., *Twilight in the Forbidden City*, London: Victor Gollancz Ltd., 1934; reprint, Hong Kong: Oxford University Press, 1985.

Ma Yin, ed., *China's Minority Nationalities*, Beijing: Foreign Languages Press, 1989.

Miyazaki, Ichisada, *China's Examination Hell: The Civil Service Examinations of Imperial China*, New Haven and London: Yale University Press, 1981.

Scott, A. C., *Chinese Costume in Transition*, Singapore: Donald Moore, 1958.

Vollmer, John E., *Decoding Dragons: Status Garments in Ch'ing Dynasty China*, Eugene: University of Oregon Museum of Art, 1983.

Williams, C. A. S., *Outlines of Chinese Symbolism and Art Motives*, Peking: Customs College Press, 1931.

Illustration Credits

Photographs in this book were provided by, or reproduced with the kind permission of, the following individuals or organizations. Care has been taken to trace and acknowledge the source of illustrations, but in some instances this has not been possible. Where omissions have occurred, the publishers will be happy to correct them in future editions, provided they receive due notice.

Asian Art Museum of San Francisco, The Avery Brundage Collection (1990.214): **Plate 12**
Hugh D. R. Baker, London: **Fig. 13.8**
Eric Boudot, Hong Kong: **Plate 78**
British Library: **Fig. 11.7**
China Tourism Photo Library: **Fig.** 14.3, 15.5, 16.3, 16.4, 16.5, 16.7, 17.2, 17.3, 17.4, 19.2; **Plates** 53, 65, 79, 84, 86, 92, 93
The Commercial Press Ltd, Hong Kong: **Fig.** 2.4, 2.5, 2.6
Gary Dickinson, London: **Fig. 5.2**
FormAsia, Hong Kong: **Fig. 18.3**
Valery Garrett, Hong Kong: **Fig.** 3.4, 5.8, 5.9, 5.11, 5.12, 5.13, 5.14, 5.15, 6.4, 6.5, 6.7, 6.9, 6.10, 7.2, 7.7, 7.10, 8.2, 8.5, 8.6, 9.1, 9.5, 9.7, 9.9, 10.6, 10.7, 11.6, 12.1, 12.6, 12.9, 13.3, 13.5, 13.6, 13.7, 14.2, 14.7, 14.9, 15.3, 15.4, 15.6, 20.3; **Plates** 19, 21, 25, 32, 38, 39, 40, 41, 42, 43, 44, 46, 47, 49, 51, 52, 54, 55, 59, 60, 61, 62, 63, 66, 67, 68, 69, 70, 71, 72, 73, 74, 75, 76, 89, 90, 91, 95, 96
Imperial Wardrobe, Gary Dickinson & Linda Wrigglesworth, 1990: **Plate 26**
Joint Publishing (HK) Co.: **Fig. 2.12**
Kwong Sang Hong Ltd, Hong Kong: **Plate 48**
Liaoning Provincial Museum, Shenyang: **Plate 94**
Library of Congress, Washington: **Fig. 12.8**
Keith Macgregor, Hong Kong: **Plate 50**
Metropolitan Museum of Art, New York: **Fig.** 4.7, 4.13, 5.5
The Estate of Hedda Morrison: **Fig. 20.2**
Museum of Dingling: **Fig.** 1.4, 1.7, 2.3, 13.1; **Plate 13**
Museo Oriental, Valladolid, Spain: **Fig. 11.2**
Nanjing Museum, Nanjing: **Fig.** 1.10, 1.13, 1.14, 1.17; **Plates** 2, 15
National Palace Museum, Taipei, Taiwan, Republic of China: **Fig.** 1.1, 1.5, 2.1, 2.2, 3.10, 3.13, 4.5, 4.11, 14.1; **Plates** 3, 5, 56
The Nelson-Atkins Museum of Art, Kansas City, Missouri (Nelson Fund) 35-275: **Fig. 4.8**
Cornelius Osgood: **Fig. 10.2**
Palace Museum, Beijing: **Fig.** 1.9, 2.1, 2.2, 2.8, 2.9, 3.2, 3.11, 3.12, 3.14, 4.12, 4.14, 4.22; **Plates** 16, 23, 24, 57
Plum Blossoms (Int'l) Ltd, Hong Kong: **Plates** 88, 99
Private collections: **Fig.** 1.16, 1.18, 2.11, 12.4, 12.5; **Plates** 4, 6, 9, 10, 11, 14, 17, 27, 29, 30, 33, 34, 36, 58
Public Records Office, Hong Kong: **Fig.** 8.4, 10.4, 11.10, 13.2, 15.1, 15.2
Royal Ontario Museum, Far East Dept., Toronto: **Fig.** 3.3, 3.5, 4.6

Royal Ontario Museum, Textile Dept., Toronto: **Fig.** 3.6, 5.10; **Plate** 28
Sotheby's, London: **Fig.** 7.8
South China Morning Post, Hong Kong: **Fig.** 12.10
Spink & Son Ltd, London: **Fig.** 1.8; **Plates** 7, 8
Teresa Coleman Fine Arts, Hong Kong: **Plates** 18, 20, 31, 98, 100
University of Oregon Museum of Art, Eugene: **Fig.** 3.9, 4.15, 4.16
Urban Council of Hong Kong, the Collection of the Hong Kong Museum of Art: **Fig.** 13.4; **Plates** 1, 22, 35, 37
Urban Council of Hong Kong, the Collection of the Hong Kong Museum of History: **Fig.** 9.8, 10.5; **Plates** 52, 64
Victoria & Albert Museum, London: **Fig.** 3.1, 4.1, 4.3, 4.9
Franck Vassal, Paris: **Plate** 97
Bernard Vuilleumier: **Fig.** 1.15, 3.7

Index